D1139432

Fighting Flotilla

Fighting Flotilla

RN Laforey Class Destroyers in WW2

Peter C. Smith

Pen & Sword
MARITIME

This 2nd edition first published in Great Britain in 2010
by Pen & Sword Maritime
an imprint of
Pen & Sword Books Ltd
47 Church Street
Barnsley
South Yorkshire
S70 2AS

ISBN: 978 1 84884 273 1

1st edition published in 1976 by William Kimber, London

A CIP catalogue record for this book is available from
the British Library

Typeset in Palatino by S L Menzies-Earl

Printed in the UK by MPG Books Group

Pen & Sword Books Ltd incorporates the imprints of:
Pen & Sword Aviation, Pen & Sword Maritime, Pen & Sword Military,
Wharncliffe Local History, Pen & Sword Select, Pen & Sword Military
Classics, Leo Cooper, Remember When, Seaforth Publishing and Frontline
Publishing.

For a complete list of Pen & Sword titles please contact:
Pen & Sword Books Limited
47 Church Street, Barnsley, South Yorkshire, S70 2AS, England
E-mail: enquiries@pen-and-sword.co.uk
Website: www.pen-and-sword.co.uk

See all Peter C. Smith's published books at:
www.dive-bombers.co.uk

Contents

Foreword

by
Mrs R.M.J. Hutton

It is an almost overwhelming task for me to write the foreword to Peter Smith's book about the 19th Destroyer Flotilla. I have been asked to do it because, as the wife of R.M.J. Hutton for forty-five years, it had been thought that I would know what made him tick.

'Tubby' was captain of *Laforey* and D.19 for most of that gallant ship's life. He stood by her when she was building in Yarrows yard and served in her from her commissioning on 12 August 1941 until he was relieved on 28 November 1943. Sad as he was at leaving her he was delighted to hand over to 'Beaky' Armstrong, a distinguished destroyer captain for whom he had the highest regard but who was to lose his life in her so tragically only a few months later.

This book is about the birth, life and death of the ships of the 19th Flotilla, but at various times 'Tubby' found himself as Captain (D) for many other destroyers that were attached to his command. He was, therefore, well known in the destroyer world of many nationalities and he believed very much that those who commanded should be known to those under their command. He never liked serving in big ships – he complained that they were too impersonal. He liked to know his lower deck almost as well as he knew his wardroom, and I know those who served under him knew him as a good mixer.

He was a professional. All the officers of his rank, at that time, were. There were no short service commissions in those days. After World War I the Royal Navy was cut to the bone and only the professionals, aided by a good deal of luck, managed to survive in the service. He went to Osborne at the age of thirteen and was brought up in the traditions of the Navy. On 3 August 1914, when he was fourteen, he solemnly wrote to their

Lordships requesting an immediate sea posting – something their Lordships decided to defer for eighteen months!

He had three spells at the Staff College and was well indoctrinated with the theory of waging war, but above that, he was quite sure the spirit of the men who fought was the most important thing. He, himself, was a very simple, very devout Christian. Whenever possible he held Sunday services aboard and he tried never to go into action without a brief prayer himself. Talking to *Laforey* survivors in 1974, I was delighted to know how much they appreciated this side of his character.

There were never any grey zones in his life – things were good or they were bad. He hated war but, in spite of endless self-criticism, he knew it was the result that mattered.

He kept his finger very much on the common pulse, believing the best could only be achieved through the goodwill of men; he was able to be friendly without being familiar, considerate without being soft-hearted. Throughout his life he managed men without misgiving or mistrust.

Laforey, and the 19th Flotilla, were the epitome of his life – that `grey mistress' of which I, his wife, could only be immensely proud. May his spirit and example, and that of the men of the Laforeys, live on in this book.

Lois Hutton
Oak Lawn, Wootton Bridge, Isle of Wight,
March 1976

Acknowledgements

This book owes a great deal to the many people who knew and loved the Laforey Class destroyers during their brief life span; to those who willingly answered my many questions; the firms who provided me with detailed information and photographs; the many official departments which extended every aid and co-operation, in particular the Naval Library and the Public Record Office; and the ex-serving members of the L Class Survivors' Association who raked their memories and told me story after story of destroyer life in those far-off days.

In particular I would like to thank the following: Rear Admiral P.N. Buckley and the Naval Historical Branch; Miss V. Riley and the Naval Library; Mr S.G.V. Smith and the Public Record Office; Lieutenant David Lyon and Mr Antony Preston and the National Maritime Museum; the Ministry of Defence (Navy) at both Whitehall and Bath; the Controller of Her Majesty's Stationery Office, London; Mr R. Squires of Imperial War Museum, London; Mr P.A. Vicary, Cromer, Norfolk; Messrs Yarrow and Company, Scotstoun, Glasgow; the Planning Department, H.M. Dockyard, Chatham; Swan Hunter Shipbuilders Ltd, Newcastle; Cammell Laird & Company (Shipbuilders) Birkenhead; Richardsons, Westgarth & Company, Wallsend and Scotts Shipbuilding Company Ltd, Greenock.

Among the many enthusiasts and researchers I wish to acknowledge the help and advice of Edwin Walker, Jim Colledge and Joe Fama of California.

Outstanding among the L Class survivors have been David Braybrook (*Lookout*), Alf Brenchly (*Lookout*), Bob Burns (*Laforey*), Captain J.C. Cartwright (*Legion*), J. Hall (*Lightning*), Rear-Admiral D.H.F. Heatherington (*Lookout*), Rear-Admiral Geoffrey Henderson CB, (*Laforey*), Commander R.F. Jessel

(*Legion*), Tom King (*Lightning*), Captain C.N. Lentaigne (*Gurkha*), F.W. Moore (*Legion*), J.W. Martin (*Legion*), M.H. Sayers (*Legion*), Eric Smith (*Legion*), Lieutenant Commander G.W. Style (*Lance*), W. Turton (*Lookout*), V.J. Vine (*Legion*), L.G. Williams (*Loyal*) and V. Wilson (*Lightning*). Further thanks are also due to Ronald Sired and William Kimber & Co. for permission to quote from *Enemy Engaged* and Eric Smith for permission to quote from *Seaman Crusher*.

Introduction

When I was approached by Eric Smith on behalf of the L Class Survivors Association and asked whether or not I would consider writing a book on the history of the Laforey Class boats of World War II I was delighted. I had always considered the big ships of this class, with their half-sisters, the Milne Class, to be the most beautiful warships of that period to fly the White Ensign. Certainly they combined that beauty with power; they were working and fighting vessels and they were considered by many to be the most successful destroyer type to serve with the Royal Navy in combat.

Some excellent books have appeared which sing the praises of other classes of destroyer, the Tribals, the Battles and the V and W Classes, and I would be the first to admit that all these designs had their outstanding merits. The V and Ws were certainly the longest-serving destroyers in the fleet; although perhaps chary re-armament could claim the credit for this fact, the Battles, although woefully undergunned for their size, had great beauty, while the Tribals were also powerful ships for a surface engagement and their arrival, with their resounding names, just prior to the outbreak of the war, gained them immense publicity.

However the Laforeys were far superior ships. They mounted only six 4.7-inch guns instead of eight as the Tribals, it is true, but the Laforeys were given a higher angle of fire to enable them to engage aircraft and they mounted their guns in weatherproof shields, while the Tribals open mountings were no advance in operational conditions to those of twenty years before. Also the numerical superiority of their guns was more than nullified by the fact that Y mounting aft on the quarterdeck (the 'lazy' mounting as it was known in the service), could not be fully utilised in heavy weather and X mounting above it was soon replaced by a twin 4-inch gun to combat dive-bombing. The

Battles were magnificently equipped to deal with air attack but they arrived far too late to participate in the war for which they were designed; only *Barfleur* fired her guns in anger. Therefore the outstanding British destroyer design to see *combat* in the Second World War was undoubtedly that of the L and M Classes.

A history of this kind, which attempts to be comprehensive, cannot be so if it fails to mention the men who manned the ships. For as alive as a ship may appear, it is her crew which makes her so; the crew imposes on a ship its own personality, whether good or bad. In as far as I can judge the Ls *were* happy ships. The *Legion* with her band of 'Legionnaires' who used to meet annually represented what was, without any doubt, a happy ship. Now of course, most of these veterans have 'crossed the bar' and their knowledge of life when what was then still Great Britain really had a Navy to be proud of, have gone with them, so I am glad to have preserved some of their knowledge in these pages. From many accounts the *Laforey* herself was also a happy ship; certainly her survivors still have an enormous amount of affection for the memory of Captain R.M.J. Hutton, the famous Captain (D) 19th Flotilla.

To reflect these fast-fading memories in a country changed beyond all recognition from the land that they fought for, I have incorporated throughout the book a medley of comment, opinion and information supplied to me in letters and interviews by the survivors of these vessels. These snippets reflect far better than I could hope to the way of life of the Royal Navy destroyer service of some seventy or so years ago. It is not a huge gap in time but in comparing conditions and life in the Royal Navy then with the present miniscule remnant of a once great service, it seems much larger.

Although 'Hard Lying' money (extra pay for bad conditions) was paid to some of the sailors of 1942, modern sailors might care to reflect on conditions aboard these vessels as described by their crews. Remember also that the Laforeys at this time were the largest and finest destroyers in the fleet. Many people from Churchill downward considered them to be 'too large for destroyers'. What the modern occupant of the air-conditioned world aboard a 6,000-ton Daring Class 'Destroyer' of today would have felt about conditions aboard the *Lightning* off Norway as described in these pages can only be guessed at!

I have attempted then to combine a definitive history with a social commentary, and, although numerous tables and charts are included to help tell this story, much of the more detailed information is contained in the Appendices at the back of the book so as not to interrupt too much the flow of the general narrative. I therefore trust that this book will remain a valid and lasting record of these magnificent fighting machines and the breed of men who sailed them into battle in times that now seem as remote as the Napoleonic Wars in terms of warfare.

Peter C. Smith
Riseley, Beds.

Chapter 1

The Origins of the Laforeys

By the late 1930s British disarmament policies brought about by bowing to American pressure at the Washington Conference and subsequent further futile retrenchments, had forced the Royal Navy to throw away a long established lead in the field of destroyer design and it was facing a difficult problem in attempting to make up for many years of neglect beyond its control. From the destroyer's first inception with the little *Havock* of 1893, up to the superb ships of the V and W Classes, which joined the fleet towards the end of the First World War in 1918, it had been British destroyers that had been taken as the pattern for development by navies the world over, and this design had proved itself eminently satisfactory. True, during this long period, Germany had adopted several radical features for her destroyers which, on paper at least, gave their designs a better edge, but in the hard testing ground of war the British flotillas had proved to be in every way superior ships, both in their fighting ability and in their seaworthiness.

However, in the aftermath of the Washington Naval Treaties of 1922, British destroyer design, stifled of funds, appeared to stagnate compared with new developments elsewhere. Restricted as the Admiralty was by these treaties and the further adoption of the myopic 'Ten Year Rule', instituted while Churchill was at the Treasury and which envisaged no major war for that period (and was further made doubly dangerous by a 'receding' clause so that this period of no foreseeable conflict stretched forward into infinity despite the rise of dictatorships in

Europe), the Admiralty was forced to fight tooth and nail with the other two services for the limited scraps reluctantly made available by an all-powerful Treasury. Whatever monies came their way had to be carefully spread over the whole of the naval reconstruction programme and destroyers came behind capital ships and the 8-inch cruiser programme.

Therefore it was a policy directed to replacing over-age tonnage rather than any increase in power or numbers that was adopted, with the cheapest and most reliable form of torpedo carrier as its main spring. This enabled an annual programme to be initiated, after some testing of the two prototypes, *Amazon* and *Ambuscade* built in 1927, of eight destroyers and an enlarged Flotilla Leader. Thus were the A to I Classes produced in the period 1930–37. By the latter date the British Government had become further embroiled with even more limitations in the London Naval Treaties and thus this continuation of the A to I line found further favour in providing numbers of small destroyers and leaving special developments to the province of the heavier units of the fleet.

The average destroyer of this period then carried four single 4.7-inch guns in open shield mountings very little changed from the old V and W boats of two decades earlier. Arrangements of the most primitive kind had allowed the elevation of this weapon to be increased from 30 degrees to 40 degrees but they were designed as surface weapons and were therefore naturally of only limited value against aircraft. For close-range defence it had been decided to reject the 40-mm Bofors and the 20-mm Oerlikon quick-firing cannon, both of which appeared in the late thirties and were available to the Royal Navy, in favour of the traditional pom-pom developed during the First World War, and the 0.5-inch multiple machine gun, a weapon with neither range nor weight of shell. It was as torpedo carriers that the 'Standard' British destroyer of this era was built and they each carried twin sets of quadruple 21-inch torpedo tubes, but no re-loads.

In view of the criticism to which these flotillas were later put it is perhaps interesting, and not irrelevant to the origins of the Laforeys, to quote the opinion of seasoned destroyer officers who served in these boats, both at the time they were built and during the war. These were the men to whom the Admiralty was to turn when designing the Ls and they were the men who would have to fight the coming war in ships that they designed. The answers to questions on the merits or otherwise of the A to I Class destroyers from a selection of these officers therefore bear some study.

Among those who submitted valuable opinions to me were Admiral Sir Richard Onslow, Admiral Sir Deric Holland-Martin, Rear Admiral C.D. Howard Johnston, Captain Edward Gibbs, Captain F.S. de Winton, Commander The Rt Hon. Sir Allan Noble, Commander W.K. Cornish-Bowden and Commander C.A. de W. Kitcat.

It was my old friend Captain Gibbs who wrote that:

> There are three essential qualities in a destroyer; sea-worthiness, battle-worthiness and habitability. *In that order*. An otherwise battle-worthy ship is useless if she is only a fair-weather ship; a habitable ship is useless unless she is battle-worthy.

With this we must surely agree, and certainly the Italians and Germans greatly neglected sea-worthiness in order to concentrate on heavy guns or higher speeds, and they paid the price with ships that proved of little fighting value. The Americans combined the qualities of habitability and good modern armament with endurance, but their sea-keeping left much to be desired. Likewise the Japanese built the best destroyers in the world, and the most advanced in the 1930s as we will see, but they had the advantage of only having to concentrate on the Pacific Ocean, which made their problems of design much simpler than that which confronted the Admiralty. Nor were their hands tied by treaties as they had the good sense to withdraw from them in the interests of their own national security.

It is a much-quoted fact that British warships were built to fight anywhere in the world and despite becoming a hackneyed saying it none the less still had some validity in the 1930s although not so

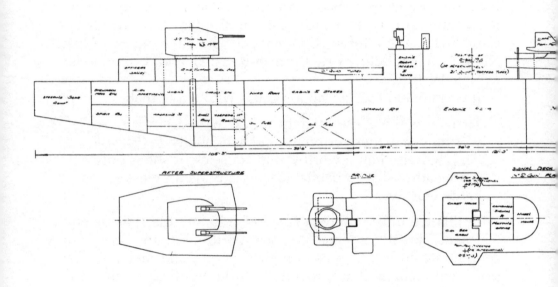

L Class Destroyers, General Arrangement

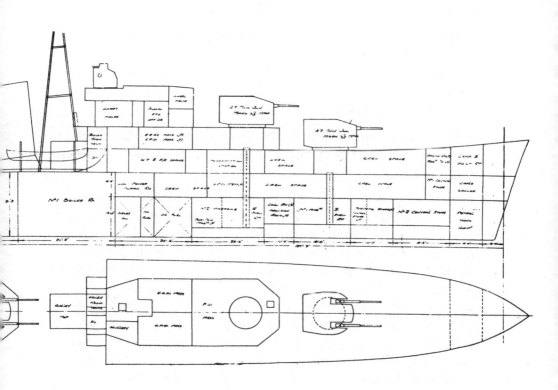

much as has since been placed on it. It was the opinion of all the above officers then that the current A to I destroyers met this condition by being excellent sea boats. 'Incomparably better sea boats than the V and Ws' was one comment.

> Their only weakness in this respect lay in the fact that they were too short and heavy for'ard. They could therefore still bump, and very heavily at that, in a head sea and could suffer considerable structural damage unless their speed was most undesirably cut down.

Another officer wrote of how the A to I could be handled in wartime on the North Atlantic convoy routes, their ultimate testing ground.

> The experiences of peacetime served me well in the war when I found myself recovering exhausted survivors out of the ocean or off an upturned lifeboat. One had to do it right and there was one moment or all was lost, the half dead men would slip out of reach. Backing up astern and edging in just so and no further did the trick, using the wind to help as all these destroyers flew into the wind when going astern and they had to be held so in one position, whereas with an approach bows-on, once the speed was down to four knots there was no control by the helm and the ships' bows just fell off with the wind.

With regard to battle-worthiness the following varying opinions were expressed on 1930s destroyer types.

> For their day I think the A to I Classes were very fine ships in every respect. Their gun, torpedo and ASDIC equipment, and control thereof, were excellent; their W/T and R/T equipment, their boilers, engines and all-round freedom from any kind of breakdown were excellent; in fact they were, for their day, very fine fighting machines, not as fast as some (as for example the Italians), but better all-round fighting machines in any kind of weather than most, and possessed of a good range of action. By modern standards of course their AA armament was pathetic, 0.5s

and Lewis guns, though the 40 degree elevation of their main armament of 4.7s did make long-range barrage fire possible. In this connection however two things should be remembered (a) the aeroplane of those days was not what it later became, and (b) destroyers were designed to work with the fleet where the big ships did have controlled long range AA fire at their disposal.

Another officer wrote: 'They all remained useless against high-flying attackers.'

A third officer writing on this subject was asked whether or not he felt that this lack of AA firepower was discussed in the fleet before the war broke out in any depth, bearing in mind the Japanese system had by this time been developed far beyond what the British were not to achieve until the 1950s. He wrote:

> I am sure that at times this was commented on, but no one seems to have taken it seriously. Although the Fleet Air Arm carried out many torpedo attacks it was assumed that the close-range armament was a sufficient defence. The danger of air attack on the fleet, apart from torpedo-carrying aircraft, was, I am quite certain, hardly considered by most officers. There may have been far-sighted men who realised the lack of co-ordinated defence, but like some of the minor prophets, their voice was not heard! I remember the whole Mediterranean Fleet at Alexandria in 1936 firing at a 'Queen Bee' pilotless aircraft with marked lack of result. I had understood something of high-level bombing having been in 1933–34 at the receiving end in the-target ship *Centurion*, but I do not think that before the war I had ever heard of the Stukas. I do not suppose that I was alone in that, and I think you can take it that air defence was sadly neglected.

The Stuka dive-bomber certainly was to do more than any other weapon in Germany's armoury to destroy the ranks of the A to I Class destroyers during the first two years of the war, but it was a short-range aircraft and the thought that France would

collapse after only a few days of warfare and thus provide the
Luftwaffe with bases on the Royal Navy's doorstep was of course
beyond consideration before the war. However it had already
demonstrated its effectiveness against ships in Spanish ports
during the Civil War in 1938–39 and it is therefore surprising to
learn that although the Navy was caught up on the fringes of
this war the potential of the dive-bomber escaped it. AA defence,
or rather lack of it, was of course *the* major fault of these pre-war
vessels as it later turned out, but at the time the opinion at
command level seems to have been that they were adequately
equipped.

> Although the Germans, Japanese and Americans had
> slightly larger destroyers I do not think our ships were
> really at a disadvantage there as the lighter shell was easier
> to handle from the shell room to the gun breech and I think
> our rate of fire compared quite favourably.

The difficulties experienced by the Germans in the Arctic
certainly confirmed this viewpoint. The Italians with their
closed-in bullet-proof bridges also suffered, the open-topped
British bridges being far more suited to night fighting in those
pre-radar days as numerous examples showed during 1940–41.
In this respect the design of the destroyers was perhaps
compensated for by the excellent seagoing training which the
pre-war flotillas underwent.

> I think the flotilla system provided excellent training and I
> can confidently say that the manoeuvring ability of the
> flotillas pre-war was at a high peak pretty well throughout
> the thirties. A series of brilliant officers commanded the
> flotillas during that time. It should be noted that the loss of
> the Flotilla Leaders *Codrington*, *Keith*, *Exmouth*, *Grenville*
> and *Hardy*, all within the first nine months of the war was
> the main reason for the break-up of the system, which had
> proved ideal in peacetime. I can't think of a superior
> system.

Yet another opinion expressed was:

It has been said that in the early thirties we were preparing to fight World War One all over again. This is an extremely unfair and misleading statement with a germ of truth in its origin. The final objective of a fleet is to fight and destroy another fleet, and it isn't doing its job if it isn't prepared to do so. A fratricidal war with the Americans was unthinkable but war with, and a fleet action against, the Japanese was not; and in those days our Home and Mediterranean Fleets were trained and ready for a fleet action. Now, in being ready for this, it should be plain to any thinking man that the battle efficiency of every individual ship must be as near 100% perfect as possible, and that if any given ship is ready for a fleet action then she is ready for any other kind of action as well. In fact, in the last four years or so before World War Two, when it was as plain as a pikestaff that Germany and Italy were going to be our first enemies (and that very soon), emphasis in the Mediterranean Fleet in which I was serving shifted from fleets during fleet exercises to personal initiative and the taking of risks with one's ship at the highest speed on the darkest of nights. It was splendid training.

However not *all* aspects could be covered as another officer pointed out when discussing convoy work.

Had we taken convoys seriously between the wars something might have been organised on the lines of the later Escort Groups which developed rather than on flotilla lines, but there is no doubt that convoys were relegated to a poor relation and far too little thought to them.

ASDIC (sonar in today's American-based parlance) was thought to hold the key to defence against the submarine but its performance was vastly over-rated pre-war, as was perhaps to be expected with a new weapon. On habitability the comments of the officers who served in the pre-war boats were all similar.

This was a vast improvement on all that had gone before,

for the first time destroyers had a forced draft ventilation system through a punkah-louvre system, larger scuttles and a refrigerator room which would hold, as far as I can remember, about ten days' supply of fresh meat. In earlier destroyers all these hot-weather blessings had been totally lacking.

Another detailed reply revealed:

The mess decks were very slightly roomier, with a better galley and washing facilities, and the officers' quarters were provided for the first time with a long bath in the after superstructure. There was no plumbing of any sort below upper deck level where all cabins and half the messdecks were situated. Nor should there have been – a fractured drain pipe would have resulted in a flooded compartment. The galley was improved but, in the earlier classes at least, still burnt coal.

There were, however, two great improvements made to living conditions. (1) The stinking, noisy old steam capstan engine, which in earlier classes had sat unadorned in the middle of the upper messdeck, was moved to a watertight box on the forecastle deck where it drove two cable-holders and (2) auxiliary electric lighting, powered by a diesel-driven generator situated on the upper deck was installed for use in harbour when boiler fires had been drawn. This supplemented, but did not replace, the oil lamps fixed to the bulkheads in living quarters and passages. The 'wheezy-diesel' as it was universally known, was an animal of very uncertain temperament. Moreover it made the nights in Sliema Creek when the flotillas berthed at Malta, hideous with its unsilenced putterings.

These are the impressions of the pre-war destroyers from the pens of the men who commanded them. How does their viewpoint fit in with the contemporary scene as it appeared to the layman and to the experts locked in the fastness of the Admiralty? What discussions and factors influenced them in those eventful days when the world marched towards war?

British design, as we have seen, was content with only small improvements over the ships that had gone before, but meanwhile the major nations of the world had been going their own way in destroyer design. The French and Italians had found, from experience with ex-German destroyers they had run after the Great War, that an enlarged hull and armament coupled with high speed suited their needs on the Mediterranean sea routes. The French Chacal Class of six ships in the 1922 programme were of 2,126 tons with a designed speed of 35.5 knots and a gun armament of five 5.1-inch guns. Between 1925 and 1929 destroyers were laid down in French yards with tonnage increased to 2,441 tons and the size of gun carried went up to 5.4-inch. In 1930 the six ships of that programme provided a further increase to 2,569 tons and a designed speed of 37 knots while finally the *Mogador* and *Volta* came out with a tonnage of 2,884 tons, a speed of 38 knots and eight 5.4-inch guns, almost in fact light cruisers.

The Italians also had been going for speed and incredible claims were made for some of their destroyers. Critics in Britain decried these speeds as false trials, but experience during the Abyssinian crisis, which later was to be proved over and over again during the war, was that the Italian boats, as heavily armed as our own, could also show British destroyers a clean pair of heels. In Germany rearmament came late but when it did the Germans went straight for 2,170-ton ships armed with five 5-inch guns.

In response finally to this threat the Admiralty, after much discussion, decided to stiffen the traditional destroyer flotillas they were still producing with two flotillas of an enlarged type. These became the Tribals and were hailed as super-destroyers, or destroyers of destroyers, when they were announced. It is a sad fact, however, that despite the ballyhoo which attended their design (on a nominal 1,870-ton displacement and carrying eight 4.7-inch low angled guns), when they entered service they were still far outclassed as surface fighting units by the French ships and easily still outclassed by the Japanese destroyers they had been designed to combat.

The fact was that the Japanese were at least a decade ahead of the Tribals. The twenty units of the Fubuki Class each displaced 2,090 tons and carried six 5-inch guns in splinter-proof turrets. In later units of this class a special 5-inch gun was carried in these turrets, which had an elevation of 70-degrees, thus making it as efficient against aircraft as against surface targets. They also carried nine torpedo tubes with the 24-inch torpedo and in 1933 the introduction of the new 'Long Lance' torpedo with a range of 43,500 yards with a 1,100-lb warhead made the Japanese flotillas the leaders in destroyer design. The Japanese boats carried re-loads for all tubes, which could be readied for firing again in fifteen minutes. All this was achieved by 1930 and subsequent classes saw only further improvements.

By contrast the Tribals carried only four torpedo tubes, and in common with all British destroyers, no re-loads. Their main armament was doubled by twinning the 4.7s but no increase in elevation was obtained and the old system of open-backed shields was continued.

It was not that the British were not alive to the problems of anti-aircraft defence so much but that in every case the priority of the surface role was emphasised to the detriment of heavy AA potential. It was freely admitted at this time that six torpedo-bombers attacking a destroyer of the F Class (built in 1935) was almost certain to sink her. Repeated attempts were made to get at least one or two of the single 4.7-inch mountings carried adapted to elevate higher than 40 degrees but British designers seemed to find the difficulties insurmountable even though the Japanese and Americans had overcome the problems years before. At the same time as the Tribals were being built (to loud cries that they were 'too big for destroyers'), the Americans had the ships of the Porter Class on the stocks carrying eight 5-inch guns in turrets with eight torpedo tubes. Nor was the heavier armament carried by these vessels, and others built earlier, carried at the expense of other factors. In endurance, for example, the British 'Standard' boats were outclassed. Taking the ships completed in 1935 as an example we find the following:

Nation	Destroyer	Tonnage	Guns	Range in knots
Great Britain	Fearless	1,405	4–4.7 (LA)	6,000 miles @ 15
United States	Craven	1,500	4–5 (DP)	9,000 miles @ 15

Following the Tribals, the demand was to revert to a smaller unit again for the fleet, but it was by this time obvious that repeats of the A and Is would not do. After further lengthy discussion with conflicting objectives, the J Class appeared, which as a standard type showed enormous advances over the A to Is. Longitudinally framed for extra strength, single-funnelled and with a low silhouette, on a tonnage of 1,690 tons they carried six 4.7-inch guns, and ten torpedo tubes. Even so, advanced though they were, they were still deficient in anti-aircraft armament. The 4.7-inch twin mountings had been developed but could still only elevate to 40 degrees. The close-range weapons still remained the pom-pom and the machine gun, although almost every other navy had turned away to automatic weapons and the Dutch were developing a fully stabilised automatic anti-aircraft mounting (the Hazemeyer); in Britain the opinion was still that 'eye shooting weapons are sufficient'.

Nevertheless the experience of the Spanish Civil War was not completely ignored and a few muted cries began to be heard by the Admiralty for guns that could cock up higher than 40 degrees and it was belatedly realised that, despite its small size, a destroyer would have to mount (a) a dual-purpose main armament and (b) more efficient close-range weaponry. Thus it was that Vickers Armstrong were told to proceed, as a first step, to design a gun in a closed-in mounting which could elevate to 50 degrees; even now British designers could not obtain the higher elevations common to Japanese destroyers for ten years. Meanwhile Mountbatten was fighting valiantly for the rejection of the old close-range weapons and the adoption of their foreign automatic counterparts. Both battles were eventually won, but both were won too late to prevent grievous loss to British destroyers from aerial attack in the early years of the Second World War. To a great extent the story of the Laforey Class destroyers, in their design, eventual construction and use, is the story of these fights to enable destroyers to stand up to air attack.

But it was quite a different consideration that weighed upon the designers when the Laforeys came to be thought out early in 1937.

On 12 February A.P. Cole, the Head of the Destroyer Section of the DNC, was asked by the Controller if he was underway with the design of the destroyers to be ordered in August 1937. Cole replied that he was still awaiting details of the proposed armament from the DNO's office and that he expected this information the following month. The Controller revealed that these destroyers would be delayed three months, which would give DNC's office sufficient time, and he wished to know whether the new class would be much altered from the Js. The weight of the new 50-degree mounting and guns was considered by Cole to be the crucial factor in determining this and he replied that DNO thought, so far, that each mounting would be about four tons heavier than the twin Mk X, and that in addition they would be HA.

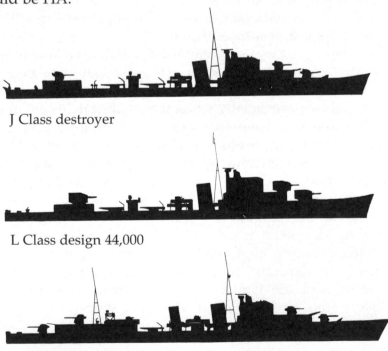

J Class destroyer

L Class design 44,000

Tribal Class destroyer

L Class design 77,000

However, it was not until April that some preliminary work was completed. On the 22nd of that month J.A. Stansfield of the DNC informed Cole that DNC would also wish to know, before the next New Construction meeting to be held on 5 May, by what date tenders could be invited for the L Class destroyers.

In his reply of 29 April Cole incorporated the following points:

> 1. According to a rough outline received from DNC the weight of the new gun, inclusive of the shell hoists, would be forty tons as compared with twenty-nine tons for a J. On a three-turret ship this would involve an increased weight in mountings of some thirty-three tons.
> 2. Because the new mounting was designed for a 62-lb shell, as against a 50-lb shell in the Js, a further additional weight of eight tons per ship would result, plus a similar increase for the heavier cordite charges used, giving a total of fourteen tons per ship.
> 3. Another weight consideration was that of the revolving bulk of the new mounting, which would need heavier pumps of approximately five tons. The total increase in deep condition over the J Class he estimated as fifty-nine tons.

Nor was this the end of the matter for he revealed that Captain Roger Bellairs (ADSJD), had indicated that there was a strong call from the fleet for an increase in speed; a figure of 33 knots in deep condition was suggested, which was one knot more than allowed for the J design.

Finally, the large increase in deck weight gave rise to concern, Cole felt, on account of the rise in G.[1] To ensure reasonable stability it would be necessary to increase the weight of the machinery, quite apart from the speed requirement, and he felt a three boiler design was essential.

Cole summed up by saying that these considerations made it clear that a larger ship than the Tribals would be required if the new weatherproof mountings as were then being designed were to be fitted. These, *in themselves*, would not necessarily increase the length of the vessels, but to accommodate them the beam would increase by two feet and the length in proportion must therefore also go up. He considered therefore that the Laforeys would mean a complete departure from the J design and would require detailed investigation. He added that until the Tribals were finished in early 1938 this could not be seriously considered and that an estimated nine to twelve months would be required to produce the drawings and specifications.

Initial work was also expected to be modified to examine the current ideas being utilised in the construction of a new design of destroyer that Messrs Yarrow had under construction for the USSR. On 1 July Sir Harold Yarrow took these designs to show the Controller. He also promised to provide particulars of the French *Le Triomphant*, which was attracting much interest, with particular respect to their propellers. Should an enlarged destroyer be finally decided upon for the Royal Navy such details were essential.

At the end of the same month DNC instructed that the legends and silhouettes for two designs be prepared.

Because of the various treaties which we had become embroiled with, the need to achieve a desirable balance was the most difficult problem faced by British designers in the late 1930s and silhouettes for two designs were prepared. These were:

| L.44. | 44,000 SHP | 36 knots Standard | 32 knots Deep |
| L.70. | 70,000 SHP | 40 knots Standard | 35 knots Deep |

There was not time to prepare sketch designs but the silhouettes of both compared with a J and a Tribal were submitted (see Diagram 1, page 26, and on 30 July 1937 Mr Stansfield for the DNC submitted the Legend forms.

He added the following points:

1. In the L.44 the oil had been fitted abreast the after magazine and shell room and also abaft the cut-up. He did not consider this desirable in a longitudinally framed ship because of the complicated structure at the cut-up. The L.44 design had no margin of stability or of trim for any possible increase in armament weight. (This, it was known from previous experience, was inevitable and was to provide the DNC with many headaches before the Laforeys took to the water.)

2. In L.70 he considered that a complete re-design of stern would be necessary to take the propellers and the larger rudder. It was thought that this might adversely affect the speed.

In both designs, on account of the height of the centre of gravity of the ship because of the heavier gun mountings, the heel on turning at full speed was thought likely to be excessive, especially in the L.70 at forty knots! These ships would be uncomfortable in a seaway due to the shallow draught and high CG. It was also felt that the modified stern and great length of the L.70 would also reduce manoeuvrability at moderate speed and it was expected that her turning circle would be far greater than a normal destroyer.

Commander Hughes-Hallett of the DNO stated unofficially on 31 July that his department would be in favour of a two-mounting design to enable them to reduce the weight of mountings as it would then be necessary to make them blast-proof.

The following figures were also given with regard to the 40-knot destroyer called for.

Stability

GM	3.12 ft (2.55 ft Deep)
Max GZ	1.16 ft at 340
Range	60 degrees

Weights (estimated)

	Standard	Deep
Hull	1,200	1,200
Machinery	935	935
Equipment	105	170
Armament	260	290
Oil fuel	–	600
R F W	–	70
Giving totals of	2,500	3,265

Speed

On the basis of the Tribal form estimated speeds were:

Standard	40 knots at 70,000 SHP with PC = 0.52
	" " at 72,500 = 0.50
Deep	35½ " at 70,000 = 0.50
	36 " at 70,000 = 0.52

The E-in-C stated unofficially 'that he might be able to get 72,500 out of machinery'.

Owing to the high speed called for it would be necessary either to adopt twin rudders or, alternatively, a semi-balanced rudder. The ordinary spade rudder of the dimensions required would be difficult to fit in the ship. It was estimated that 122 feet diameter propellers would be required. In this case it was thought likely that a cruiser stern would have to be adopted, which would in turn affect the speed. With regard to the layout of armament the forward guns were 10 feet further aft from the bow than the Tribals or the Js but were otherwise similar.

In a letter to the Controller enclosing these figures DNG emphasised the particular problems as unearthed by the preliminary investigation.

With the L.44 stability was the principal trouble especially the need for the Leader's increased topweight on what was described as 'an already neat arrangement'! It was thought that the support of the after mounting should be fitted further forward than in the Js.

Regarding the L.70 it was stated that the E-in-C 'helped us tremendously' by agreeing to a three-boiler arrangement. He also modified the engine-room scheme to provide two engines abreast, 'instead of a nasty staggering arrangement'. With regard to the propeller problems DNC was confident 'We can do what the French have done but I want to go one better...'. Seaworthiness they felt would compare with a First World War Arethusa Class cruiser for dryness, but was expect to roll more.

The estimated costs were £685,000 for the L.44 and £905,000 for the L. 70.

On 8 September two further designs were considered to reach the high speed demanded and were submitted to the Controller.

	SHP	Equipment	Machinery	Armament	Hull
L.72	72,000	110 tons	960	335	1,320
L.90	90,000	130 ton	1,200	395	1,480

This gave the totals respectively of 2,745 and 3,205 tons.

This placed L.72 into Sub-Category C of the Washington Treaties and L.90 in Sub-Category B.

Other details were:

Length	420 ft	475 ft
Speed	35 Deep	36½ Deep
	39½ Standard	40+ Standard

	L.72	L.90
Armament	Four twin 4.7-inch One quad .661" M.G. Two quad 21" TT	Four twin 4.7-inch Two Mk-M quad pom-poms Two quad .661" MG Two quad 21" TT

There was no TSDS or minelaying in either.

On seeing these figures the Controller immediately 'ruled L.90 out of court', because the 1937 Programme provided for Destroyers, Sub-Category C, not Light Cruisers Sub-Category B.

This is an interesting point for the L.90 would have been an ideal vessel as things turned out, especially from an anti-aircraft point of view. It was equipped with eight dual-purpose 4.7-inch guns in weatherproof mountings, two quad pom-poms and two heavy multiple machine guns, as well as a strong torpedo armament and an excess of 40 knots.

It is interesting to note that the 1930 London Naval Treaty, to which earlier destroyers had been bound, laid down that they were not to have a standard displacement exceeding 1,850 tons nor to carry a gun above 5.1-inch. However, the 1936 Treaty allowed, under Sub-Category C, not destroyers as such, for they were not listed, but *Light Surface Vessels*, which did not carry a gun exceeding 6.1-inch and a standard displacement not greater than 3,000 tons. One gets the impression that here the Treaty was being used as a smokescreen to cover the dismay at the enormous cost such a ship as the L.90 would put the nation to.

With regard the L.72 design the Controller was told that the design had not yet been gone into. The opinion of the Fourth Sea Lord was generally favourable and ACNS, (Commander Holland), also expressed a favourable opinion. He asked if the necessary wireless for a cruiser function by these ships in the A–K line could be added to the design and was told it could. The draught to the tips of the blades was estimated at sixteen feet. With L.90 out of the way DNC submitted the following:

Length of Machinery

Type	SHP spaces	Breakdown	
L.72	72,000	80 (Engine Room)	2 Engine Rooms
		101 (Boiler Room)	4 Boiler Rooms
L.60	60,000	70 (Engine Room)	2 Engine Rooms
		95 (Boiler Room)	3 Boiler Rooms

L.56	56,000	57½ (Engine Room)	1 Engine Room 82 (Boiler Room)
		1 Gearing Room	3 Boiler Rooms
L.44	44,000	56½ (Engine Room)	1 Engine Room
		65 (Boiler Room)	1 Gearing Room 2 Boiler Rooms

On 20 July E-in-C had stated that he hoped to get 60,000 (and possibly 63,000 SHP) in a single engine room thereby reducing the length by twelve feet. It was also recorded that these boiler-room lengths were guaranteed but that as a result of forcing trials in *Imogen* and *Icarus* it might in the future be possible to reduce by about one foot in each.

The E-in-C also stated that he had been consulted with regard to Yarrow's side-fired boilers as fitted in the Russian destroyer design. A request to inspect the drawings had been refused by the company although E-in-C, Commander Maclean had noted that the *Grenville*'s boilers were too large to be fitted in such a side-by-side arrangement as that utilised by Yarrow.

On 16 August the Controller had sent ACNS a covering letter with the first two legends. He stated that his object in calling on DNC for the two designs was that, on looking ahead, he saw a reasonable possibility of the MTB type of small craft appearing in large numbers. He compared this development with that of the rapid increase of torpedo boats towards the end of the nineteenth century, which led to a counter in the form of the torpedo gunboats, the forerunners of the modern destroyer. Should such a development occur he wished to survey the type of ship needed to counter it in the same way.

He made two points: 1) that as the speeds of battleships were increasing destroyer speeds must also rise to achieve rapid tactical dispositions; 2) that the cost of an enlarged destroyer type would be beyond the financial reach of the Royal Navy if 5,000-ton cruiser types were also perpetuated. The estimated cost of the L.70 design destroyer was put at £905,000 compared with £1,850,000 for a new Dido Class cruiser. The Navy could therefore have more L.70s for the same cost as additional Didos and he felt that the former would be more suitable to perform with the existing A–K line.

This policy he felt was economical both in initial cost and in maintenance as personnel for L.70s would be less than for Didos and he envisaged a time in the not too distant future when the rearmament programme would taper down to about ninety million pounds. He considered the Dido Class cruisers 'the most valuable adjunct to the Fleet, but, having got them I think we should confine ourselves to the L.70 Class.'

He anticipated the criticism that these destroyers would be held to be too big and suggested calling them light cruisers or something similar. He concluded that he would be glad of early remarks as there was a large amount of work in DNC's department to do once the design was chosen and he was anxious to avoid the situation which arose with the J Class when in effect orders were placed with problems still outstanding.

Ten days later ACNS added his comments. He identified the main problems as:

1. What were the consequences of the destruction of the speed balance of the Fleet due to the high speed of the projected capital ships?
2. If as a result of this first point it was decided to build faster, and therefore necessarily larger, destroyers, could this be offset by a reduction in the number of Didos?
3. Which was the most suitable design for adoption, L.70 or L.44? With regard to the first point he confirmed that the Staff had been concerned for some time about the speed balance of the fleet. The existing battle tactics had been evolved in a large measure from experience gained in a fleet in which cruisers had an excess of speed over battleships of about 8 knots and destroyers 10 knots. Quoting from CB 1815, he gave the following table to explain how that in the future this margin would no longer exist.

Country	Estimated future battlefleet speed (deep)	Average margin of speed over (ii) of their own – battlefleet		
		Cruisers	Destroyers	Aircraft Carrier
Britain	27	+4	+4.75	+2.75
France	28	+3.25	+4.0	
Germany	27	+2.75	+4.0	
Italy	29	+4.8	+3.6	
Japan	25	+6.5	+5.0	+2.8
USA	26	+5.75	+5.9	+5.2

In order to implement the present tactical theories it was considered that the deep speed of future ships should be:

Carriers	35 knots
Cruiser	35 knots
Destroyers	36–37 knots

He pointed out that the margin of speed over potential enemy capital ships was equally important as over our own. While realising that such deep condition speeds would be difficult to obtain for the carriers and cruisers they were perfectly attainable in the 'ships of the large destroyers (light cruiser) type'.

This speed margin was especially essential in the day torpedo attack. This exercise was still the backbone of all British destroyer exercises in the late thirties and it was to fulfil precisely this function that the destroyers of the A to K Classes (with the exception of the Tribals) had been built.

The absence of a speed margin, he pointed out, greatly increased the already high degree of risk attached to such a manoeuvre. While this tactic was reducing in value as battle fleets became sparser and speedier and the role of the destroyer would ultimately be taken over by torpedo-bombers and enlarged MTB types, these were at present not available in sufficient quantities, nor were they reliable enough; therefore the old tactic must be that on which the design had to be based.

This was by no means the only consideration in fleet working where high speed was vital, therefore a higher speed in future destroyers was of the greatest moment.

The Dido Class cruisers were then analysed as to their performance in the role of fleet cruisers whose duties would be:

Reconnaissance
Screening
Shadowing
AA defence of the Fleet
Support of light forces

The Didos were of limited use in the first role, e.g. to fight their way through enemy cruiser opposition, as in a surface capacity they were inferior to all foreign types except the Japanese Natori Class. (It should be noted, however, that the Japanese used their smaller cruisers not in this role but as flotilla leaders, in much the same way as the British had before the First World War.) Air reconnaissance, it was felt, would enable cruisers of the Dido type to form some effective *concentration* prior to undertaking this task in a future conflict.

In consideration of the L.70 destroyers, only in the last two requirements did they fall below the Didos in the roles outlined above. Therefore if they were to replace the small cruiser the L.70s were not large enough. In AA performance the adoption of the 62-pdr gun and 50-degree elevation was an advance over the Tribals, but fell far short of the Didos (which mounted ten 5.25-inch guns), but for surface fighting the reduction to six guns meant a comparable broadside of 372 lbs for the L.70 to 400 lbs in a Tribal. This was regarded as unacceptable. The design of the large French destroyers was considered and the conclusion reached was for the Ls to mount an ideal armament of six 5.25-inch guns in twin turrets. The minimum armament was listed as:

Eight 4.7-inch 62-pdr guns in four twin 50-degree mountings
    eight torpedoes in two quadruple tubes
Eight 2-pdr Mk M pom-poms
Twelve 661-inch machine guns in two six-barrelled
    mountings

The possibility of such a ship being adaptable for minelaying was also brought forward.

It was suggested that the design of such a ship be considered and that if it was practical from a Treaty tonnage point of view then the dropping of three Didos from the 1938 and 1939 programme be considered. With the improved armament the 'Modified L.70s' would meet both the fleet cruiser requirement and form a speed margin flotilla. Ten such ships costing one million pounds each would cost less than eight improved Js and the three Didos and he considered the fleet would be stronger by having ships of the required speed. Having thus put the cat among the pigeons, the following detailed comments were made on the L.70 design as specified other than the main armament.

The single .661-inch mounting was considered inadequate for close-range armament. On G.03774-36 it was pointed out that unless trials of the new six-barrel .661-inch gun proved that it was of a definite superiority over the Mk M pom-pom then the retention of the pom-pom was preferred. Even if it was so proven at least two equipments of the new mounting should be carried. He agreed a 22-degree depression of No. 2 mounting when firing ahead could be accepted because of blast problems on No. 1 gunhouse but thought that an increase in endurance would be welcomed. He concluded thus:

> If the Light Cruiser is not accepted as a type, the L.44 design produces a better ship than the J Class since her new weatherproof gun mountings should be workable under more exacting conditions than those of a J and save a total of 17 personnel per ship.

The class was, however, at a disadvantage with regard torpedoes and close-range AA weapons and the reduction to eight torpedoes was depreciated.

This led to the introduction of the L.72 and L.90 designs as mentioned earlier. On 7 September Hughes-Hallett wrote that he had looked into the question of giving the L.70 an extra twin 4.7-inch mounting. This could be done on a standard displacement of 2,750 tons – '...could not be made into a minelayer'. Also, her cost was estimated at £1,150,000. Taking into consideration the cost of personnel, two of these vessels could be built for the same cost as one Dido. He considered it very urgent to get a decision as he feared the flotilla allowed for in the 1937 Estimates would not be laid down in the financial year.

The Director of Plans, Rear-Admiral Philips, added a note to ACNS's minutes that submitted that the whole argument of a 'speed balance' which had to be maintained was open to question.

'The tactical conceptions which underlie our present Battle Instructions did not arise from absolute and immutable laws.' Quite the reverse applied, he continued; the tactical considerations had in their origin the practical fact that for the past fifty years or so it had been technically convenient to build flotillas which were substantially faster than their contemporary line of battle. It did not follow that because modern capital ships had almost caught up that it was automatically essential to 'burst ourselves trying to maintain a speed balance appropriate to an epoch which is passing'. He thought that the soundest and most economical policy would be for a revision of the tactics. 'Battle Instructions are made for ships, not ships for Battle Instructions.'

He argued that to try and maintain this speed balance at the cost of a million pounds per ship was possible, but was it the correct course? He felt it might be more sensible to ignore 'the high speed freaks', of foreign navies and build more capital ships ourselves. They could only be threatened by expensive and larger light vessels which were in themselves vulnerable. An enemy would find construction of such vessels expensive while we would find that the greater our margin in capital ships the more risks we could expose them to. Any paper increase in speed of future light craft would in any case always be nullified in heavy weather, where the large ships of the line could always maintain their 27 knots but light craft would have to fall behind.

By constructing large expensive light craft, which would always be exposed to superior fire power, Britain automatically restricted the resources available for constructing the most powerful ships possible upon which the ultimate conclusion would always rest. 'It would indeed be an expensive luxury to pay nearly half a million pounds for an extra 3½ knots.' He did not rule out the merging of the large destroyer and light cruiser types. This was, however, a problem for next year's flotilla as the urgency of proceeding with rearmament would not permit waiting for yet another design. He considered the practical choice was that of repeating the Js or going ahead with either L.44 or L.70. He favoured the L.44 but with improved close-range armament.

The CNS commented on 9 September that he had read all these papers and asked his DCNS to 'consider them during my absence.' He thought a joint discussion with Controller and ACNS would be valuable. He considered it 'distinctly disturbing' that they were now being asked to consider building destroyers of 2,750 tons. 'This seems to be rather going off the deep end.' It had already been decided two years before that a destroyer must be a destroyer and a cruiser a cruiser and that hybrids were always failures. The only thing gained, he felt, was an additional 4 knots available only in good weather. He thought ACNS arguments on speeds 'fallacious'.

He drew attention to the fact that fast battleships (Queen Elizabeth Class – 25 knots) had been in service for twenty years and that battle-cruisers with speeds of 28 to 32 knots had been available for a similar period of time without any serious difficulty with regard to the speed of their escorts. Further, with regard to stopping craft of the MTB type, 'numbers of guns were needed', and yet, he pointed out, no increase was expected from L.44 or L.70 and the 2-pdr was given up for the .661 machine gun. He ended by stating:

> The purse strings are going to close; bigger ships mean more men (it was overlooked that the new 4.7-inch mounting would save 17 men per ship), more maintenance, more fuel. The more money we put into small ships the less we shall have available for big ones.

Before leaving for Geneva CNS arranged for a meeting to be held to thrash this problem out and it was fixed for 14 September 1937.

The discussion was duly held and in it a number of varying problems that had been talked over before were again brought out and dusted. The Controller opened the discussion by referring to the time when the Naval Estimates would be back to 'ninety millions' again once re-armament was completed. 'At present time including the 1937 programme we had 196 destroyers. In 1914 – 220.'

He could not visualise a repeat of the Battle of Jutland with either Germany or Japan. He questioned the value therefore of both light cruisers and the A–K line, which had been built for solely this threat.

DCNS agreed. He thought the day torpedo attack, 'if not mythical, is fading out of the picture'. He foresaw that the combination of faster capital ships and manoeuvrability of the battle line would soon force the destroyers to revert to their original role, that of night torpedo attack. For this role small handy ships were more suitable. He saw destroyers as night vessels rather than day vessels, excepting in their anti-submarine role. The Controller thought speed was essential and stated that a recent meeting with officers of the Fleet on destroyer policy had resulted in a universal cry for speed. There followed a long discussion on the value of the extra 4 knots speed in attacking an undamaged enemy fleet by night or a crippled fleet by day.

During this DCNS asked whether British design was to be influenced by foreign vessels.

ACNS pointed out that during the Abyssinian crisis the Italian destroyers as typified by the *Alfredo* with 39 knots could not have been caught. DCNS thought this traditional as the enemy had always built for speed and we for strength. (Nobody at the meeting at this point mentioned Jackie Fisher!)[2]

He asked if we could afford to merge destroyers into the cruiser class and have nothing smaller left for night attacks. The Controller replied that we should have plenty of the larger type.

DCNS then said that if it was then accepted that sufficient were on hand should the cruiser type be kept or replaced by

larger destroyers? Should the L.70 type be built and admitted as
light cruisers? He asked what essential work the Didos carried
out that L.70s could not do. ACNS said that because the Didos
had some protection they would not be vulnerable to destroyer
fire as would the L.70. In addition, the Dido had a better AA
capability. He admitted that with regard to the reconnaissance
role there would not be much between the two. In reply to
further questioning on what function the Didos were capable of
better than destroyers ACNS replied again, 'AA defence of the
fleet.'

The Controller asked whether for the general purposes of
war it would be preferred to have three or four smaller
destroyers rather than one Dido. ACNS replied that he would
prefer to keep a balance between the types, although he would
prefer three or four destroyers to one Dido, in a straight choice.
There was the problem of manning a vast number of large
destroyers. On the basis of wars with Japan and in Europe being
waged at the same time the number of destroyers needed was
sure to be high. He did not foresee a large-scale action against
the German fleet and the modern ships would go east leaving
the older flotillas to see the trade in. He thought that an L.70
would be the best type of destroyer afloat. 'The Tribals are not
superior to everything else; they are about as good.'

DCNS thought it was the old question of whether Britain was
to build with foreign construction in mind or decide on what
would be our most valuable vessel. The Controller rejected the
idea that L.70 was designed with foreign types in mind. He
thought that two L.70s would, for example, be more useful than
one modern equivalent of a C Class cruiser. DCNS thought that
it would be better to drop the Dido concept in future and build
strong cruisers and allow destroyers to grow naturally in size.

The discussion then veered round to the close-range
armament and the Controller emphasised that the new .661-inch
machine gun was definitely only a short-range weapon. He
summed up by stating that in the 1938 programme we were
scheduled to get another sixteen of the smaller type destroyer
with more the following year. He saw little chance of a Jutland

against Germany and only a slim chance of such a fleet action against Japan. He thought they should begin to plan for twenty years ahead. ACNS finished by saying that six L.70s could be built instead of three Didos and would be the best destroyers afloat. He preferred building the Dido but whether this was the best destroyer policy was another matter.

DCNS added a note for the Controller to the typescript of this conversation. He reiterated that the same problem of when to call a halt in growth of small warship types had always beset the Admiralty. The present case with the destroyers he felt was an extreme one. He thought the decision would always ultimately rest on the capability of the type to perform the function allocated to them in war. He could not agree with the prominence given to a daylight attack on an enemy fleet. He stated that Fleet opinion had always been divided on this subject and although an immense amount of thought and work had been given to perfect this manoeuvre it was likely that a first-class maritime war would be waged without it ever taking place successfully.

The day of battle lines that were miles long and misty conditions with flotillas massed ahead for the delivery of this blow were gone. Even in the last war the long awaited massed torpedo attack never occurred. At present with small fast battle lines it was even more unlikely to take place. He concluded that the destroyer must therefore revert once again to a night attack role.

It is a far cry from the Russo–Japanese war, but it is for consideration whether Admiral Togo's tactics are not more in line with today's conditions than they were in the conditions in which the German war was fought. He reserved his night fighting force for night fighting with the results which are familiar to us all.

He repeated that destroyers had other functions to perform but he did not feel at all confident that decisions on tonnage and speed should be influenced by requirements for day attack, nor did he place much faith in the MTBs to take over this role in view of their size and availability. He concluded that he felt it was therefore wrong to allow any large growth in the size of destroyers. They could not in his view replace the fleet cruiser.

These notes were forwarded with the cryptic remark, 'I cannot claim that we have taken the matter very much forward, but the discussion has served to a certain extent to clear the air.' It was decided to send a telegram to the C-in-Cs of the Home and Mediterranean Fleets, wherein were concentrated the bulk of the Fleet destroyer strengths, asking for the viewpoints of all concerned.

This was promptly complied with. The emphasis was to be on whether an improved J was the most suitable type or whether the Fleet thought that something faster, and therefore larger, would suit them best. The message was sent out coded on 27 September.

It stated that the type of destroyer to be built for the second of the approved flotillas for the 1937 programme was under review. In view of the factor of the high speed of current capital ship design, it stated that the question of the speed of existing types of destroyer was questioned. The number of destroyers built or building was listed as eighty-nine of the A and later types, and sixteen of the Tribals, all of which were suitable for working with the existing battle fleet.

Consideration was being given to a design, 'speed 39.1 knots standard or 35 knots deep condition, eight 4.7" guns, 62-lbs projectile, two quadruple tubes, four .661" machine guns or other close range weapons.'

The silhouette was specified as similar to the Tribals except for length, and ability to steam in a seaway as good as an Arethusa. (Although originally taken to be a World War I Arethusa, this was not here stated and could have been taken to mean the 1936 *Arethusa*!) Tonnage was 2,750 and the estimated cost £1,150,000, half that of a Dido cruiser or twice that of a J destroyer. Relative complements were given as Dido 485, Large destroyer 234, Improved J 201. The telegram requested the C-in-Cs' very early views on whether they regarded such a ship as a desirable unit, 'having due regard to its ability to carry out many of the duties now assigned to a small Fleet cruiser'. If they thought the design was a handy ship to have, consideration would be given to reducing the number of Didos building from ten to eight. The alternative was to go for an improved J Class destroyer and accept the relatively low speed of 32 knots in deep condition.

Admiral Sir Roger Backhouse replied from HMS *Rodney* on 4 October. He did not favour the larger ship, which, despite its assets, could be easily disabled by a single hit from a 4.7-inch gun. 'She is not a cruiser and yet would have to do cruisers' work and I think our experience shows that cruisers must be able to stand up to some hitting.'

He thought that the absolute limit for increase in the size of destroyers was around 2,000 tons and preferred a ship with eight guns and six tubes to one with six guns and eight tubes – in other words he favoured a Tribal type ship for gun power. He thought that there was a modern tendency to put too much into destroyers. This resulted in cramped deck space and loss of efficiency as numerous subsidiary duties like TSDS placed too much strain on a limited crew. He thought that if such unnecessary weights could be removed more important things like endurance could be increased. He was against any reduction in the number of new cruisers and drew attention to the fact that the old C Class cruisers were at the end of their value.

He thought that what was required was two types of destroyer, one for fleet work and one for escort duties. He therefore came down in favour of an improved J.

C-in-C Mediterranean Admiral Sir Dudley Pound sent in his reply two days later. After full consultation with his flotilla officers he thought that the premier consideration was to have large numbers of destroyers, as, in the Great War and the Abyssinian Crisis, there were never enough. 'In certain war plans which are now under review the same shortage of destroyers is apparent.' If the 2750 type were built this would only accentuate the shortage.

Nor was he convinced that the 'Super-Destroyer' as a type was particularly of merit and he stated that the French Liaison Officer with his fleet had told him that they were ceasing construction of these vessels after the Mogadors as they had been found too unwieldy to handle in flotilla attacks. He thought that the introduction of 29-knot battleships was nothing new and cited the battle-cruisers. 'The destroyer will never be able to keep up with capital ships in all weathers however large they may be.'

He preferred a large number of improved Js so that he could station half his destroyers on either wing with certainty of getting half of them in the van after deployment.

First Sea Lord Admiral of the Fleet Sir Ernle Chatfield minuted that the views of the two C-in-Cs were similar to his own as expressed earlier: 'We must keep a cruiser a cruiser and a destroyer a destroyer.' He thought that Admiral Backhouse made a valid point on the two different types of destroyer and that this question required careful analysis. He thought that one half of the destroyers built would be directly attached to the Battle Fleet and that the others would be mainly used as anti-submarine escorts or on patrol duties. By building solely with Fleet duties in mind we had incurred a great expense. He thought the conference should consider the following points:

1. Whether the Tribals should be repeated.
2. Whether the Js should be repeated.
3. Whether an improved larger and faster J was required.
4. Whether a reversion to the I Class should be considered.
5. Whether two separate types were now feasible.

He went on: It seems to me therefore that a decision has to be made on principle first. *What do we want*, and what can we afford?'

A further meeting was arranged, but a note by Hughes-Hallett dated the 6th anticipated the result: 'DNC is working at the design of the improved J.'

The final meeting took place on 13 October and present were the First Sea Lord, DCNS, Controller, ACNS, DNC and DNO. It was generally agreed here that the 'powerful gun type' of destroyer would have to be limited to four flotillas and it was also agreed that this was the type which was needed at the

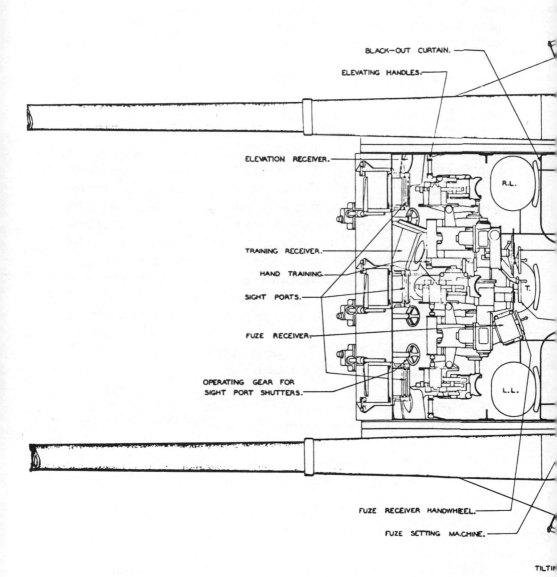

BLACK—OUT CURTAIN.

ELEVATING HANDLES.

ELEVATION RECEIVER.

R.L.

TRAINING RECEIVER.

HAND TRAINING.

SIGHT PORTS.

T.

FUZE RECEIVER.

OPERATING GEAR FOR
SIGHT PORT SHUTTERS.

L.L.

FUZE RECEIVER HANDWHEEL.

FUZE SETTING MACHINE.

TILTI

Plan of Gunhouse

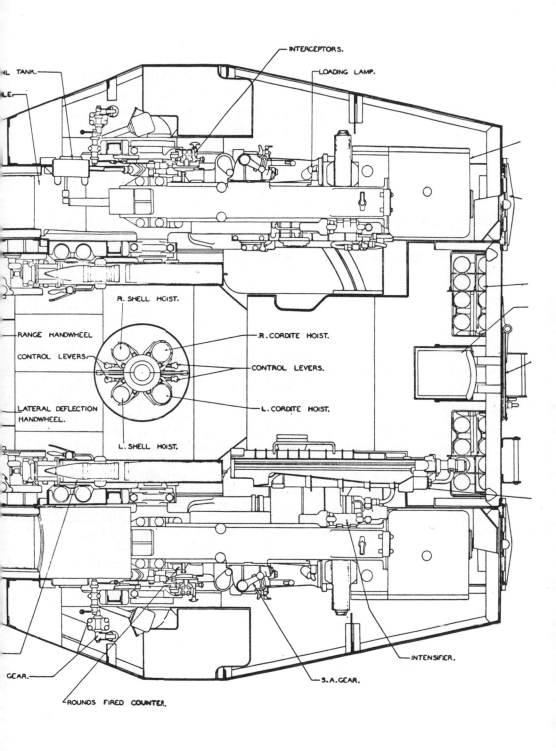

INTERCEPTORS.

LOADING LAMP.

L TANK.

LE.

R. SHELL HOIST.

RANGE HANDWHEEL

R. CORDITE HOIST.

CONTROL LEVERS.

CONTROL LEVERS.

LATERAL DEFLECTION HANDWHEEL.

L. CORDITE HOIST.

L. SHELL HOIST.

INTENSIFIER.

GEAR.

S.A. GEAR.

ROUNDS FIRED COUNTER.

moment. The L.40 was considered suitable with the exception of the .661-inch machine gun, which would not cover the gap between the high and low-level bombing. Nor was it as handy as the pom-pom as an anti-MTB weapon. This probably decided the fate of this mounting, which never saw production.

Opinion was divided on the torpedo armament, one quadruple mounting being thought sufficient by First Sea Lord, DCNS and ACNS, DNC undertook forthwith to complete the design for the first of the L flotillas to be armed accordingly and for the design to mount two pom-poms or one pom-pom and a .661-inch mounting. And so it was arranged, but the arguments were far from over.

Notes

1. G refers to the stability of the ships. The vertical distribution of the weight, guns, machinery, torpedo tubes, determine the ship's centre of gravity (CG). The higher this CG the more 'top-heavy' becomes the ship and the possibility of capsizing increases in heavy weather. This is controlled by the designers fixing the metacentre (M) at the most appropriate level to compensate for these top weights.

This can be done by changes in hull design (i.e. giving the ship greater beam etc.). The distance between this metacentre and the centre of gravity is calculated from the initial detailed drawings and gives the Metacentric Height (GM). These factors relative to the stability of the ship and various compromises required to achieve it are often loosely referred to as G.

A higher G factor gives a more unstable ship and a poor gun platform. A lower G factor makes the ship squat in the water, which is obviously the better gun deck but results in a loss of speed and increased displacement. This latter point is important as displacement was restricted by numerous international treaties.

2. Admiral 'Jackie' Fisher was a very famous naval officer of the early twentieth century who reformed the Royal Navy in time for the First World War. One of his most controversial ideas was 'speed is armour', embodied by the battle-cruiser concept. It may seem strange to some naval historians that, just a mere two decades on from this, his view of things was not even mentioned in these discussions.

Chapter 2

Planning and Building the Ships

While the design was being worked out during the last three months of 1937 several factors arose which necessitated the readjustment of the final decisions taken at these conferences.

It had already been noted that the rise of G coupled with the increase in speed in the submitted designs would increase the tendency to heel on turning. In comparison with the *Greyhound* this was worked out at a 50 per cent increase in the L.60 design and involved a large metacentric height, which was estimated to be 4 feet in the L.60 compared with 22 feet in *Greyhound*. This metacentric height was also necessary to maintain the one foot GZ in light condition. Stability problems were by no means lessened with the final design. Everything depended on the final weights of the new mountings and the final decision on boilering arrangements for the machinery. During September discussions and exchanges of correspondence took place with Yarrows on a four boiler arrangement to give 70,000 SHP but with the adoption of the smaller design these came to nothing.

The C-in-C Home Fleet, Admiral Backhouse, also had second thoughts and wrote to the Controller that although he and Admiral Pound were more or less in agreement on the new destroyers, he felt that '1650 [tons] was sufficiently large for a destroyer'.

On 25 October Mr Stansfield and Mr Cole visited Vickers to inspect a mock-up of the new 4.7-inch gun, which was being worked-out at Barrow. Also present were the DDNO, Engineer

R.A. Little, Engineer Captain Whyham, Engineer Captain Johns, Commander Hughes-Hallett and the Gun Mountings Overseer. They decided from the inspection that the height of the shield could be reduced by three inches by a re-arrangement of the roof supports, thus gaining a slight concession on weight.

The unhappy 0.661-inch machine-gun mounting was also studied on this date. The weight of this mounting in its mock-up form was given as four tons, 15-cwt and this compared very unfavourably with the original figure of 2.75 tons given by DNO and the 3.4 tons estimated in the L.48 design. The weight of ammunition came out at 7½ cwts for 1,200 rounds. Other figures produced for calculation were a roller path diameter of 64 inches, working radius of gun muzzle of 74½ inches and a platform radius of 74 inches. The CG of the mounting was given as four feet above the roller path and a crew number was put at five. The seating was the same as for the 2-pdr pom-pom.

No other details are given and it would appear that these high weights for the same weight of fire as the 0.5-inch machine gun, coupled with reservations about the production time of the new weapon, finally killed off this gun.

Similarly, E-in-C was informed on 22 October that the Controller had decided to allot Yarrows an L Class destroyer to build with side-fired boilers. This was also subsequently dropped following detailed studies and a note dated 4 December was passed to DNC which stated that the margin of stability in the L Class destroyers was not sufficient to permit any increase in weight or rise of the CG of their machinery. The further additional weights of boilering also involved a loss of 1-knot in speed in light and ¼-knot in deep conditions. It concluded that neither of these two proposals could therefore be accepted in the design.[1]

However, it was the new weight of the gun mountings then revealed by Vickers which caused the most heartburn at the Admiralty. On 25 November it prompted the question from Stansfield that perhaps the L.48 design should be abandoned and the Ls then built as repeat Js until the Mark XX mounting was more nearly approaching a state of production.

The view given by Vickers was that they could not state precisely the final weight and this was remarked upon at the Admiralty as 'disturbing'.

Goodall reached a temporary solution in a memo dated 10 December. Vickers were to be instructed to work to 41.65 and 42.4 tons' weight on the new mounting. The firm was told that this was a critical figure due to weight and centre of gravity considerations and that if, as work progressed, they felt liable to exceed these figures then they were to forward an immediate report.

Almost immediately Goodall was advising the First Sea Lord, on 14 January 1938, that 'further particulars concerning the 4.7-inch weatherproof mountings have been supplied, with the result that it has been found necessary to increase the size of the ship'. This entailed, he continued, a reduction in speed from 33 to 32½ knots in deep condition. Thus even before the design was finalised the high hopes earlier expressed of a high-speed vessel were rudely cut down.

On 31 December it was stated that the general arrangement of the 0.661-inch mounting was still not available, but the outline of the new combined DCT for destroyers, also to be built by Vickers, had been received unofficially on 6 November and that the new design of destroyer bridge was being worked out. Mr Harris had agreed to 10-foot 9-inch diameter propellers and the stern lines were being worked out in this respect while a further design of the stern for fitting twin rudders had been completed and was being studied.

A proposal was received on 25 October to fit the Denny Stabiliser in one L Class destroyer. Figures supplied were:

1. Period of roll – G Class 8 seconds; Tribal 9 seconds;
   L   Class – 9½ seconds.
2. Speed for stabilising – 28 knots.

The reply received from S.V. Goodall said that there was no point fitting stabilisers until trials with *Wakeful* were over. With regard to welding to save weight the following information appeared on 31 December on the welding of the oil-tight bulkheads.

Prior to the Tribals it was stated that firms were allowed a practically free hand in welding bulkheads, the bulkheads being designed and specified as riveted bulkheads. Longitudinal bulkheads were of 6 and 5.5 lbs and traverse bulkheads of 7 and 6.6 lbs. When defects in the long segments of the G and H Class destroyers were found, overseers were requested to arrange for the longitudinal bulkheads of the I Class to be riveted. Only two vessels were in the stage of construction that allowed this to be done. A conference was held between the shipbuilders and the DDNC in January 1936 when the policy of welding bulkheads was discussed and it was there agreed that the boundary bulkheads of oil-fuel tanks, fresh-water tanks and reserve-feed tanks for future destroyers should be welded. The minimum weight of plate for welding was to be 7 lbs. Anything thinner than this was to be riveted.

This still held good for the Ls.

The sketch design and proposed armament were submitted on 10 January 1938. In working out the design it was stated, DNC found that, as a result of more detailed particulars of the 4.7-inch weatherproof mounting, the standard displacement would now come out at 1,905 tons. (The Tribals were given as 1,885 tons.) The exact provision to be made for the HA armament and the torpedo tubes was stated as being 'still not clear'. The drawing (see page 26) enclosed with the report showed the ship carrying one four-barrelled Mark M pom-pom and one .661-inch multiple machine gun, but provision was made to enable a set of quadruple tubes to be quickly fitted in place of the .661-inch mounting.

The following points, it was revealed, had made themselves clear since the decision on the design.

1. The quadruple pom-pom mounting allowed for in the design could not be delivered, without robbing the other services, until nine to twelve months after the flotilla was completed.

2. The six-barrelled .661-inch machine gun was still an untried weapon and its ability to stop aircraft was in doubt, although the chances of hitting were considerably greater than the four-barrelled pom-pom. The conclusion

reached was that it would have been better to allow for an extra pom-pom in lieu. Anyway, neither the second pom-pom nor the .661-inch would be available until 1942!

The conclusion reached in this depressing summary was that the Ls would be in commission for a year without any short-range weapons at all and would not be fully equipped for a further year. Hughes-Hallett therefore proposed that the initial close-range armament should be two .5-inch machine gun mountings and that two quadruple torpedo mountings should be shipped. The ships could subsequently revert to short-range HA as originally intended or be fitted with at least one pom-pom. Such an initial armament would have the merit of not adding to the difficulties in deciding the proportion of gun-type destroyers to battle-type destroyers to be kept immediately available for peacetime duties. One final word of cheer for the Admiralty was that the complement of the L as it stood would be at least thirty less than that of a J.

The note on the .661-inch machine gun was not favourably received. 'It is considered that, if aimed in the right direction, the .661-inch m.g. will get many more hits than an equally well aimed 4 barrelled pom-pom.' It was conceded, however, that the aiming apparatus of the .661-inch was inferior to the pom-pom and the effect of hits very considerably less. It was therefore suggested that, subject to any change in view resulting from the .661-inch machine gun trials, it would be preferable to mount two quadruple pompoms rather than one pom-pom and one .661-inch.

With regard to the production difficulties, a seemingly insurmountable obstacle, the following armament stages were put forward:

1. Two quadruple torpedo tubes and two 0.5-inch machine guns.
2. Two quadruple torpedo tubes, one quadruple pom-pom with directors (the .5-inch machine guns to be removed if necessary).
3. Forward tubes be removed and a further quadruple pom-pom fitted.

If Stage 1 was adopted there was the question of fitting power-worked torpedo tubes. This was seen as desirable if Stage 3 was implemented but not essential if *both* sets of tubes were ultimately retained. This would be a question answered by the performance of the Tribals with only one set of tubes. The summing up was strangely optimistic considering the gloomy forecasts on armament difficulties. ACNS wrote:

> These ships should be fine fighting units, and adverse criticism is only likely to be directed to their large silhouette, unavoidable with the weatherproof mountings, and to the poor W/T performance, unavoidable if the main mast could not be fitted.

The Controller replied in a note to First Sea Lord on 21 January 1938. The term 'poor' as applied to the W/T performance he felt was hardly the correct one. The W/T performance might admittedly be improved if there were a mainmast fitted. In theory there should be a 5 per cent loss of efficiency in transmitting and more in reception, 'but that the loss actually exists in fact has yet to be proved'. As the weatherproof mountings had raised the CG to the limits the acceptance of an extra 1¼ tons in the ships was unacceptable. The absence of a mainmast had already been accepted in the Js and Ks. The First Lord approved on the 25 January the design as proposed in the hope that production possibilities in the future would overcome the black outlook of the close-range armament. S.V. Goodall added the standard 'Noted for compliance', on 4 February.

The Drawings and Legend were submitted for Board Approval together with the General Description on 26 March. It was noted that the remaining Building Drawings would not be completed until about 9 April. This involved difficulties in placing the tenders with the firms concerned but Goodall was able to overcome this problem as will be related.

The following points were made in the General Description. The leader and the destroyers of the L flotilla, as in the case of the Js, were to have the same dimensions and thus form a homogeneous flotilla. The leader would have a slightly greater displacement owing to increased complement, larger cabin accommodation and more extensive W/T equipment.

The main difference between the Ls and the Js was of course the adoption of the main gun armament, which was to consist of six 4.7-inch guns in three twin weatherproof mounting with central hoists power-worked. The guns were capable of 50-degree elevation instead of 40 and firing a 62-lb projectile (which incidentally was heavier than the standard German 5-inch shell then being mounted in their current programme), instead of 50 lbs. The heavier armament was the reason for the increased size of the ship but involved a smaller complement. It was added that due to the considerable weight and high centre of gravity of this type of mounting which formed a critical feature of the design, should the estimated weights as supplied by DNO be exceeded it would be necessary to consider compensating for the extra by reduction of topweight. How this was to be done was not specified at this time.

It had been decided as we have seen that the armament would consist of two quadruple pom-poms instead of one pom-pom and one .661-inch machine gun but that two quadruple torpedo tubes be shipped until the pom-pom supply situation had cleared itself.

The control of the main armament was provided by the new combined HA/LA director control tower, which incorporated the rangefinder. Positions had been arranged for directors to control the pom-poms, but until these were available provision had been made to ship 0.5-inch machine guns in their place.

To accommodate the heavy armament it had been necessary to increase the beam over the J Class from 35 feet 8 inches to 36 feet 9 inches and the freeboard compared with the Js was reduced by 7 inches. It was held that owing to the vessels being of larger size and the complement less, the accommodation should prove superior to that of previous destroyers.

The Board finally approved the Legend and Drawings for the Laforeys in a minute dated 7 April, 1938.

As the final drawings were not completed at this time

however (Goodall approached the firms who would be invited to tender in similar letters written on 7 January and in them he explained that the orders had to be placed before the end of the financial year but that completed drawings would not be ready before at least the end of March). Therefore the Official Letters of Invitation to Tender would be sent out on 8 March and they would contain an invitation for the firms concerned to send representatives to the Admiralty in the period 9–17 March to take such notes and information as they required for tendering. The tenders themselves would have to be submitted by 19 March.

Goodall conceded that the scheme as outlined above would not give the firms involved sufficient time, and he therefore proposed that they send someone to the Admiralty on 18 January where they could receive proof copies of the Specification Parts I and V and take such particulars of the drawings as they required so that they could make preliminary enquiries regarding sub-contracting work. Thus armed they could put in their tenders a week after receipt of invitation, on 9 March. The Engineer-in-Chief promised to supply the full machinery details at the same time. The following firms took the details:

Alexander Stephen	Cammell Laird	Swan Hunter
J.S. White	Hawthorn Leslie	Scotts
J.I. Thorneycroft	Fairfield	John Brown
Vickers Armstrong	Parsons	Yarrow

The following firms applied for machinery contracts:

Wallsend Slipway Co.	Parsons Marine	John Brown
Vickers Armstrong	J.I. Thornycroft	Alexander Stephen
Hawthorn Leslie	Scotts	Yarrow
Cammell Laird	J.S. White	William Denny

The lowest tenders received in order of price (lowest first) were: Yarrow; Parsons (with Hawthorn Leslie's built hulls); Scotts and Cammell Laird. The extra quoted for the Leader was £5,000 (Yarrow); £5,200 (Parsons); £5,225 (Scotts) and £5,250 (Cammell Laird). The orders were placed as above solely on costs, although there is still a tale going round the L Class survivors that Parsons pointed out that they always supplied the turbines and never got a whole ship and that hence they were allowed two destroyers, with hulls sub-contracted out, in way of acknowledgement.

The Official Letters of Acceptance contained the following paragraph, which every other nation in the world was blatantly disregarding:

> Under the conditions of International Treaties the hulls must not be laid down until after 10th June, 1938. 27 months to complete. This letter may be regarded as granting in respect of the work mentioned herewith, the licence required by Section I, Subsection (I) (a) of the Treaties of Washington Act, 1922.

A final amendment followed on the official documentation of the Planned Design well in keeping with the previous discussions and frustration. In it Mr Simon of the DNO minuted the Controller about the close-range armament and submitted, on 22 April:

> As the production situation regarding 0.5-inch is likely to be even more acute than the four-barrelled pom-pom, at the time the L Class is due for completion, it is proposed that we should work to Stage 3 in the first place and omit the 0.5-inch altogether.

S.V. Goodall noted and submitted the above on 4 May and added: 'If approved, action will be taken with shipbuilders accordingly.'

Hughes-Hallett the next day initialled 'Approved'.

Thus, as it stood in early 1938, the Laforeys were due to be completed with no close-range weapons whatsoever! Happily the 'Completed Design' was in fact far from completed at this stage.

What was fondly thought to be tying up the ends of the *Laforey* design was later listed in the Schedule. The launching ceremony was specified to be 'a simple ceremony for the naming of the vessel ... The choice of a lady to perform the Ceremony is left to Controller's discretion.'

On the international front it was announced that:

In accordance with Article 12(b) L.N.T. 1936 to inform the High Contracting Parties that the design would comprise the following particulars in respect of eight Light Surface Vessels, sub-category (c) included in Naval Programme for 1937. S.D. 1920 Length waterline 354 ft; extreme beam at or below waterline at S.D. 36 ft 9 ins. Mean draught 9 ft 11 ins. Designed H.P. 48,000. Speed 36 knots. Six 4.7-inch guns. Eight Torpedo Tubes. No minelaying or aircraft.

However, less than a month after this, it was proposed to increase the scantlings of the keel and upper deck amidships in order to reduce stress in the upper deck coamings to 8.6 tons/sq in. The increase in the hull weight was estimated at five tons. This, and other factors, increased the time allowed for construction to 2+ years, which was, as Edgar March rightly recorded '... about the same time as that taken to construct the battle-cruisers of the Lion Class and the Queen Elizabeth battleships in pre-war days.' This, and a comparison of the respective HP, was a good example of how the complexity of warships had increased in a twenty-year period, a complexity which was to accelerate as the war years came on.

Other facts mentioned were that sixteen tons of paint was to be allowed for painting the ship. The 148 detailed drawings were to be distributed among the four builders when completed.

On 22 November it had also been decided at a meeting, attended by the First, Second and Third Sea Lords, DCNS, ACNS, DNC and E-in-C, that, in order to increase the oil-fuel stowage and consequently the endurance of the ships, one multiple pom-pom only should be mounted in the L Class and the following M Class. This enabled the magazine stowage to be reduced and an extra 67 tons of fuel could be carried, thus increasing endurance from 3,550 to 4,000 miles in deep condition at 20 knots with clean bottom. The average cost per ship of this alteration was put at £120.

While the design of the Ms was under consideration both the C-in-Cs opposed the L Class as being too big – the old cry again. The DCNS objected to the Ls as, 'being neither gun boats nor Fleet destroyers'. However, ACNS repeated his earlier opinion that as gun boats, 'the Ls were superior to the "Tribals" as mountings were weatherproof and a heavier shell was fired'. The Second Sea Lord thought British ships should be as heavily armed as foreign ships. DNO and DDNO confirmed the Controller's figures on the mountings – the work involved on the L Class was 1.8 times more than that of a K. The time to complete mountings for two flotillas was a year and four months and the bottleneck of fire control systems was in a similar condition. None the less the M Class were decided upon as repeat Ls. (It is of interest to note that four of the M Class still survived in service with the Turkish Navy in the 1960s, after being modernised a decade before. They not only justify the soundness of the basic design and strength of construction, but vie with the V and Ws for long service, some thirty years.)

On 13 March a memo to Cole from the *Vernon* establishment at Portsmouth resulted in the decision that the depth charges of the Laforey Class, which were to be arranged on two rails, were each to be protected by a 12-lb bullet-proof box. This box was to be arranged with the sides portable to allow access to the pistols and primers. Also, the depth charges to be stowed at the throwers were to be in bullet-proof boxes designed to carry four charges adjacent to the thrower and plumbed by a davit. The carrier was to be stowed on the screen bulkhead; the boxes were designed as protection against machine-gun fire from aircraft and MTBs.

Further weight problems were brought to light in May, Stansfield reporting that the total weight of two power-worked quadruple tubes as given by DTM in T0585/38 was 2.3 tons greater than estimated earlier and that the new DCT would come out at least a ton heavier. The final weight of the 4.7-inch guns could still not be accurately forecast until the completion of the first in 1940.

In July there was an exchange of correspondence during

which it was proposed to check on the advantages or otherwise of a new bow form for destroyers which had been put forward by Hawthorn Leslie. It was designed to throw the bow wave further from the ship's side. Tests in the experimental tank at Haslar found that although it worked on the model at simulated speeds of over 20 knots, at this speed, or below, the new form made no difference. They concluded that the advantages of the chine bow were so small on the model that it might well be non-existent on the actual ship itself. No further action was taken.

The heavy delays in the completion of the new gun housings and mounts continued to be the main source of frustration and, although the hulls proceeded apace on the stocks, the outbreak of war in September 1939 only highlighted the slow rate of progress being made. It was quickly clear that a large number of destroyers would not be ready in 1941 let alone 1940. This led to some drastic rethinking of policy. On 14 November 1939 the Controller was noted as having under consideration the finishing of the L Class with 'A' and 'X' mountings only. (The original note stated with 'B' and 'X' mounting but this was changed on the 16th).

As yet the scale of air attack was not great but was sufficient enough to bring forth the following note from Stansfield in February 1940, while still in the phoney war period of low-scale activity: 'Proposals are now under consideration to arm four of the L Class with three twin 4-inch HA/LA mountings.' This entailed lengthening the forward deckhouse to enable the forward mountings to be supplied with ammunition, as the 4-inch was an open-shielded gun loaded from the rear and not a trunk-fed mounting like the new 4.7-inch. The bridge would have to be redesigned to take the T/S and the opportunity was to be taken to simplify the layout of the new structure on the lines of the Hunt Class destroyers. It was expected that the ships would be very light and stiff. It was thought that a much better arrangement would be for four twin 4-inch guns but this would mean further serious structural delay and alteration and the whole object of the exercise was not brought on so much from fear of air attack as the need to get the ships to sea early.

This provoked a heated discussion. The Director of Plans was

strongly opposed to rearming brand-new Fleet destroyers with
4-inch guns only. Nevertheless it was proceeded with. At the
Controller's New Construction Meeting on 12 March 1940 it was
recorded that the L Class was proceeding normally but it was
added that the completion dates for ships with 4.7-inch
mountings ('A' and 'X' only) varied from December 1940 to
August 1941. 'Proposals under consideration to arm some with
8 x 4-inch guns.' The nett effect of the revealed increased weight
of the 4.7-inch compared with the 1937 estimate was an addition
of 8.63 tons at 17½ ft above the keel. It was not, however,
proposed to land any topweight in compensation until the
results of the preliminary inclining experiments at the first vessel
due for completion (*Lightning* was launched on 22 April 1940).

Within a few days the proposals on the 4-inch ships was
defined. A description of the proposed armament was given on
29 March.

Four 4-inch Mk XIX mountings with Mk XVI* guns (250
rounds per gun + 50 star.)[2]
Two quadruple 0.5-inch machine-guns
Two quadruple 21-inch *hand-worked* torpedo tubes
Depth charges:
    Throwers – Eight in number, four port and four
    starboard
    Traps – Three (six charges carried per rail)
Total number of charges carried – 110

This showed an emphasis on the anti-submarine role. This was
brought about because it was felt that 4-inch gunned ships
would only be able to operate in the North Atlantic as they were
under-gunned for surface actions.

More detailed analysis of the armament followed. The gun
weight of the 4-inch twin was given as:

	Tons	Cwts	Gms	Lbs
4-inch XVI+ – Eight	16	1	–	8
Mounting – Twin XIX – Four	41	4	–	–
Spares	–	–	10	–

Total ammunition stowage was put at 2,623 rounds and the original 4.7-inch shell rooms were to be arranged as W/T compartments. Torpedoes 21 inch Mk IX* – Eight.

On 23 April came a further notice that in view of the proposed acceleration of the 4-inch gun ships an improved form of torpedo sight was to be fitted. It was also noted that in lieu of metallisation it was proposed to coat the weather decks, except in the way of the deck conveyors, with two coats of international matt surface topside paint. It was not until 9 July 1940, however, with the grim lessons of Norway and Dunkirk behind them and the ascendancy of the Ju.87 Stuka dive-bombers being demonstrated over the Channel daily, that the decision was confirmed to arm four of the Ls as 4-inch gun ships. New general arrangement drawings had been forwarded to the firms concerned. The next day S.V. Goodall was noting that two of the L Class and all the M Class would not complete until *after* May 1941, which seemed an incredible way off but even so was to prove optimistic. This drew a blast from Churchill and a demand for smaller destroyers to be got to sea quickly.

The actual improvements in delivery were given by the respective firms as:

Ships re-armed with 4-inch	Original completion	New date
Lance (Yarrow)	April 1941	February 1941
Lively (Cammell Laird)	June 1941	February 1941
Larne (Cammell Laird)	January 1941	November 1940
Legion (Hawthorn Leslie)	December 1940	October 1940

On 12 September the following action with regard the Ls was noted.The *Lance* and *Lively* were to be fitted with ASV. It was proposed to fit this set in the main W/T Office in the space originally earmarked for Type 274 radar. It was also noted that as a special D/F outfit was to be fitted in the *Gurkha* (as the *Larne* had now been re-named) and in the *Legion* the ASV and MF/DF would *not* be fitted. It was proposed to experiment with a new

metallised process in *Lookout* which had been developed by the Schori Metallisation Company. It consisted of a spray coating of polymerised shellac and zinc. In CAFO/305 of the same date it was also decided that the 4-inch Ls should be re-classified as AA Destroyers and the 4.7-inch Ls remain as Fleets.

At the New Construction Meeting of 26 September the question of the close-range armament was brought up and it was proposed at that time to fit two 0.5-inch machine guns on extensions of the signal decks of the 4.7-inch Ls. In view of the mounting loss rate from dive-bombing it is difficult to think of the further statement as anything but naive! 'As a matter of very long term policy DTSD will raise the question of gradually dropping the 0.5-inch and turning over [to] the Oerlikon.'

Even with the increased AA potential the 4-inch Ls now luckily had, not everyone agreed that it had been the correct policy. Director of Plans stated that by so arming them thus, 'what should have been magnificent fighting destroyers have had to be relegated to purely defensive duties in areas which they are unlikely to come up against serious low-angle opposition.' (The exploits of these ships in Force K and at Sirte were later fortunately to nullify this despondent assessment of the 4-inch gun's capabilities.) In fact it has been argued quite convincingly that the adoption of the 4-inch gun in all war-built destroyers might have been a good thing. Although it was hard to accept that British ships should be 'undergunned' with regard to calibre, the fact that the 4-inch was in full production, had a high angle and anti-aircraft capability and also had ease of use and rate of fire count as plus points against the newer heavier marks of 4.7 and 4.5-inch guns.

The Vice Chief of Naval Staff appreciated this point at the time and expressed himself in favour of dual-purpose guns for destroyers in opposition to his contemporaries. He recorded that 'The demand for HA was resisted on the plea that it would interfere with the LA efficiency, the point was conceded in the complicated mountings in the L and Ms.' The decision to continue with 40-degree mountings was fundamentally wrong he felt for 'this war has shown quite clearly that for each day in which a destroyer is likely to engage her opposite number there are fifty on which she wants to engage aircraft.'

The cost factor was another point in the favour of the adoption of the 4-inch mounting. Four 4-inch twin mountings cost £24,000 whereas three 4.7-inch twin mountings cost £60,000.

However, the advantages of the Mk XI gun including the firing of a 62-lb shell which showed against all other destroyer mountings in 1941 a shortened time of flight, better armour-piercing qualities, larger lethal range of burst and reduction in personnel, coupled with the natural advantages of the weatherproof mounting.

The Standard War-built destroyers reverted back to the old single 4.7-inch guns of the A to I line, heavily reinforced by light weapons. However, it was recorded that the new commanding officer of the *Quiberon*, one such equipped ship, was far from pleased with this backward step. '...wants to exchange his 4.7-inch for twin 4-inch HA', reported the DNO on her commissioning report, in which it was also stated that an all 4-inch gun ship was the one to go for, 'due no doubt to the four Ls giving a good account of themselves in the Med.' At a meeting chaired by Admiral Somerville in May 1940 improved AA for destroyers was strongly recommended, and this no doubt influenced the final decision with regard the four Ls as much as hopes of a speedier completion date.

On 8 October it was further emphasised by the fact that the L and M Class destroyers armed with 4.7-inch mountings were to be rearmed. The after bank of torpedo tubes were to be taken out (in actual fact this meant that they were to be completed thus for none were in the water finished at this time), and a 4-inch single gun fitted in their place. It was also recorded that no time improvement would result if the four 4-7-inch Ls were sent to sea with 'A' and 'X' mountings only so they were to be completed fully armed. Consequent on loss of EC hoists *Lance* and *Lively* were to be arranged with whip and bollard ammunition supply and RDF (radar) was being arranged for these boats.

In November came a series of conflicting decisions regarding the arming of the Ls. On the 10th of that month it was noted that power worked quadruple mountings were to be installed in the Ls but a month later the Controller's meeting notes for 11 December stated that as a result of the *Javelin* action there was a strong desire to return to an armament of two sets of torpedo tubes. (The *Javelin*, under Captain Lord Louis Mountbatten, with four other J and K destroyers had intercepted three German destroyers in the Channel without any decisive result, but the Germans had hit the *Javelin* with two torpedoes, blowing her bows and stern off, and made good their escape although handicapped with a deck load of mines.) The Controller decided that the HA already installed in these classes, and to be fitted to Ls, could not be given up, for the danger from the air was too great. The only alternative was a single set of tubes, power worked. The DNG said a compensating weight would be necessary.

That the 4-inch Ls were still viewed with a certain lack of confidence was revealed in a note dated 12 November in which it was stated that these four destroyers were earmarked for the Red Sea (where aerial and surface opposition was negligible). 'It should be seen that they are equipped for the Tropics; awnings etc ...' Needless to say they never got there.

On 19 November the pit trials of the 4.7-inch gun were held but four days later the first of the class was near full completion. The *Legion* was inclined at Hawthorn Leslie's yard at Hebburn. Gun trials were held on the 17th and full power trials on the 19th. The time to stop from the order full astern at full speed was recorded as seventy seconds.

In December came a further setback to the 4.7-inch boats. It was recorded that Scotts, already heavily bombed and damaged (one of the Ms building there was cut in half on the stocks), had further difficulties. Requests to get the Dido Class cruiser *Scylla* completed quickly had resulted in a shortage of electrical labour and the work force for *Lookout* and *Loyal* was therefore not fully manned. This meant yet further delay in the completion of these vessels. (It is ironic to note that the *Scylla* herself was being rushed to completion with an inferior armament to that designed, as were half the Ls. Due to the appropriation of her 5.25-inch guns to supplement London's AA defences she was due to complete with 4.5s.)

Lightning was the first 4.7-inch gun armed L to complete and she was inclined. As a result of this it was found that stability was not as bad as had been feared all along. Indeed it was stated on 20 April 1941 that twelve extra depth charges could be carried, stored on the upper deck. Because of this the twelve depth charges which had been displaced in the warhead room by ammunition for the single 4-inch HA could thus be re-sited. As the first ship operational with the new mounting the *Lightning* was subjected to critical examination. Commander Brown of the *Excellent* gunnery establishment reported on the Mk XI: 'The advantages of the central hoists were wasted as they did not revolve with the mounting.'

This, he felt, would result in a slow rate of fire and spoilt what would otherwise have been an eminently satisfactory mounting. He thought the existing rate of fire was hardly likely to exceed eight rounds per minute at its best position and at the worst bearing would only be four rounds per minute, 'owing to the supply party having to run round the top of the hoist.'

It was noted, however, that in the early stages of the design of this mounting a revolving hoist was considered and was turned down on account of the difficulty of supply and magazine stowage arrangements. The *Lightning* carried out her gunnery trials on 19 May 1941, off the Tyne. Tests in the gunhouses for carbon monoxide showed that it was at no time a hazard. 'Atmosphere notably free from fumes and no complaint was received regarding state of air in gun house.'

Test trials showed the following comparisons with three 4-inch armed Ls:

	Lighting	*Lance*	*Gurkha*	*Legion*
Displacement	2,430	2,440	2,383	2,300
Mean speed	33.8	33.43	33.73	33.5
SHP	48,200	48,000	50,123	48,074
RPM	341.4	336.6	336.16	336.3
PC	.57	.56	.534	.58

The Red Sea forgotten in the growing concern at the U-boat campaign, the Ls were due to join the Western Approaches as they were completed. In June 1941 after meetings held at Bath and in London the C-in-C Western Approaches wished to ensure that 'at least one ship, preferably two', should be fitted with the new HF/DF (Huff-Duff) to combat the Wolf Packs and the homing systems used to draw the submarines to the convoys. This equipment it was proposed to fit on a pole mast aft and *Lively* was to be used as a seagoing testbed for it. The 4-inch gun equipped ships were now operational; *Lance* ran trials in the Firth of Clyde on 1 May and on the Arran course turned in 33.43 knots against *Gurkha*'s 33.73 knots on the same course on 18 February. The ship's officers of *Lance* were very satisfied with the ship 'especially with regard to fitting out'. *Gurkha*'s Commanding Officer was also very pleased and considered his new command to be 'a sturdy, very stable, well-armed and business-like' ship. Despite these accolades it was reported that a vibration was found in the 4-inch Ls which started at 23–24 knots from which the *Lightning*, with the heavier armament, was apparently free.

On 8 July 1941 the situation with regard the L Class can be summarised as follows. The 4-inch quartet were in the Western Approaches as a Special Escort Group, the 11th. (*Gurkha* was being taken in hand at this time at Rosyth for repairs to a damaged bow which was due to be completed on 24 June.) *Lively* was to complete on 20 July. Their depth charge throwers had been altered to fire a fourteen charge pattern. *Lance* and *Lively* had, after all, been completed with EC hoists, the arrangement of whip and bollard having been dropped. RDF, ASV and MF/DF were fitted in these two vessels while *Gurkha* and *Lance* were fitted with separate HF/DF gear forward to locate submarines accurately as a special operation. *Legion* and *Lively* were approved to be similarly fitted out but with HF/DF aft and ASV retained forward.

The 4.7-inch Ls were to have the full main armament as originally approved, plus the 4-inch HA in lieu of the after set of torpedo tubes and these were to be power worked in *Lookout* and

Loyal, plus 0.5-inch machine guns. Twin Oerlikons had been arranged for in these ships following *Lightning*'s good results from her inclining experiments and two further Oerlikons were being considered and had, indeed, already been arranged for in *Laforey*.

This showed a remarkable acceleration from the previously stated 'long-term' requirement of the previous year, but by this time Greece and Crete had been added to the bitter experiences of Dunkirk and Norway. To compensate for this topweight V-type bilge keels two feet in depth were being fitted in all the ships. It was also recorded that full exchanges of information of the British 4-inch and 4.7-inch HA mounting were being made with Captain Cochrane of the USN for details of the new American 5-inch mounting.

On 15 July it was asked that the *Lookout* be weighed, as she was by this time the only one of her class to which this could be done.

In August the *Laforey* commissioned with the extra 20-mm mountings. She was to set the pattern for the remaining 4.7-inch Ls and all the Ms and the arrangement of these guns was made in consultation with Captain (D) 19, Captain Hutton, and concurred by DTSD in P05231/41. It was noted that the extent of the 'wooding'[3] of the searchlight in the *Laforey* due to the fitting of the Oerlikon abreast the searchlight platform, 'appears from office information to be a reduction of depression to approximately 32 degrees on the beam and is acceptable.'

Lightning was accepted on 28 May and *Laforey* on 26 August and both were inclined.

In view of the many conflicting statements as to the displacement of these vessels given in reference books over the years, most of which took the original designed displacement and made no allowance for structural alterations during construction, the most accurate indication of this as the vessels were completed is likely to be the Suez Canal Tonnage Certificates issued to the ships. As money was involved it is likely that these figures are the closest we will ever get to actual tonnage.

Certificate Number	Ship	Date	Tonnage
P50979/41	Laforey	7.8.41	2,160.06
P3134/42	Lookout	18.2.42	2,123.41
P20267/42	Loyal	18.11.42	2,123.41
P44205/41	Lightning	7.5.41	2,119.34
P37543/41	Gurkha	5.2.41	2,158.54
P40748/40	Legion	22.11.40	2,158.58
P3951/41	Lance	3.3.41	2,158.54
P48777/41	Lively	7.7.41	2,158.54

The pattern of armament as revealed in a Controller New Construction meeting in January 1942 revealed just how much the original specification had changed under the hard testing ground of actual war. The 4.7-inch Ls were thus to be equipped with: three 4.7-inch twin; one 4-inch HA; one 2-pdr pom-pom; two twin 0.5-inch machine guns (power worked Mark V); six 20-mm Oerlikon (two twin, two single); one quadruple 21-inch power-worked torpedo tube; two depth-charge throwers, two chutes (No. 5 pattern only).

So the ships went to war, all but the two Scotts boats which were long delayed. By the time they commissioned their 4-inch gunned sisters had been sunk. The final torpedo armament of the *Loyal* was given on 13 October as:

Forward mounting 21-inch QR Mk X* Admiralty type No.4.
After mounting 21-inch QR Mk X* Admiralty Type No. 3.

Loyal ran trials on the Arran course and it was reported that her tripod foremast suffered vibration and would require staying from a point below the crow's nest. The whip of the mast as it stood would otherwise result in damage to Type 286P aerial array and transmission.

The ships were now embarking fresh equipment with every refit and just how much the displacement of these vessels could grow in a very short time is demonstrated in comparisons of inclining tests carried out on the *Lightning* in No. 2 basin at Chatham some eighteen months after the first experiment.

Comparison	24.4.41	9.11.42
Deep condition	2,661	2,743
Light condition	1,973	2,058

This showed an increase of 82 tons of which 38 tons was unaccounted for. *Lightning* in November 1942 was fitted for tropical service, had twenty-three extra crew and shipped Type 285 radar. Her armament consisted of six 4.7-inch; one 4-inch HA; one 2-pdr pom-pom; two 0.5-inch machine guns; six single 20-mm Oerlikons; one quadruple 21-inch torpedo tube; and she carried thirty depth charges.

On original completion the vessels compared with a 4-inch gun equipped ship thus: *Laforey* – 23 tons light; *Lightning* – 13 tons heavy; *Legion* – 18 tons heavy. The metacentric height for all was .11 to .21 less than was calculated. The maximum GZ was .06 to .12 less than calculated.

Despite the trials and tribulations we have found, from the time when the design was first mooted to the time the ships commissioned, most of the men who served aboard the L Class destroyers would agree with the comments of Captain (D) 19, Captain R.M.J. Hutton, and his officers when they took delivery of the *Laforey* after builders' trials in August 1941: 'The ship was considered as exceptionally steady and well finished.'

Now they had to earn their keep.

Notes

1 E-in-C's figures on this, following the Controller's verbal instructions to Yarrow to investigate the fitting of four side-fired boilers into a L.48 design, showed the following increases in weight:

Scheme 1: two side-fired boilers in the forward boiler room and one Admiralty boiler in the after boiler room.
Scheme 2: four side-fired boilers in the ship only.

Weight of Machinery – total increase		Forward movement Rise in mean GC	main GC
1	44 tons	4 inches	3 feet
2	21 tons	2 inches	2 feet

These figures were conclusive enough to stop further testing.
2 Star shell – a type of ammunition used to illuminate targets at night in pre-radar days.
3 'Wooding' is a hunting term which indicates that the sighting of the gun toward the target has been blocked by trees or other obstructions. It was adopted in the Royal Navy to likewise indicate that the line of sight of a gun or a searchlight had been blocked, i.e. by adjacent ships superstructure, masts or other gun turrets etc, on a particular bearing. In other words it indicated a blind spot in the field of fire.

Chapter 3

The Tradition of Victory

The naming of the eight powerful destroyers of the new Laforey Class flotilla was not just a haphazard gesture by the Admiralty. The names selected were honourable ones in the history of the Royal Navy and most had special connections with the destroyer service itself.

Over the long centuries of maritime dominance the British Navy had established a fine and enviable tradition of victorious service in every corner of the globe. The actions, both large and small, on which its unique position was founded were reflected both by the battle honours of the ships themselves and by the handing down over the years of the proud names of the ships and men that had fought in them to their successors, which in turn, added additional lustre to them.

Not all the Laforey Class had names with long ancestries behind them to be sure, but in the Destroyer Service the names they took had already established themselves as proud ones.

Perhaps the most traditional of the eight names finally selected was that of *Lively*. This name dates back to the seventeenth century and first appeared in the Royal Navy lists in 1689, when a prize vessel was thus named. She was a 5th-rate vessel, but during the unhappy period of the Ango–Dutch conflict she disgraced herself in that she surrendered in turn during the same year. However, the name *Lively* itself stuck and became increasingly popular for the smaller ships of the fleet. The second *Lively* was a 6th-rate of 1709 and she saw service during the War of the Austrian Succession, being awarded the battle honour 'La Guayra' in 1743. She was sold out of the service seven years later after a life-span of forty-one years, which is an indication of the longevity of warships in those far-off days when technological change proceeded, if at all, at a very slow pace indeed. Nowadays so-termed multi-million pound destroyers are discarded after less than seven years of service and several multi-million pound refits!

Another small craft bore the name for a while, but in 1756 there was put afloat a sloop which became the fourth *Lively* to serve under the White Ensign. The Seven Years' War was underway with its almost traditional tale of initial muddle and reverses marking the fortunes of British arms after the usual period of peacetime retrenchment had left her sadly unprepared for such a conflict. She served for twenty-eight years during which she added a second honour to the name, that of 'Ushant' in 1778. She was sold in 1784.

Three more small vessels continued the name between that date and the launching of the eighth *Lively*, a 5th-rate, in 1794. War with the French Republic was underway, a war that was to last with brief intervals for another ten years and which saw Great Britain reach the heights of her naval supremacy after innumerable victories over her old rival on the Continent. Holland was subjected to French occupation and Spain joined the alliance against Britain. Once more things went poorly for this nation at first, but *Lively* herself was present at the first great turning point in the struggle when she took part in the Battle of St Vincent in February 1797. Here the British fleet under the inspiring leadership of Admiral Jervis thrashed the Spanish fleet under Cordova in their own waters. Alas, poor *Lively* did not long survive this triumph for she paid the endless price of Admiralty the following year when she was wrecked.

Once more a series of small ships took up the name, four in all, between the years 1798 and 1804, and thus the next 5th-rate launched in that latter year became the thirteenth *Lively* to serve with the fleet. She gave six years of service during the war with Napoleon and the period after Trafalgar, but she shared the fate of one of her ancestors when she was wrecked in 1810. A fourteenth *Lively* put to sea in 1813 and she was also a 5th-rate, but she saw little active service and during the long peace that followed Waterloo she was finally converted into a receiving hulk.

Yet again the name was revived for small craft, no fewer than five more ships graced the Navy List with the name *Lively* between that time and the twentieth century.

One of these was a small gunboat, a large number of which were hastily built during the war with Russia in the mid-1850s. As well as the Black Sea, naval operations were carried out in the Baltic and, in March 1854, a large fleet had been despatched thither under Admiral Sir Charles Napier. It was a magnificent array consisting of nineteen battleships and twenty frigates and steam ships. The battleships, however, had changed but little since the days of Nelson, wooden walls, hearts of oak and broadsides. Equally, the Admiral, although a very gallant officer with a magnificent record of service, was in his dotage and his command proved uninspiring. The crews of this fleet were poor in the extreme, consisting largely of landsmen. Thus this fleet, which the little *Lively* later joined in the Baltic, proved itself a great disappointment to all and it achieved little or nothing. Only the bombardment of the fortress of Bomarsund could be counted against the cost of despatching such an armada. Despite this the *Lively* made her own small contribution and added the honour 'Baltic 1855' to her others.

The next *Lively*, the twentieth ship of the name, brought the story into the twentieth century, and also into the Destroyer Service. She was a 385-ton vessel built by Laird Brothers and launched in September 1900. A four-funnelled ship, low, sleek and painted black, with the distinctive turtleback forecastle of the first British destroyers, she was among the swiftest of that initial group. Only 213 feet in length, this tiny ship was a racing wonder in her day and, at an average cost of £60,000, she could just about reach her designed speed of 30 knots. Her armament consisted of a single 12-pdr forward, five 6-pdr and two 18-inch torpedo tubes and she was built to perform the original function of torpedo boat destroyers, the catching and the destruction of enemy torpedo boats; at that time the French and Russian navies were building them in enormous numbers as a challenge to offset the numerical superiority of the British battle line.

These were mainly experimental vessels but they performed well although they were of a multitude of varying types according to individual builders' conceptions of what was required. They were eventually lumped together into classes for identification according to the number of funnels they had, the *Lively* becoming one of the B Class.

When the Great War broke out in 1914 she was already obsolete, having been overtaken by larger and faster vessels over the intervening thirteen years. By all accounts, she should have been ready for the scrap yard only. As it was, the war saw every available hull being pressed into service, no matter what the age or condition, and so *Lively* sailed away to war as a lowly coastal patrol vessel whose duties were the routine ones of protection of the fishing fleets off the east coast of England. But the *Lively* was to show her mettle against the mightiest ships of the German High Seas Fleet and to have a closer look at these elusive vessels of the Kaiser's Navy than many a mighty *Dreadnought* or modern destroyer.

Her great moment came on a cold, misty morning off Great Yarmouth, on 3 November 1914. Under the command of Lieutenant H.T. Baillie-Grohman she sailed with the torpedo-gunboat *Halcyon* to take up her usual uneventful patrol position. Unknown to these two puny and ancient little ships, steaming at full speed towards them through the murk and gloom of that winter's day were the huge shapes of Admiral Hipper's Scouting Force, the battle-cruisers *Seydlitz*, *Moltke*, *Blucher* and *Von der Tann*, together with four light cruisers and a flotilla of modern and fast destroyers. The intention of the German Admiral was to carry out a bombardment of the defenceless towns of Great Yarmouth and Gorleston in a tip-and-run raid and then to quickly scurry back to Germany before vengeance in the form of the British Grand Fleet could intercept them from their distant bases far to the north. The population of these peaceful fishing towns was labelled a 'target of military importance' for the German Admiral and against its houses were to be levelled the huge 11-inch guns of the battle-cruisers.

Only two ships stood in the path of the oncoming German giants, the *Lively* and the *Halcyon*, two ancient little tubs that should not have been still at sea, let alone at war.

As the great bulks of the German ships loomed up out of the morning mist, intent about their task, they stumbled upon the two patrol boats. *Halcyon* flashed a challenge and her reply was several broadsides of giant shells, any one of which could have blown her asunder. Great fountains of spray deluged her decks as the shells pitched into the water all around her in giant geysers, and within minutes she would have been completely annihilated but for the bravery of her compatriot. Heedless of the suicidal task he had set himself, the *Lively*'s commander unhesitatingly took his fragile craft into the danger area, steering a course that placed his ship between the *Halcyon* and those huge, fire-spitting monsters on the horizon, laying down a thick smokescreen as he did so. It was the first time in war that a smokescreen had been thus used and it proved a triumphant vindication of its effectiveness.

Nor was this all, for, as the damaged gunboat limped away as best she could, *Lively*, by then joined by her equally old and frail sisters, *Leopard* and *Success*, hung on to the coat tails of the German fleet and tried to report their subsequent movements by wireless.

Their gallantry had its just reward. Fearing that these four tiny vessels could not possibly have acted so courageously unless they were merely the forerunners of a much larger and more powerful force, Admiral Hipper turned his great ships and their guns thundered out against Great Yarmouth from ten miles' range instead of the intended two. Probably as a result of this many of the shells exploded on the beach rather than in the towns and, although some houses were demolished and civilians killed, they were spared a much greater horror. Thus the lives of hundreds of men, women and children were spared as result of the action of the little *Lively*; it is little wonder then that when the names of the new flotilla were being considered *Lively* would hold a pride of place.

Happily the twentieth *Lively* survived the remaining years of the Great War and was finally broken up in 1919. If ever a warship deserved to have been saved as a floating monument to the Destroyer Service and moored at Great Yarmouth then it was she, but in those days no such thought saved this gallant vessel from the shipbreakers' yard.

With her departure the name passed to another minor vessel and then, in 1938, was selected for the new ship.

Equally famous, although in a different way, in the annals of the Destroyer Service was the name *Lightning*. Again it had a very ancient lineage, dating back to 1681 and had always been carried by the very smallest craft in the Royal Navy in the succeeding centuries – fireships, gun vessels and bomb ketches, the mosquito craft of the days of James, George and Victoria alike. The first *Lightning* was at the battle of Barfleur in 1692 when the Royal Navy under Russell defeated the French fleet under Tourville during a day's bloody combat that May and finished off the remnants the following day at La Hogue under the eyes of the assembled French army. This victory dashed forever the hopes of poor King James of reclaiming his lost kingdom.

Another *Lightning* battle honour was awarded at Vigo in 1702 when Sir George Rooke destroyed the Spanish treasure ship fleet together with its escorting French naval escort in Vigo Bay. A new *Lightning* took part in the Seven Years' War, as did a *Lively*. Pitt had sent Admiral Boscawen to Canadian waters to seize Louisburg on Cape Breton Island, the key to the St Lawrence seaway and the key also to the conquest of French Canada itself. With his fleet, and the army under General Abercrombie, went a *Lightning* and after participating in the long siege operations the town was finally subdued and the way lay open to Quebec and the climax of the campaign.

Like *Lively* again, another *Lightning* took part in Napier's ill-fated Baltic Campaign during the Crimean War in 1855. Here it was that the British fleet approached the main Russian naval base of Kronstadt in a great show of force and the *Lightning* was sent ahead of the main fleet to reconnoitre the defences of that great base. Under the command of Captain Sulivan she carried out a daring probe into the bay but found that the defence works there were too powerful, in Sulivan's opinion anyway, to be attacked and reduced by anything other than mortars. The British fleet had none at this time and so no attack took place. *Lightning* also reported that a Russian fleet of eighteen battleships lay low behind these fortifications but nothing the British could do would tempt them to venture out and give battle; so the British fleet retired to Baro Sound without accomplishing anything.

It was the eighth vessel to bear the name *Lightning* that was the most famous vessel for she was the very first torpedo boat to be constructed for the Royal Navy. With the arrival of the 'Whitehead' torpedo in the 1860s the development of naval armaments took on a new look. The old established supremacy of the battleship and the biggest gun took a knock from which it never recovered fully, and, although the Royal Navy remained the largest fleet in the world, many felt that its power was challenged by continental rivals who set out to construct swarms of small craft armed with this new weapon, to which initially there appeared no antidote.

Thorneycroft was a leading firm constructing fast vessels of this nature for foreign governments and finally, in 1877, the Government were sufficiently alarmed at the potential of such craft that they allowed the Admiralty to purchase outright from the firm one such boat, which they christened *Lightning*. The name has stuck with torpedo craft ever since and indeed is a natural one for swift vessels, the fastest ships in the fleet, packing a powerful punch out of all proportion to their size.

This *Lightning* was a low-lying craft, merely an elongated steam launch, only 84 feet long but with a speed of 19½ knots. She was originally fitted with a spar torpedo mounted on a long pole forward. The simple concept was that the *Lightning* should use her speed to rush in under the heavy guns of the conventional battleship and ram her, escaping as best she could, if she could! Later in her life she was modified to carry two Whitehead torpedoes in upper deck fixtures and this reduced her speed to 18 knots. Even so trials proved her satisfactory and another twelve 'First Class' torpedo boats were ordered to a similar design. From this modest beginning sprang the hundreds of torpedo boats and destroyers that bore the brunt of two World Wars at sea. As such the name *Lightning* will for ever be famous in the Navy List.

Despite the experimental nature of her work and her early obsolescence the tiny *Lightning* remained in service with the Royal Navy until 1910, a period of thirty-three years, although of course she was not in full commission all of that time, and she was renamed T.B.1 well before then. By that time the ninth *Lightning* had joined the fleet.

She was one of the original 27-knotters, the very first torpedo boat destroyers, which appeared on the Navy Lists in the last decade of the nineteenth century. They added a new dimension in spice and excitement to the somewhat stereotyped autocracy of the late Victorian navy, which was only then beginning to feel the first faint stirrings of momentous change. The appearance of these low-lying, black-painted vessels with their high speed gave fresh opportunity to young officers to enjoy the thrill of their own commands and the ships caught the public imagination and held it.

Poets stirred the hearts of naval traditionalists among the nation's youth with Kipling-like odes testifying to the gallant deeds and dash of these new types of warships. They were the fastest things on the seas and in the Great Britain of the 1890s the Royal Navy not only really ruled the seas without challenge but was high in the estimation of a public yet untutored in the disdain of nationalistic pride and achievement as is the current vogue.

Lightning herself was the product of the shipbuilding firm of Palmers. Charles Palmer had set up his shipbuilding slip at Jarrow-on-Tyne, as early as 1851, and had commenced the construction of iron ships. The yard was already a well-established one and many a sleek frigate had taken shape and seen birth there during the half-century prior to this; with the construction by Palmers of the *Terror* in 1854, a floating battery and forerunner of the monitor type warship, the company became a leader in the utilisation of rolled steel armour plating.

Lightning, with her two sisters, *Janus* and *Porcupine*, were the first destroyers constructed by the firm. At this time it was the policy of the Admiralty to place their contracts with as great a number of firms as possible in order that the widest selection of shipbuilders available should acquire the expertise necessary to turn out large numbers of flotilla craft in the years ahead. Not all the firms early on in the race to build such intricate and complicated craft were able to stay the pace however, and many yards bankrupted themselves in their efforts to meet the high standards of construction insisted upon by the Admiralty. But Palmers were one of those that did come through with flying colours and *Lightning* and her sisters were the first of more than forty other destroyers to come from their yards until their closure in 1930.

Lightning was launched on 10 April 1895 and she cost the then astronomical sum of £37,000. Just 200 feet in length, with the typical turtle-back fo'c'sle of her type, her maximum beam was under 20 feet and she displaced 280 tons.

The armament of these early destroyers was not much more than the very torpedo boats that they were designed to destroy. Indeed, on such a limited displacement and within such tight dimensions every ounce of weight saved contributed towards their vital factor of speed. They were initially described as 27-knotters and in fact on their trials with clean bottoms, best Welsh coal and a picked team of stokers, most of these early boats did achieve this speed; *Lightning* herself exceeded it by almost a knot. It is doubtful, however, whether any of these boats were good for much more than 25 knots flat out in actual service, and then in a reasonably flat calm. In any sort of a seaway their speed naturally fell away considerably, although as the same applied to the torpedo boats so long as they maintained their margin they could still fulfil their designed functions.

Many were powered by three-stage compound engines with twin screws, although the majority were finished with triple-expansion engines and carried a coal bunkerage of about 65 tons. This limited their range to an average of 1,000 nautical miles at an economical cruising speed of 11 knots. But it was not originally intended that they should be deep-water craft anyway, their function was to ward off the swarms of torpedo boats that were expected to attack a British battle-fleet blockading an enemy coast in the grand-old style of the Napoleonic wars. The enormous strides in gunnery ranges and accuracy, however, soon made this doctrine obsolete and the 27-knotters were very soon made out of date in the frantic naval building programme of the early nineteenth century.

The armament of the *Lightning* at this time consisted of a single 12-pdr gun forward around which was assembled the flimsy bridgework – a canvas screen! She also carried five 6-pdrs and had two single 18-inch torpedo tubes. To achieve their required speeds their construction was flimsy in the extreme and early photographs show clearly that the frames and longitudinals of their hulls were plainly visible behind the paper-thin plating of their delicate hulls. Life aboard these racing craft, with their white-hot engines spewing thick black smoke from their stubby funnels upon the white corticine decks was no holiday cruise either. Their crews were paid extra allowance to compensate for the hardships of life aboard ('Hard Lying' money as it was termed) and no money was more hardily earned. Despite this the early destroyers never lacked for volunteers to man them. Young officers found a chance to shine and to develop their own ideas on attacking instead of drilling some outdated manoeuvre on the spotless deck of a battleship in the Mediterranean. Little wonder then that those who first went to sea in the 27-knotters remembered them with great affection.

They were run hard in the early years of the century as great efforts were made to ascertain exactly what roles they were capable of and how best to organise them. *Lightning* spent much of her life working out of Portsmouth and her constant employment did much to ensure that she was one of the very few survivors from that early group of eighty-two ships that were still in service on the outbreak of the Great War, almost twenty years after launching.

Naturally their capability was extremely limited by this time but, as we have seen from the story of the twentieth *Lively*, they performed valiantly although their ancient hulls were sorely tried by the vicious North Sea gales and by their increased top-hamper.

Alas, *Lightning* did not long last the test of war for she fell victim to a mine off the East Coast while on patrol duties and sank on 9 August 1915, after a lifespan of two decades. But she and her sisters had laid down a convincing precedent for the naming of a new destroyer *Lightning* at the first opportunity. Another two decades were to pass before this arose.

The name *Larne* has a much more recent origin, dating back to the last years of the Napoleonic war. The original name is of course geographical and comes from the township of the north-eastern coast of County Antrim in what is now Ulster.

The first ship to carry the name in the service of the Royal Navy was a sloop built in 1814. She saw service during the Burma War of 1824–5. This was the first of three campaigns that added that country to the Empire and, although the fighting was on a small scale, it was at times very ferocious. The British troops fought and defeated the Burmese deep in their home country, fighting in the steamy climate dressed in their traditional red serge uniforms and full equipment. It was by the skilful use of the great river systems of that land that the Royal Navy was able to penetrate right into the country to land the attackers and give them overwhelming fire support.

Under the overall naval command of Commodore Grant, the naval forces assigned to the expedition of 1824 consisted of the *Larne*, *Liffey*, *Slaney* and *Sophie* (all sloops), four Indian Navy cruisers and numerous brigs and schooners fitted out as gunboats. Rangoon was taken on 11 May that year after a brief bombardment. As the flotilla pressed higher up the Irrawaddy they were counter-attacked by fire-rafts but, despite this, Kemmendine fell after heavy fighting. With the illness of Grant, Commander Marryat (the novelist) assumed temporary command and the operation continued, although the ghastly climate took a heavy toll of seamen and soldiers alike.

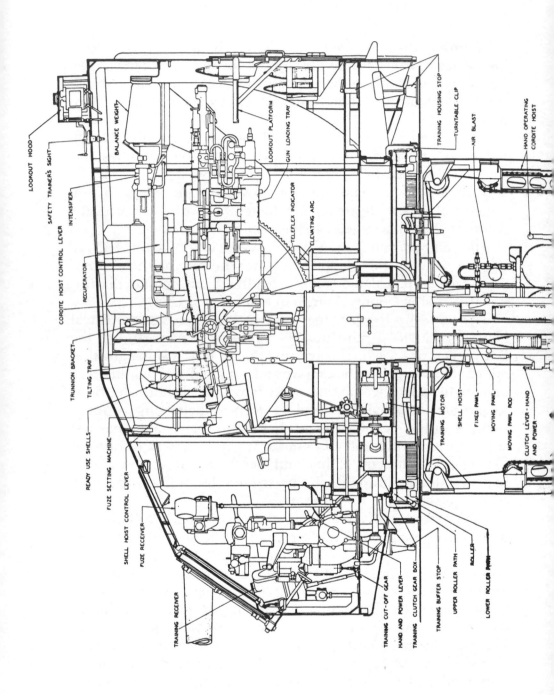

Arrangement of Mounting: Mark XX Side Elevation

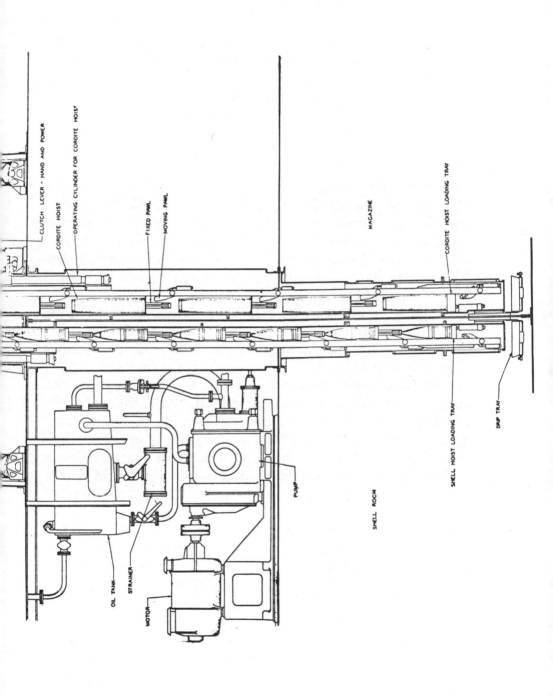

CLUTCH LEVER - HAND AND POWER

CORDITE HOIST

OPERATING CYLINDER FOR CORDITE HOIST

FIXED PAWL

MOVING PAWL

MAGAZINE

CORDITE HOIST LOADING TRAY

SHELL HOIST LOADING TRAY

DRIP TRAY

PUMP

SHELL ROOM

OIL TANK

STRAINER

MOTOR

At Dalla, for example, the gunboat *Kitty* was threatened by a large force of the enemy and saved only by the timely arrival of the *Larne*'s boats upon the scene. During Sir Archibald Campbell's final drive on Prome in February 1825, during which Bundoola was killed and his followers dispersed, the *Larne* featured largely in the escapades of the covering naval squadron. Soon after this was finished the *Larne* was sold out of service in 1828.

The paths of two ships of the flotilla cross with the re-naming of the *Lightning*, a gun-vessel, as the *Larne* in 1832. The second *Larne* also saw service in the East and her most distinguished period of operations was during the China War of 1839–41. This gallant old vessel was finally sent to the breaker's yard in 1866 and there ensued a long gap before the third *Larne* joined the service, but this time she was a destroyer.

This third ship to carry the name was one of the ships of the Acorn Class, later known as the 'H' class after the re-organisation of the destroyers of the fleet and their names carried out in 1913.

Pretty and petite ships, the Acorn Class destroyers were a delight to the eye and, when first built, a delight to handle according to a report from one of their first commanding officers. Later on, during the early winters of the Great War, their seaworthiness and their endurance came in for sharp criticism. Nonetheless the class as a whole was soundly built and served right through the Great War with some considerable distinctions.

At the time they first took to the water, in 1909–10, the naval arms race between Great Britain and Germany was approaching its dizzy climax and after several years of experimentation with boats of varying designs and capabilities a period of standardisation was called for. There was much concern in the country and the press that the Germans were apparently turning out destroyers at a faster rate and with higher reputed speeds. The previous class of British destroyer, the Beagles, had reverted to coal burning, but with the Acorns oil fuel returned once more to the flotillas and remained thus ever since, save for a few craft laid down for foreign countries and taken over later.

The third *Larne* then was a vessel of 760 tons, a tiny ship by the standards of the fourth destroyer, but already twice the displacement of the first destroyers described in these pages, *Lively* and *Lightning*. She was armed with two 4-inch and two 12-pdr guns and a much improved torpedo outfit of two of the new 21-inch torpedoes. Oil fuel saved weight and their Yarrow boilers made them good for 27 knots, although this was normally exceeded on trials; *Larne* herself touched 28 knots. She was built by that most famous of all flotilla craft constructors, Thorneycroft, the firm that with Yarrow did the most to pioneer the destroyer type in the Royal Navy. Thorneycroft has had a long association since with the type for no fewer than 101 destroyers have been built by this firm since, including two for the Royal Canadian Navy. Their yard was originally at Chiswick in London, but the destroyers came from Woolston in the main after the move there in 1904.

Larne was put afloat in August 1910 and cost £91,424. She had an overall length of 246 feet and carried Parsons turbines as her main mover.

She served with her sisters throughout the war of 1914–18, as a Grand Fleet destroyer until 1915, and then she, with others of her class, went out to the Mediterranean theatre where they spent most of the rest of the year. In 1921 they were considered surplus to requirements and they were sold to Ward's Shipbreaking firm in June of that year for scrapping.

It is interesting to note that when *Larne* was re-named *Gurkha* there had already been two previous destroyers carrying this name in the fleet. The name *Larne* was immediately re-instated for another small vessel, one of the Algerine Class minesweepers built in 1943, which subsequently served at Normandy and in the Mediterranean before being sold to Italy in 1946. So the name itself did not die when the re-naming of the destroyer took place.

The four 'new' names adopted for the flotilla had only been carried once before, but even so the first ships to bear them had already built up their own tradition in the Royal Navy, and one that was enviable. All these boats, *Lance*, *Legion*, *Lookout* and

Loyal, had been destroyers of the L Class, which were the last destroyers to be completed before the outbreak of the Great War in 1914. Being the front-line ships at the outbreak of hostilities they were much in the news during the opening battles and frequently made the headlines.

They were originally to have been named after characters from Shakespeare, Scott and other literary masters, while others had old small ship names dating back many years; they were to be known as the Florizel Class. Thus *Lance* was first known as *Daring*, while *Legion* was to have been *Viola*. *Lookout* was originally *Dragon* and *Loyal* was *Orlando*.

On what was to become the standard displacement for the bulk of the destroyer tonnage built during the Great War, 900 tons, these vessels were designed to carry three semi-automatic 4-inch guns and featured also the new twin torpedo tubes, which doubled their firepower in this important arm. Most of them joined the service with Parsons Geared Turbines, another feature that was to become standard. Their boilers were Yarrow and they were either two- or three-funnelled. Their average cost worked out at around £120,900, or half as much again as equivalent German boats then completing, and on trials they turned in a sound 30 knots.

On completion these four vessels joined the bulk of the flotilla, the Third, and became part of the Harwich Force whose exploits became legendary. *Lance*, *Legion* and *Loyal* belonged to the 1st Division and *Lookout* the 2nd Division. Being the naval force closest to the enemy-held ports it was natural that they should be in the thick of the fighting.

In fact it was the *Lance* that actually fired the first British shot of the Great War. The gun itself is now on display at the Imperial War Museum, London, SE1. This was on 5 August 1914, when *Lance*, in company with the *Landrail*, opened fire on the German minelayer *Koenig Luise* off the Suffolk coast. In the ensuing action the German vessel was quickly sunk, and the destroyers rescued forty-three of her crew.

Their second taste of action came during the Battle of the Bight on 28 August 1914. A bold penetration by the ships of the

Harwich Force right into the Germans' backyard started to roll up the local defence boats and in response to this they soon drew down upon their heads heavy reaction from German light cruiser forces from the Elbe and the Jade. The Ls were in the thick of the subsequent hard fighting and eventually the timely intervention of Admiral Beatty's vast battle-cruisers turned a hard scrap into a massacre. It was a timely British victory at the beginning of a frustrating war at sea.

On 17 October 1914, *Lance*, *Legion*, *Loyal* and *Lennox* were at sea with the light cruiser *Undaunted*. They were again close in to the Germans' main bases, in the vicinity of the Dutch Island of Texel, when they came upon a German destroyer patrol, which immediately turned to flee. The four destroyers formed line ahead and, with the *Undaunted* providing long-range supporting fire, they soon overhauled the enemy division. The *Undaunted* then sank *S.117* and *S.119* in quick succession while the British destroyers engaged the other two German boats. During this brisk action *Loyal* was hit aft and had one gun put out of action and *Legion* was hit in the bridge, but neither ship was badly damaged. The two remaining German destroyers, *S.115* and *S.118*, soon joined their sisters on the seabed.

During the bombardment of Great Yarmouth by Hipper's force on 23 November as related earlier, again it was *Undaunted*, with several Ls including the *Legion*, who very nearly precipitated a more general action as they passed in close proximity to the Germans without realising it. In February of the following year the *Loyal* was again in the news when she made a gallant attempt to tow home the cruiser *Arethusa*, which had struck a mine. But she failed to save this famous ship. In a similar manner the *Lance* came to the succour of the crew of the *Lassoo* when she was mined off the Dutch coast.

Mines were indeed the major hazard at this time and the *Legion* fell victim to one in November 1916, and her stern was wrecked. Despite this she was got home. Her subsequent refit lasted six months and, when she emerged from the dockyard, it was as a special minelaying destroyer. Her after guns were landed and mine rails, like narrow rail tracks, were built on her deck aft with stowage on them for forty mines. To preserve secrecy a painted canvas screen shielded this part of the deck and from any distance at all she resembled a normal patrol destroyer. So successful was she in this role that the *Loyal* was treated in a similar manner. As fast minelayers they later served in the famed 20th Flotilla and many were the daring and highly secretive operations in which these little vessels were engaged during the long nights of 1917–18, working close in to the German ports and harbours. These exploits justified a book to themselves,[1] and so suffice it to say here that it was far and away the most dangerous of missions, and also one of the most successful and skilful, carried out by the Royal Navy in this conflict.

Later in the war many of the other Ls transferred to the Dover Patrol. After the Armistice, although only eight years old, they were considered worn out because of the very strenuous service they had given and were put on the sales list.

As was befitting, the destroyer with by far the most distinguished name was both the name ship of the class and the flotilla leader, the *Laforey* herself. It was indeed a pleasing custom that had come about whereby the Admiralty named the flotilla leader of each class after one of their most distinguished officers of the past, and this continued throughout the 1930s and 1940s.

Laforey was named after the famous son of an equally famous father, both of whom served the Royal Navy well.

The name *Laforey* derived from the original French Huguenot family of La Forêt who fled their native land and settled in England, victims of one of those periodic upheavals and pogroms that France suffers from regularly. The persecution of the Huguenots took place at the time of William III and he encouraged their settlement in the freer atmosphere of England. The first of the family to enter the service of the Royal Navy was John Laforey, the second son of Lieutenant-Colonel John Laforey, who died in 1735. John Laforey was born in 1729 and entered the Royal Navy being promoted to Lieutenant in 1748 and appointed to commander in the *Ontario*. He was serving under Commander (late Admiral) Keppel off North America at this time and he and his son were to make their names on this side of the Atlantic Ocean in the years ahead.

The next command of John Laforey senior (as we shall now describe him) was the *Hunter*, which he was appointed to in 1756. Under his command this vessel served with distinction at the action off Louisbourg under Admiral Holbourne in 1757 and at the subsequent capture of that place by the British Fleet under Admiral Boscawen the following year. John Laforey senior particularly distinguished himself on 25 July when he was in command of a division of boats which penetrated the harbour and burnt or cut out the French ships *Prudent* and *Bienfaisant*. In recognition of his conduct on that day Boscawen appointed him to the frigate *Echo*, a much sought after command.

In 1759 the *Echo* was attached to the fleet of Sir Charles Saunders during the spectacular campaign in the St Lawrence, which finally culminated in the capture of Quebec from the French. After this John Laforey senior was transferred to the West Indies and was present at the reduction of Martinique by a squadron, under Admiral Rodney, in February 1762.

While at Antigua John Laforey senior had married Eleanor, the daughter of Colonel Francis Farley of the artillery and he was appointed to the frigate *Levant* the same year, 1763. In this ship they returned to England and their first child, a daughter, was born in London in March 1764.

A period of no naval appointments followed as the Laforey family moved to America and it was here, in December 1767, that their son Francis was born in Virginia. From an early age he determined to follow his famous father to sea and indeed their lives were to be entwined to a remarkable extent in later years. They fought well for their ancestors' adopted homeland against their family's original country, which had rejected them so scornfully.

This period of stable home life was terminated in 1770 with the appointment of John Laforey to command the frigate *Pallas* but he stayed with her only a few short months before transferring to the command of the big 2nd-rate battleship *Ocean*, 90 guns, which had been launched in 1761.

In command of this formidable warship John Laforey was present at the skirmish off Ushant on 27 July 1778, under his old mentor Admiral Keppel. At the subsequent court martial of Keppel which followed this action, John Laforey fearlessly defended his old commander in no uncertain terms.[2] Although Keppel went on to become First Lord of the Admiralty, Laforey's defence of him was not forgotten or forgiven by some. Perhaps as a result of his forthright attitudes, Laforey's next appointment was to waters he knew well and which he was to come to know even better. He was appointed Commissioner of the Navy at Barbados in November 1779, and in the Leeward Islands. He set up residence at Antigua where he had first courted and won his wife and was instructed to act in the capacity of Commander-in-Chief on that station.

In February 1783, he returned to Plymouth but his actions earlier had not been forgiven. In September 1787, a general promotion of flag officers took place, including the elevation of many officers of junior seniority to Laforey, but John was himself passed over. The lame excuse given for this unjustified treatment, was that as he had accepted a civilian position he was no longer eligible. True to his tradition John Laforey fought. As at sea he fought both hard and well and, after two years, he was justified by the appointment of himself to Rear Admiral of the Red, with a seniority dated September 1787. At the same time he was created a baronet and, a few days later, he returned to the Leeward Islands once more as Commander-in-Chief.

Meanwhile, young Francis was also carving a name for himself in the Royal Navy. He entered the service in 1780 and was promoted to Lieutenant in 1789 and the next year became a commander. His command was the *Fairy* from 1791 to 1793 and she was stationed in the West Indies, under command of his father. Both were therefore in a fine position to further win themselves new laurels and enhance the family name when war again broke out with France in 1793.

As soon as news of the declaration of war reached him, Sir John organised an expedition to take Tobago from the enemy. Tobago, part of the Windward group of islands, duly fell on 15

April, 1793, and Francis who was present in the *Fairy*, returned home with the despatched and was promoted to Captain. His father was likewise promoted, to Vice Admiral, and he returned home that July.

Francis took command of the 28-gun frigate *Carysfort* and off Land's End on 9 May 1794, recaptured the 32-gun frigate *Castor*, which had been taken by the French just three weeks before. In this brilliant little fight, Laforey lost just seventeen men killed and nine wounded in an hour and ten minutes' fierce action. Among the British prisoners released was a certain Captain Troubridge who likewise went on to gain the highest honours.

In May 1795, Sir John was again re-appointed Commander-in-Chief of the Leeward Islands and sailed to take up his position there once more in the 3rd-rate battleship *Scipio*, 64 guns, commanded by Francis Laforey – a fact that must have delighted both!

Under his command the Dutch Islands of Demerara, Essequibo and Berbice were all captured during 1796 and Sir John became a full Admiral. He also very successfully put down a negro revolt in St Vincent, Grenada and Dominica and ended it with typical firmness. By this time he was feeling the effects of his years and of the climate and was relieved by Sir Hugh Christian. He sailed for his beloved homeland for the last time, but sadly he did not live to see England again. He contracted yellow fever while aboard the *Majestic* and died on 14 June 1796, two days before she made landfall.

Sir John was buried at Portsea on 21 June and Francis then succeeded to the title becoming the Second Baronet.

Sir Francis took command of the new 38-gun frigate *Hydra* and searched the English Channel for the enemy. During an action off Le Havre in 1798 he pursued and destroyed the French frigate *Confiante*, but his most famous command was the ex-French battleship *Spartiate*, a 74-gun ship captured at the battle of the Nile that same year.

Together the *Spartiate* and Laforey were to inflict a terrible price on the country from which both once sprang. *Spartiate*'s own history is given in *The Trafalgar Roll* by Colonel Mackenzie.

She was built at Toulon, being launched there in 1793. Under the command of Captain Emeriau she was at the Nile battle when Nelson destroyed utterly the French fleet, thus reducing Napoleon's Egyptian conquests to ruins. The *Spartiate* herself was the third ship in the French line that lay anchored ready for battle on that fateful day of 28 July and she was initially engaged by the *Vanguard* and then by the *Audacious, Minotaur* and *Theseus*. Completely dismasted she struck her colours and Lieutenant Galway of the *Vanguard* and a Royal Marines boarding party took possession of her, later presenting Emeriau's sword to Nelson.

Repaired and commissioned into the Royal Navy the *Spartiate* served two commissions under Captain Pierrepont in 1799 and later under Captain Stuart. When first taken over by Sir Francis Laforey she was in the West Indies, serving under Admiral Cochrane. She returned home in 1805 where she joined the weather column of Lord Nelson's fleet, and, on 21 October 1805, she took part in the great and decisive battle of Trafalgar.

Being one of the rearmost ships into the action did not prevent *Spartiate* distinguishing herself. She exchanged broadsides with several of the enemy, and then with the *Minotaur* managed to cut off the big Spanish 84-gun *Neptune* and get alongside her. The Spanish vessel defended herself valiantly for more than an hour in this unequal duel. Eventually, having lost her mizzen and fore and main topmasts, she hauled down her flag at 5.10, being the last enemy ship to surrender that day. Laforey's command had lost three men killed only, with twenty wounded. *Spartiate* had her own foretopsail yard shot away and sustained heavy damage in her yards and rigging, but was nonetheless seaworthy.

For his conduct in the battle Sir Francis received a gold medal, a sword of honour from the Patriotic Fund and the thanks of Parliament. At the funeral of Lord Nelson Sir Francis Laforey carried the standard in the first barge up river from Greenwich.

The *Spartiate* soon repaired her slight damage and was back in the war; Sir Francis took her to join the flag of Sir Richard Strachan at Rochefort during the blockade of Allemand's ships during 1807–8; the following year she was part of the force that took the islands of Ischia and Procida from Napoleon's followers. Promotion to Rear Admiral took place in 1810 and the following year, no doubt to his immense satisfaction, Sir Francis was given the task which his father had carried out with such success before him. He was appointed as Commander-in-Chief of the Leeward Islands, a position he held until the end of the war with France. He became a KCB in 1815.

With the coming of peace scope and further chances to prove himself on the field of battle passed. In 1819 he became Vice-Admiral and attained the rank of full Admiral in 1830 at the age of sixty-four. Full of his years and honours he died at Brighton in 1835. Eighty years were to pass, however, before the Royal Navy honoured such a famous son by bestowing his name on one of their fighting vessels.

The first ship to be called *Laforey* was a destroyer of the same class as those mentioned earlier, *Lance*, *Legion*, *Lookout* and *Loyal*. She was built by the Fairfield Shipbuilding Company and was launched on 28 August 1913, completing just before the outbreak of the Great War. Her original name was *Florizel*, the name ship of the class. Like her sisters she displaced around 990 tons and carried three 4-inch guns and four torpedo tubes. Her cost was £98,000. Her main power unit was Brown Curtis turbines and on her trials she almost touched 30 knots.

The outbreak of the Great War found her serving with her sisters in the 3rd Flotilla at Harwich where she led the 3rd Division under the command of Commander G.R.L. Edwards. Now, Commander Edwards was one of the most famous of those 'characters' with which the Destroyer Service abounded. Unconventional and a born leader of men, he was a much-loved figure with his own unique style. In the service he was affectionately known as 'Father' because of his habit of disregarding the orthodox signals when leading his ships at sea. Instead of the normal order 'Proceed in execution of previous orders' the signal halyards of *Laforey* when steaming out of Harwich harbour would carry simply 'Follow Father'.

Another famous destroyer man, Captain Taprell Dorling,

knew him well and he described several of 'Father's' other signals in his book *Endless Story*.

On another occasion at sea, when one of his flock was badly out of station, he rather horrified the flotilla by signalling the offender in broad daylight by semaphore, 'If you don't keep better station, Daddy will come over when you are in your bath and smack your fat little !' mentioning a portion of anatomy which is not, as a rule, talked of in polite society.

Led by such a personality *Laforey* was never long out of trouble. She shared the dangers and excitements of her flotilla and added a few more of her own during her very brief life span.

Perhaps one of the most thrilling of these escapades came on 1 May 1915. Word was received at Harwich that the destroyer *Recruit* had been torpedoed and sunk by a German submarine off the Galloper Shoal in the Thames Estuary. The trawler *Daisy* had rescued some of the survivors from this destroyer and then called for help in finding others. At once the duty division, which happened to be *Laforey*'s 3rd, composed of herself with the *Lark*, *Lawford* and *Leonidas*, raced south in the hope of flushing the U-boat and avenging their comrades.

They searched long and hard but were unrewarded with any sign of the submarine, but, while approaching the vicinity of the North Hinder lightship they heard firing and came upon two German torpedo boats, *A2* and *A6*, which had sped over from Zeebrugge intent on a hit and run raid against the helpless drifters and trawlers of the patrol zone. Against negligible opposition they had sunk one trawler and were firing into a second, when nemesis came upon them in the form of the dark, lithe shapes of *Laforey* and her consorts. Their creaming bow waves must have indicated to the Germans as they turned to run that they had no hope.

Under Edwards' able leadership the 3rd Division soon overhauled the German vessels and well-placed salvos from their 4-inch quick-firers quickly sent both enemy ships to the bottom. Some fifty-seven survivors were picked up by the British ships afterward, in marked contrast to the fate of the British crews from the trawlers the Germans had left to die. It was rather as if the school prefect had caught the school bully in the act of mistreating a junior and had administered a dose of his own medicine!

Laforey was engaged on a similar errand on the night of 17/18 March 1917, while working with the Dover Patrol. With the *Llewellyn* she was sent out to rescue survivors from the destroyer *Paragon*, which had been attacked and sunk by a German squadron. Busy in this humane task they had their searchlights switched on searching the dark, cold waters for wounded men. They knew the risks of such a course of action but carried on, for another of the unwritten laws of the Destroyer Service was never abandon a shipmate. On this occasion they paid the price for the Germans returned, attracted by the lights, and put a torpedo into the *Llewellyn's* bows. Despite the subsequent damage the *Laforey* managed to get her sister ship home to port to repair.

Within a week, however, *Laforey's* time had come. On 23 March 1917, she was mined and sunk in the English Channel. She had not disgraced her illustrious name.

Thus we have seen from this brief examination of the history of all the names allocated to the new *Laforey* flotilla that, even before they put to sea they were all heirs to the proudest fighting examples. To the crews that came to man these eight powerful units during the most desperate actions of the Second World War this heritage was an imposing precedent for them to follow. We shall now examine just how well they upheld those traditions, and indeed, even excelled them.

Notes

1 See author's book on the work of the 20th Minelaying Flotilla and the part it played in two World Wars, entitled *Into the Minefields*, also published by Pen & Sword.
2 For the full details of the results of the Keppel and Palliser court martials please turn to this author's forthcoming book *Sailors in Dock*.

Chapter 4

The Leaders of the Flotilla

'It seemed that the whole of his life up to that time had been spent in preparation for that moment', wrote Lois Hutton about the day that Captain Reginald Maurice James Hutton took command of the *Laforey* as Captain (D) 19th Flotilla. 'Tubby' Hutton, as the first and much-loved commander of the L Class destroyers, had indeed a unique and enviable record of dedicated destroyer experience to give to his new command.

He was born in 1899, the son of Reginald Hutton of Wootton Bridge, Isle of Wight, in sight almost of Britain's premier naval base across the Solent. A naval career was his early ambition and he was educated at Osborne and Dartmouth and first went to sea as a Midshipman in 1915 aboard the battle-cruiser *Indomitable*.

In this mighty vessel as part of Admiral Beatty's Battle Cruiser Fleet, the spearhead of the Royal Navy in the Great War, he served at the Battle of Jutland. 'Tubby' gained his first taste of small ship life while undergoing his Sub-Lieutenants' courses during which, as Acting Sub-Lieutenant, he served aboard the little patrol vessel *P.48* from March 1918. These little 600-ton vessels were mass-produced to meet the growing threat of the U-boat and proved an ideal training ground for his future service.

As a Sub-Lieutenant, 'Tubby' joined the brand-new destroyer *Trojan* in November 1918 and while serving his two-year commission in this fast lively craft, gained his promotion to Lieutenant. From now on Reginald Hutton was to be a 'Destroyer Man', and was never away from these ships for long, while his heart always remained with them.

He gained his promotion to Lieutenant in October, 1919 and the following year joined the 'V' Half-Leader *Valkyrie* in which he served for a year before joining the S Class destroyer *Somme* as her First Lieutenant in October 1921.

These were the final days of the old Royal Navy, which was still far and away the world's largest and finest fleet. Destroyer flotillas still numbered twenty ships with a Flotilla Leader and a Half Leader and massed torpedo attacks by several such flotillas formed the basic fighting tactic by night and by day. But in 1921 came the harsh dictates of the Washington Naval Treaty, which resulted in wholesale scrapping of warships, among them over 200 destroyers. Many men were discharged from the service early and promotion for those that remained was slow and competition fierce. Against such odds the professional ability and dedication of 'Tubby' Hutton ensured that he not only continued in the service, but that he saw continual service afloat.

His next ship was the *Witch*, another of the V and W Class destroyers, which at that time represented the peak of destroyer development on which the bulk of the Royal Navy's strength in this type of vessel was based for more than ten years. As Lieutenant he served two eventful years aboard the old *Witch* before joining the battle-cruisers once more, this time aboard the famous *Renown*, which he joined in March 1926.

Promotion to Lieutenant Commander followed the next year and in April 1928 he realised his most cherished ambition with the announcement that he was appointed 'In Command' of the destroyer *Truant*. Two happy years were spent in this little vessel, a 35-knotter built in 1919.

In 1930 he married Lois, daughter of MP Griffith Jones, CBE, and for a time he left his beloved destroyers. A Staff Course was followed by his appointment as Staff Officer, Operations, 4th Cruiser Squadron, in the East Indies in the Flagships of that force, initially the cruiser *Effingham* from January 1931 and later her sister ship, *Hawkins*. This period was followed by a spell ashore in the Admiralty Plans Division. By this he time he was Commander Hutton and in this rank he was next appointed Executive Officer 3rd Cruiser Squadron, serving aboard the light cruiser *Despatch* in the Mediterranean from July 1935.

This was at the time of the Italian invasion of Ethiopia and the ineffectual policy of sanctions that the League of Nations applied with complete lack of result. The Mediterranean Fleet at this time was at the very highest pitch of training and efficiency under the magnificent leadership of Admiral Sir William Fisher, and were supremely confident of their ability to deal with Mussolini's bully-boys. Unfortunately, a weak and vacillating Government at home did not share their faith in themselves. None the less the fleet which assembled that summer in the Western Mediterranean was outstanding, in its size, capability, training and leaders. Among the many great seamen of the day were officers, like 'Tubby' Hutton, who were shortly to make their names famous by their exploits and courage. Admiral Sir Andrew Cunningham was there as Rear Admiral (D) of the four flotillas; Max Horton of submarine and Western Approaches fame was there as Commander of the 1st Cruiser Squadron of 8-inch heavy cruisers; William Whitworth, later to achieve fame off Norway was there as Captain of the Fleet; and Rear Admiral Raikes was Chief of Staff. Among the more junior officers were such outstanding men as Captain Philip Vian, Commander Warburton-Lee, Commander Lord Louis Mountbatten and Commander G.N. Oliver.

Admiral Cunningham took passage in *Despatch* and with Commander Hutton joined the fleet at Alexandria. He later described the scene:

> One day during the dinner hour a large transport crammed with two or three thousand soldiers arrived, all cheering defiantly at our two ships. As they passed they broke into the Fascist anthem *'Giovinezza'*; but were considerably put out by the loud shouts of 'Encore!' from the hundreds of sailors on the forecastles of the *Despatch* and *Resolution*. It is impossible to describe the withering contempt the British bluejacket can put into his applause if he dislikes the entertainment or entertainer, and on the occasion their sarcastic shouts penetrated even the thick hides of the Italians.[1]

After this anticlimax Commander Hutton remained with

Despatch until 1938 when he returned home to take up another shore appointment at the Staff College before joining the Operations Division at the Admiralty in the autumn of 1939. Here he spent the first two years of war and was promoted to Captain in December, 1940. Finally on 10 March 1941 came the crowning moment, his appointment to command *Laforey* as Captain (D) 19.

Never was a more apt choice made. Under his able guidance the 19th gained the reputation as the most efficient and happy flotilla in the fleet. Captain Hutton was particularly admired by the lower deck, in war as in peace, the only true judge of a commander's merit for good or ill. Under their scathing and unbiased scrutiny 'Tubby' came out on top. Bob Burns was a leading light in reuniting *Laforey*'s survivors after the war through the offices of the local paper of Northampton, the *Chronicle & Echo*, and he is well qualified to recall the feelings of the crew for Captain Hutton. He wrote:

> I had been in the Navy from the age of fifteen, and served proudly with many of the top ranking naval officers who made history in World War II, but I never came across anybody with the warmth and understanding of R.M.J. Hutton. His DSC and two bars spoke well of his brilliance as a flotilla leader skipper, but I was, and never will be, not qualified to comment of those qualities. All I know is that those officers and men of the *Laforey* would have gone to hell and back for him, and the saddest day but one of my time on *Laforey* was when he said goodbye to us in Malta dockyard.

That this is no isolated viewpoint is clear from the correspondence received during the research for this book and in the following pages we shall see just how 'Tubby' Hutton kept *Laforey* well to the forefront of the naval war.

Captain R.M.J. Hutton had personalised the Laforeys with his inspired and brilliant leadership and his departure to take up his new appointment in September 1943 was deeply felt among the crew, and by the flotilla as a whole.

He had won two bars to his DSO with the flotilla but now he was promoted to Commodore (D) of the Home Fleet destroyer flotillas based in the *Tyne* at Scapa Flow. In this capacity he led the ships of the O, S, V, Z and Ca classes in the closing years of the war, years that included the final triumphs of the Russia convoys, air strikes and destroyer sweeps off the Norwegian coast and the final surrender of the remnants of the German fleet.

Post-war his service was equally distinguished. He served as Chief of Staff to the Naval C-in-C in Occupied Germany between 1945 and 1946. This was followed by a two-year period as Director of the Naval Staff College, where he had himself spent periods earlier in his career.

He went to sea again in 1949 as Captain of the aircraft-carrier *Triumph*. Hutton finished a brilliant naval career as the Senior Naval Member on the Staff of the Imperial Defence College. In the Coronation Year of 1953 he was placed on the retired list.

Even so, he remained an active man for in addition to time spent with his sons or fishing, his favourite pastime, Rear Admiral Hutton served as Clerk to the Governors Christ's Hospital, Sherburn, until 1964. He died in January 1973 and at his funeral were two of the crew of the *Laforey*, his secretary, Commander A. Jones, DSC, OBE, and a bridge telegraphist Roy Hazel. It was fitting that this should be so.

The great sadness and sense of loss felt by the crew of *Laforey* on the departure of the much-loved Captain Hutton was somewhat made easier by the reputation and the calibre of the man sent to replace him at the helm of the flotilla.

'Beaky' Armstrong, as Harold Thomas Armstrong, DSO, DSC and bar was invariably known, was another destroyer man from the top of the deck. Like 'Tubby' Hutton he had early lost his heart on sight to destroyers and had served in them for much of his wartime naval life.

As one of his officers was later to recall: 'To be chosen to be a Term Officer at Dartmouth when it was opened to 13 year-old entry cadets as "Beaky" was meant that you were one of a select band.'

As a Midshipman the young Armstrong joined the battleship

Warspite in 1922, when she was part of the 2nd Battle Squadron of the newly formed Atlantic Fleet under Admiral Sir Charles Madden. In her he took part in the post-war Royal Review at Spithead in July 1924. On promotion to Sub-Lieutenant, Armstrong joined the battleship *Revenge* in May, 1926. He served in this mighty vessel as a Lieutenant transferring to yet another capital ship, the battleship *Resolution*, in December 1927.

So far there was little in his record to show his inclination for destroyers and following his period at Dartmouth mentioned above from July 1928 to July 1930, he again joined a battleship, this time the newest and mightiest in the fleet, the *Nelson*.

However, at the end of his two-year stint in her, Armstrong at last found himself in the small ship navy when he was appointed First Lieutenant of the sloop *Fowey* in September, 1932. No lively ocean greyhound she. On the contrary she was a slow, ill-armed escort vessel whose principal function, that of convoy guard, was reflected in her modest size, but she was a small ship and 'Beaky' never again lost touch with that most exacting but most rewarding type of command. Command it was for he was promoted to Lieutenant Commander of the *Fowey*, in continuation as the Navy puts it, with a seniority dated from April 1934.

Another short period ashore between February 1935 and July 1937 was spent on training duties at Portsmouth Naval Barracks, a duty which his earlier years certainly prepared him for. Nonetheless it must have been with considerable relief that Armstrong was finally to shake off the dust of that establishment, the more so since his new command was one of the smallest ships in the whole Navy.

This was the river gunboat *Cockchafer*, an ancient little tub built during or just after the Great War whose duties were patrol and guard duties on the mighty rivers of China. Promoted to Commander in June 1937 'Beaky' joined *Cockchafer* that October.

Following the unique experience of self-reliance taught by command of one of these little ships hundreds of miles away from civilisation, 'Beaky' finally got the command he had always wished for, a destroyer.

True, his ship was not a brand-new leader straight from the stocks. She was, in fact, one of the most elderly of the Royal Navy's destroyers, being of the old V and W Class destroyers of legendary fame, built towards the end of the First World War. Indeed, the scrap yard should have long since claimed her, but for the fact that, with war now on the horizon the Admiralty had wisely found a new duty for this old destroyer.

Unfortunately for the *Wren* she was sunk off Aldeburgh very early on in the war but 'Beaky' had moved on to command one of the Royal Navy's most modern and largest destroyers, the Tribal Class ship *Maori*. It was in this sleek powerful vessel that the war first gave him his chance to prove himself in combat and 'Beaky' was determined to do just that. Rear Admiral Sir Geoffrey Henderson was 'Beaky' Armstrong's secretary in destroyers and he has painted a vivid picture of 'Beaky' as he knew him.

Tall, lean, a fine upstanding figure, ruddy complexion, pointed features and his hair slightly tinged with red, he had a fine commanding personality and looked every inch the active, alert, quick-thinking person he was. He loved people and was adored by his officers and men who knew they had somebody very special at their helm.

He could be quick-tempered, but it was always seen to be for a justifiable cause. Everybody knew that his standards were of the highest, but they always had absolute confidence in his justness and human understanding.

His standards in all things were high. Always immaculately dressed, even at sea he took great pains to get the staff he wanted. An avid reader, his official writings were succinct and to the point. In the long, long days at sea he would alleviate any boredom by watercolour painting.

On most evenings in harbour he would come into the Wardroom for his pre-dinner drink(s) and, sitting on desk would 'hold court', sometimes for an hour or more, talking about everything under the sun and the stories would be reeled out. In fifteen months of intensive service I never heard him repeat himself once. He had a wonderful sense of humour and could laugh at himself.

It would seem superfluous to comment on his courage; his decorations (DSO, DSC and bar) speak for themselves.

'Beaky' spent an eventful year in command of *Maori* from May 1940 and the tail-end of the Norwegian fiasco, to June 1941. His command included the *Bismarck* hunt, convoy work in the Western Approaches and operations against E-boats in the English Channel.

In July, 1941, 'Beaky' was promoted to Captain and appointed to the brand-new flotilla leader *Onslow* as leader of the 17th Destroyer Flotilla. Under Armstrong's leadership the *Onslow* and her sisters soon won fame, both as ace U-boat killers in the North Atlantic and as determined fighters on the hard-fought convoy routes to Russia and the north.

Roger Hill recalled his own initiation to the joys of 'Beaky's' humour and sharp wit (and sharper signals).[2] He wrote how, while on passage to join the fleet at Scapa Flow in his new command the *Ledbury* they came upon *Onslow*, busy about her own affairs.

> There was a single destroyer some way to port of us. Through the glasses I could see she was a Flotilla Leader; she started flashing at us and I thought, 'Now we are going to get a friendly signal of welcome'.
>
> From *Onslow*: 'Clear my range or I will use you instead of the target'.
>
> Soon after this *Ledbury* went to sea with the fleet.
>
> I started to cut across but had to steady up as I had two O Class destroyers on either side. However I hauled ahead of them, cut across their bows and came roaring down past D (Beaky), who riddled me with a broadside of 'Manoeuvre badly executed'. I bet he was laughing like a drain and it was worth while making the mistake for the excitement of getting back.

It was far from all laughter in the bleak days of 1942 on that cruel Russia convoy route but *Onslow* played a gallant part in many of these grim actions. During PQ 18 she was responsible for an attack on *U-589* that left her a smashed wreck on the sea bottom. 'Beaky' had an undiminished detestation for U-boats. Commander William Donald of the *Ulster* remembers how:

> The destroyers on patrol were a mixed lot from the various flotillas out there; one of the Captains (D) at the time was Captain Beaky Armstrong in *Laforey*, a most dynamic character who hated being in harbour, and was all for offensive action against the enemy at every possible moment.
>
> 'Come on chaps,' he would say, 'let's comb the Med. for these damn U-boats.'[3]

'Beaky' was in his element aboard *Onslow* but in December 1942 he handed over the flotilla to the equally gallant Sherbrooke who led her to immortal glory a month later in the battle against *Lützow* and *Hipper*. Armstrong was appointed Deputy Chief of Staff to C-in-C Nore (Sir George D'O Lyon) and was listed for 'Special Service' from January, 1943, in that role. In February 1943 Captain H.T. Armstrong was appointed as Captain, Coastal Forces, for the whole Nore Command; and he did a great deal to improve training and tactics.

'Beaky' as always put everything into the job, although he no doubt wished he was back at sea in his beloved destroyers. He wrote to his former secretary that March:

> I am still in these parts (HMS *Watchful* at Great Yarmouth) attempting to shake up Coastal Forces but to date have done little else but shake up my own stomach.

Coastal Forces had been operating with great bravery and panache but had achieved very poor results nonetheless. Peter Scott was to recall: 'They had even been nicknamed in some quarters "the Costly Farces".'

But 'Beaky' and his skilled staff soon made their presence felt. With great energy Captain Armstrong organised much more specialised and advanced training than had been possible in the time available, and his influence on the achievements of our MTBs, MGBs and MLs was very soon apparent. The standards of training and fighting experience, particularly of night action, in Coastal Forces had, by 1943, become second to none in the Navy, a position which was perhaps finally established for them by Captain Armstrong.[4]

In the autumn came his appointment to *Laforey*. He wrote joyfully to his No. 2, Geoffrey Henderson:

> As you have probably seen I am off to sea again. Should you get de-moted at any time and want a little more destroyer life – let me know.[5]

'Beaky' was back in harness!

Notes

1 *A Sailor's Odyssey* by Viscount Cunningham of Hyndhope, Hutchinson, 1951.
2 *Destroyer Captain*, by Roger Hill, Kimber, 1975.
3 *Stand by for Action*, by Commander William Donald, Kimber, 1956.
4 *The War at Sea*, Vol II by Captain S.W. Roskill, HMSO, 1956.
5. *Battle of the Narrow Seas*, Peter Scott, Country Life, 1945.

Chapter 5

The Destroyers go to War

The first of the Laforeys to commission for service for the 4th Destroyer Flotilla was the *Legion*, in December 1940. Her actual sailing was delayed while the RDF (radar) set was installed, a modified Type 286M with a rotating instead of a fixed aerial array. It is believed this was the first such set in any destroyer. However, she arrived on the Clyde on the 19th and lost her first motor boat the same day; it was recorded in her log as being stolen by leprechauns! Torpedo trials were then carried out in Loch Long and the *Legion* further distinguished herself by losing five with dummy warheads. During the full power acceptance trial, which was carried out in the swept channel off the Durham coast, the *Legion* at speed touched off one of the German acoustic mines at a range of about one thousand yards. On this being reported orders were received that instead of returning to Hebburn she was to land all Admiralty officials and dockyard personnel that had been embarked for the trial at Rosyth. The civilians were *not* amused.

Legion was sent to work-up at Scapa Flow but before this had been completed fully she was ordered to sea to search for possible survivors from a merchant ship torpedoed in mid-Atlantic. While returning after an unsuccessful search, *Legion* made ASDIC contact with her first potential U-boat. This encounter took place during a very dark night and the submarine escaped on the surface. Star shells were fired and these were seen by a division of Tribals, one of which claimed to have attacked and damaged the submarine.

In early 1941 the bulk of the escort forces in the Western Approaches consisted of elderly destroyers, sloops and corvettes and the C-in-C asked for the formation of a new 'Special' Group of modern fleet destroyers to be attached to his command. This started with the *Legion* and the Polish destroyer *Piorun* (an ex-British N Class boat) and was later joined by the *Lance*, *Gurkha* and *Lively* as each of these commissioned. This group was much in demand and was used to give support to the slow conventional escort forces on the vital Halifax, Sierra Leone and Gibraltar convoy routes and they were also used on all the big troop (W.S.) convoys to the Cape.[1] But they were also assigned, being the most modern destroyers afloat, to the numerous special operations that demanded powerful and fast ships.

On one of the first convoy escort operations *Legion* was involved between 8 and 12 January as part of the local escort for convoy WS 6A with destroyers *Atherstone*, *Cottesmore*, *Keppel*, Canadian *Restigouche* and *St Laurent* and Polish *Piorun*. This was followed with similar duties with convoy WS6B, along with the destroyers *Garland*, *Hesperus*, *Hurricane* and *Piorun* until the 20th. Convoy WS 7 followed, with *Legion* as part of the escort, which included the battleship *Revenge*, light cruiser *Edinburgh* and destroyers *Broadwater*, *Bedouin*, *Mashona*, *Matabele*, *Somali* and *Piorun*. She left that convoy on 26 January and returned to the Clyde and then to Scapa Flow, where she arrived on the 27th to prepare for Operation *Claymore*.

Life aboard His Majesty's newest destroyer was no sinecure however. Eric Smith recalls life below decks during this settling in period:

> Now destroyers, and in fact all small ships in those days, operated a canteen messing system. This was comparatively new to me, although the same system operated on the East Coast gun battery where I had been stationed earlier in the war. Briefly it operated as follows.
>
> One person in each mess was elected as mess caterer. It was his job to make out the daily menus and to see that sufficient food was ordered. A free issue of bread, meat, potatoes, tea, sugar and milk was made weekly to each

mess, depending on the number of persons in that mess.
Each caterer was then allowed two shillings, (10p), per
man, per day, for the purchase of all other foodstuffs, either
from the 'Pusser' or the NAAFI canteen manager. It was
up to the mess caterer to keep within this limit. If it was
exceeded, members of the mess paid so much per head to
pay off the debt to the paymaster. If it was under the
amount allowed the mess was credited with the savings,
each man receiving so much back. Bills were squared up
monthly. In my mess it was a leading seaman, who, being
the senior rating, took over as caterer for the first three
months.

The only 'second veg.' we ever had for dinner was dried
pussers' peas, which were quite cheap (about 2p per lb),
and which had to be soaked overnight. Also we seldom got
a dessert. Two 'cooks' of the mess were detailed each
twenty-four hour period and it was their duty to prepare
whatever meals the caterer decided on and take them to
the galley for the cooks to prepare.

Being a big eater in those days I was only too pleased to
learn as much as I could about preparing the various
dishes, making 'duffs' and the like, and I soon became
quite an expert. After a couple of months of practically no
other vegetable other than pusser peas or tinned carrots,
we held a mess meeting to elect a new caterer, during
which time the leading seaman was told to shove all his
pusser peas up his sail-hoch! Jack Spencer, one of my
messmates, protested that this was unfair as the poor
bastard still had twelve cold 'Chinese wedding cakes' to go
there from the day before! The leading seaman was sacked
and I was elected in his stead, a position I held throughout
the commission.

Once attached to the Clyde Escort Force we seldom had
more than a day or so in harbour before we were off to sea
again escorting another convoy. Christmas 1940 was spent
in some outlandish hamlet where the First Lieutenant
decided that only chief and petty officers would be

allowed ashore. This of course did not go down too well with the remainder of the hands, and one of them in my mess decided that it would be a good thing if we made our own 'hooch' to drown our sorrows.

He claimed to have the know-how to produce potato whisky. To this end, pounds of spuds were peeled and placed in a mess fanny full of water. Yeast and assorted ingredients were obtained from somewhere and added and the whole issue covered with a mutton cloth. After a few days, when he claimed the time was ripe, the whole smelly, bubbling mixture was transferred to stone jars to await further fermentation. By this time we were quite used to depth charges being exploded by the duty watch on deck whenever a 'ping' was obtained on a suspected U-boat. But one night we were all awakened by a terrific bang. The home-made whisky had exploded, breaking almost all the crockery in the mess-shelf above. We were still a 'dry' ship!

The first of the special sorties took place when the *Legion* was allocated as one of a force of five destroyers used to escort and provide support for the Troop Carriers *Queen Emma* and *Princess Beatrix* in the *Claymore* operation.[2] This was the first Commando raid on the German-held Norwegian Lofoten Islands. This force sailed from Scapa Flow on 1 March 1941 and proceeded to Skaalefiord in the Faeroes, arriving there at 1900 hours whereupon the destroyers refuelled from the tanker *War Pindari*. Guided into the approaches of Vestfjord by the submarine *Sunfish*, the whole Force arrived off their objective without being once sighted or reported by the German Aircraft searches.

At dawn on 4 March the force split into two groups and *Legion* accompanied the *Princess Beatrix* and *Eskimo*. Troops were disembarked and quickly occupied the ports of Stamsund and Henningsvaer at 0645 hours. All landings were unopposed and the troops feted by the Norwegians who were unaware that it was merely a raid and thought liberation had come. The German defenders put up little resistance and apart from the destruction of the armed trawler *Krebs* there was little for the destroyers to do. Ashore the naval demolition parties who had gone in with the troops proceeded with the methodical destruction of the oil tanks and other installations, necessary to deny them to the Germans but far more effective sadly at destroying the livelihood of the Norwegian population.

Legion sighted two trawlers to the southward during the day but on investigation these turned out merely to be two of the little 'puffers' returning. She was not called upon to act in support of the troops ashore. The whole force was re-embarked and assembled at 1300 hours and left Vestfjord but it was not until two hours later that the first German aircraft sighted them. However, rendezvous was made with the covering cruisers *Edinburgh* and *Nigeria* the next day without any attacks having developed.

The next item of note for the *Legion* took place when the Armed Merchant Cruiser *Rajputana* was torpedoed and sunk in the seas south of Iceland by *U-108*. *Legion* and *Piorun* arrived on the scene on 13 April. The two destroyers picked up the 177 survivors and landed them in Iceland and almost immediately were sailed, after a hurried oiling, to escort the battleship *Rodney* into Scapa Flow. A further WS convoy followed between the 24th and 29th as part of the 14th Escort Group, along with the destroyers *Beagle, Eridge, Harvester, Havelock, Hesperus, Hurricane,* Canadian *Restigouche* and *Saguenay* and Polish *Piorun,* guarding WS8A with the battle-cruiser *Repulse* and light cruiser *Naiad*.

During all the days at sea that winter the *Legion* was licking herself into shape and the crew settling down to become a highly efficient unit. Of course the principal reason for her existence was those eight 4-inch guns and Eric Smith describes the gun drill for one of the twin mountings.

The action procedure for the twin 4-inch gun was briefly as follows:

The HA director would train and lay on the target, the Rangefinder would transmit the range (this before radar assisted laying of course). The instruments in the director would transmit the range, bearing etc to the same type of instrument at the guns (see Appendix 2). All the gunlayers, trainer, sight setters and fuzesetters had to do was to follow the pointers on their instruments. Should the director be put out of action, or for some other reason the guns had to go into independent firing, the layer trainer would disregard the pointers and lay and train on the target themselves by means of their telescopes.

The crew of a twin-4-inch mounting consisted of the following:

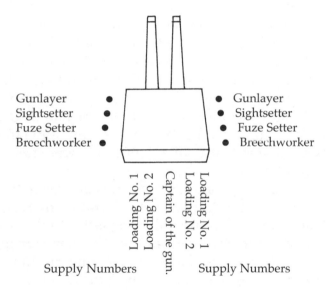

The shells would be taken from the Ready-use lockers around the guns and placed on the fuze setting tray and as soon as the fuze was set, loaded immediately. The breech automatically closed as the shell was rammed home and the contact made. The A, B, X or Y Gun-ready lamps would light up in the director and the director layer would press the trigger on orders from the gunnery officer. All the guns would then fire in unison.

For surface targets of course, the type of shell would be semi-armour piercing and would not need to be fuzed.

The month of May 1941 brought the *Bismarck* hunt. As we have seen, the *Legion* had been originally allocated, with the Canadian destroyers *Assinibone* and *Saguenay*, to the escort of the battle-cruiser *Repulse* and aircraft-carrier *Victorious* as ocean escort for troop convoy *GVS8B*. However, once it was known that the German battleship was out, these warships were sailed from the Clyde to join the *King George V* off the Butt of Lewis on 22 May. The *Lance* was at Scapa Flow working up but she was added as part of *King George V's* escort nonetheless. Unfortunately, her new engines broke down and she had to return the same day.

Legion remained with the C-in-C's screen until 2000 hours on the 24th by which time the tragedy of the *Hood* had taken place and contact had been lost with the *Bismarck*. The screen was sent to refuel at Iceland and from here they steamed to Londonderry to repeat the process. From this port *Legion* sailed to meet the *King George V*, now victorious after the despatch of the *Bismarck*, off the coast of Ireland on the 28th; at the same time the *Lance*, her defects made good, also joined, but they were not to reach Loch Ewe until next day.

During the following month *Legion* and *Lance* were twice sent out to a mid-Atlantic rendezvous with ships that had found and sunk German supply ships (mainly auxiliaries to the *Bismarck*), and they collected the prisoners and took them into Scapa. Both the *Gurkha* and *Lightning* commissioned during this time but the latter, on 18 May, was allocated to the 19th Destroyer Flotilla, Home Fleet, and did not operate with her 4-inch gunned sisters at this time. A large number of *Lightning's* crew came direct from the destroyer *Ashanti*, which was undergoing repairs after a collision off the Tyne the previous October.[3] She sailed to work up at Scapa Flow, being temporarily diverted as an extra escort for a North Atlantic convoy en route. On 11 June she was considered ready for service at Scapa.

Between 31 May and 3 June, *Legion* was part of the escort for WS8X along with the destroyers *Brighton*, *Saguenay*, *St Mary's*, *Sherwood*, *Vansittart*, *Wild Swan* and *Wivern* en route for Freetown with the heavy cruiser *Norfolk*.

The arrival of the *Gurkha* on the scene was quite an event as her first and only commanding officer, Commander C.N. Lentaigne, remembers:

Gurkha was in fact *launched* as *Gurkha* and not renamed afterwards as is often stated. The true story is that when the third *Gurkha* was sunk the Gurkha brigade telegraphed Winston Churchill and offered to buy a new destroyer to be named *Gurkha*. As the average cost of a destroyer at that time was in excess of half a million (*Gurkha* actually cost approximately three-quarters of a million), Mr Churchill declined the offer but ordered that the next destroyer to be launched should be named *Gurkha*. As *Larne* at Cammell Laird's was the next due to be launched, Mr Churchill sent his daughter Mary, then in the WACs, to launch her as *Gurkha*.

Mary Churchill and her then sister-in-law both attended the commissioning lunch on board. General Sir Ian Hamilton and one retired Gurkha officer, as well as Sir Robert Johnson of Cammell Laird's, were my guests. There was no other ceremony partly due to the fact that the ship's company did not arrive from Devonport until after midday, some five hours late, due to the train being delayed by air raids.

In addition of course it was necessary to get the ship out of the fitting-out basin as soon as possible. This basin was a prime target for frequent air raids as *Prince of Wales*, one cruiser and four destroyers were all completing in this small area. None of these ships were badly damaged by bombs, but two destroyers building on a nearby slip were hit.

The badge awarded by the Admiralty soon after launch was the crossed kukris of the 5th or 6th Gurkhas. *Gurkha* was the fourth ship of her name in the service of the RN, and, as my brother was commanding the 4th Gurkhas we mounted their crossed kukris as the badge on the bridge and either side of the after superstructure.

The *Gurkha, Lance* and *Legion* were then based at Greenock under Western Approaches Command as the 11th Escort Group specifically for convoy defence in the North-West Approaches. Almost immediately *Gurkha* was in a bad collision on 26 February, and took heavy damage to her forward hull, several compartments being flooded. She had to be immediately withdrawn from service and this brand-new vessel was placed under repair at Rosyth Dockyard, which involved a complete reconstruction forward of the bridge. She did not emerge until the end of June.

At the end of June the *Legion* and *Lance* escorted the old carrier *Furious* down to Gibraltar. She was laden with Hurricanes for Malta and the two destroyers were temporarily attached to Force 'H' during this and subsequent flying-off operations on the 27th and 29th of that month, Operations *Railway I* and *II*. On the first mission the *Ark Royal* with the battle-cruiser *Renown* and light cruiser *Hermione* were escorted by the *Lance* and *Legion*, with the 8th Destroyer Flotilla ships *Faulknor, Forester* and *Fury*. On the second mission the *Furious* and *Hermione* were screened by *Legion, Fearless* and *Foxhound* as Force 'A' while *Lance* escorted *Renown* and *Ark Royal* with *Faulknor, Forester* and *Fury* as Force 'A'.

The two Ls then returned to the Special Escort Group at Greenock on completion of these missions. *Gurkha* emerged from her repairs and underwent trials at the beginning of July, and so her first wartime duty between the 12th and 15th of that month was as part of the escort for convoy WS9C, which had assembled in the Clyde, along with the destroyers *Vanoc, Wanderer* and the Polish manner *Garland*.

On 2 August *Gurkha, Lance* and *Legion* were escorting convoy WS10 from the Clyde with the destroyers *Whitehall, Winchelsea, Witch*, Polish *Piorun*, Dutch destroyer *Isaac Sweers* and the old ex-American four-stacker *Broadway*, returning to Greenock on the 6th. A similar escort duty for WS10X followed for *Lance, Gurkha, Isaac Sweers* and the former British destroyer *Noble* now manned by Polish sailors as the *Piorun* on the 17th. On 19 August *Legion* and *Lance* were sent to joint the hard-pressed convoy OG71.

Here they employed their D/F equipment gainfully to prevent attacks from a wolf pack, which included *U-201*, *U-564* and *U-559* until the convoy reached Gibraltar.

This was followed for *Legion* and *Lively* by yet another WS convoy operation, WS11, along with the anti-aircraft cruiser *Cairo* and destroyers *Cossack*, *Highlander*, *Winchelsea*, *Zulu*, *Piorun*, *Garland* and *Isaac Sweers* until 4 September. Once this convoy was in safe waters the two destroyers left and proceeded to Gibraltar where they were to join Force 'H' under Admiral Sir James Somerville. *Lively* had commissioned in July equipped with the new FH3 HF/DF equipment, which was to prove invaluable in the U-boat war. In August she also embarked an experimental Type 271 radar set (later known as the Type 273).

Lightning was joined at Scapa by her Flotilla Leader, *Laforey*, in August after she had completed of trials and had calibrated her guns. From here on these two destroyers continued to work with the Home Fleet and this period included several grim trips in vile weather across the North Sea escorting fast minelayers like the *Manxman*.

Tom King recalls what conditions were like aboard the *Lightning* on such trips as these to the Norwegian coast.

> I can remember leaving Scapa one night early in the commission; going to action stations all through the night; and it was rough. This was the only time I can remember being battened down inside our gun turrets because of rough weather. Our guns were elevated to the full but we still managed to take in water in the gun houses.

Lightning's next foray in company with the *Manxman* took place in July. A strong convoy, codenamed *Substance*, was to be run through under cover of Force 'H' from Gibraltar to Malta. To reinforce the ships of this force the Home Fleet sent the battleship *Nelson*, cruiser *Edinburgh*, the *Manxman* and the destroyers *Lightning*, *Cossack*, *Sikh*, *Nestor*, *Farndale*, *Avondale* and *Eridge* to escort convoy WS9C down to Gibraltar where the convoy became GM1 and these were off Gibraltar heading for the rendezvous on the night of 20 July. *Lightning* was detached with the light cruiser *Manchester* and Australian-manned destroyer *Nestor* to escort the liner *Pasteur* into the Rock to embark troops for Malta.

There were seven ships in the convoy, but unfortunately one, the *Leinster*, ran aground. The other six, *Melbourne Star*, *Sydney Star*, *City of Pretoria*, *Port Chalmers*, *Durham*, and *Deucalion*, together with the Home Fleet cruisers *Manchester*, *Arethusa* and *Aurora*, joined up with Force 'H', the battle-cruiser *Renown*, aircraft-carrier *Ark Royal*, cruiser *Hermione* and destroyers *Faulknor*, *Fearless*, *Foxhound*, *Firedrake*, *Foresight*, *Forester*, *Fury*, and *Duncan* with the 6th Flotilla's *Cossack*, *Maori* and *Sikh*.

The convoy and escort forged eastward in perfect weather throughout the 21st and the destroyers fuelled from the *Brown Ranger* during the following morning. Force 'H' to the north of the convoy was sighted by Italian aircraft but the merchant ships were not sighted. At dusk an Italian submarine made an attack on the *Nestor*, which promptly counter-attacked and drove her off. The next morning the Italian shadowers were about early and despite the efforts of the Fleet Air Arm the convoy was located. A combined torpedo-bombing and high-level attack resulted in the loss of the destroyer *Fearless*. The cruiser *Manchester* was also hit and sent back to Gibraltar. Further torpedo bomber attacks were made on the *Manchester* and the convoy without result but a high-level bombing attack was made which resulted in a hit on *Firedrake*, which had to be towed back to Gibraltar by *Eridge*. At dusk the convoy pressed on to Malta but the main force turned back and *Lightning* was part of their screen and saw no subsequent action.

On 31 July *Lighting* and *Sikh* escorted Force 'X', the light cruiser *Hermione* and *Arethusa* with fast minelayer *Manxman* with seventy Army officers and 1,676 men from the grounded *Leinster*, destined for Malta. This mission into Malta, Operation *Style*, was unopposed by the Axis, but *Hermione* was ably handled and rammed and sank the Italian submarine *Tembien* en route in the early hours of 2 August. *Lightning* later escorted the *Renown* on her return to the UK for repairs sailing on 8 August in company with the merchant ship *Pasteur* and the *Cossack*, *Maori* and *Sikh*.

It was after *Lightning's* return to Scapa on 12 August, that the 4-inch gunned Ls were permanently transferred to Force 'H'; they and the Tribals were gradually replacing the hard-worked F Class boats of the 8th Flotilla and the skyward-pointing main armament of the Ls were indeed to prove welcome in that sphere of operations. The flotilla was to find its full potential in the Mediterranean, dominated as it had become by German and Italian air power.

Lightning had sailed on 20 August, escorting the battleship *King George V* with *Inglefield*, *Punjabi* and *Tartar*, and *Lively* had been working up at Scapa during July. But on 22 August *Lively* had sailed with *Lightning* after receiving reports that the Free French submarine *Rubis* was in difficulties after being damaged off Norway. They were met by the AA cruiser *Curacoa* from Rosyth and eventually located the *Rubis*, which had repaired one engine and was limping home. The British ships escorted her into Dundee. *Lightning* was next out on an anti-submarine hunt in the north-west approaches with the destroyers *Intrepid* and *Lamerton* and trawler *Regal*, with no result and this was followed at the end of the month by escort duties for the newly refitted battle-cruiser *Repulse*, along with the light cruiser *Sheffield* and destroyers *Badsworth* and *Vivacious*. Between 3 and 5 September *Lightning* escorted the fast minelayer *Manxman* and light cruiser *Kenya* on Operation *EH* off the Norwegian coast. It was here that she encountered such bad weather conditions that she was forced to undergo repairs at Greenock, which kept her out of the war until 16 September.

In September the 4-inch ships moved down to Gibraltar to join the 4th Destroyer Flotilla there in readiness for the next major Malta Convoy operation, *Halberd*. *Gurkha*, *Lively* and *Lance*, along with *Forester*, escorted the carrier *Furious* to Gibraltar at the beginning of the month and conducted another flying off operation, *Status I*, of Hurricane fighters to Malta. This was repeated with Operation *Status II* on 12 September, *Legion* escorting *Furious* with *Foresight* and *Forester*, while *Gurkha*, *Lance*,

Lively and *Zulu* escorted the battleship *Nelson*, carrier *Ark Royal* and cruiser *Hermione*.

In addition to Force 'H' the Home Fleet was again providing reinforcements to fight the convoy through and so it came about that the whole of the L flotilla was involved (the two Scotts boats were of course still building). Somerville's Report of Proceedings noted that *Gurkha*, *Lance* and *Lively* were to join Force 'H' on conclusion of *Halberd*. Beforehand, *Gurkha* and *Lance* with *Zulu* rendezvoused with the convoy coming down from the UK, while *Legion* escorted *Furious* with *Foresight*, *Forester* and *Fury* en route for a refit in the USA, before returning to take part in the convoy operation.

The convoy, WS10 (the WS convoys became nicknamed 'Winston's Specials') comprising the *Breconshire*, *Clan Macdonald*, *Clan Ferguson*, *Ajax*, *Imperial Star*, *City of Lincoln*, *Rowallan Castle*, *Dunedin Star* and *City of Calcutta* passed through the Straits of Gibraltar on the night of the 24/25 September. Their escorts consisted of Force 'H', and the Home Fleet reinforcements: the battleships *Prince of Wales*, *Nelson* and *Rodney*, carrier *Ark Royal*, cruisers *Hermione*, *Kenya*, *Edinburgh*, *Sheffield*, *Euryalus* and destroyers *Laforey*, *Lightning*, *Gurkha*, *Legion*, *Lance*, *Lively*, *Cossack*, *Zulu*, *Duncan*, *Foresight*, *Forester*, *Oribi*, *Fury*, *Farndale*, *Heythrop*, the Polish-manned *Piorun* (formerly HMS *Nerissa*) and *Garland*, along with the Dutch *Isaac Sweers*.

On 25 September the convoy, re-numbered GM (Gibraltar–Malta) 2, had its escort split into two groups in order to give the impression that only Force 'H' was out. The fuelling force, tanker *Brown Ranger* and corvette *Fleur de Lys* made contact and the destroyers topped up. The first contact came from the submarines. At 1700 hours *Duncan* obtained a contact and attacked. Her starboard thrower failed to function and only four charges were dropped. The *Gurkha* now joined in the attack, putting down a fourteen-charge pattern at 1716 hours. *Duncan* later made a second attack but after this they lost the scent. The following day was largely uneventful, although it was thought the force was sighted by Italian search planes.

The two escorting units joined up at dawn on the 27

September in preparation for the inevitable attacks. Standing patrols of Fulmars were kept over the convoy by *Ark Royal*. Radar sightings of Italian aircraft were made early but not until 1158 hours was one sighted from the fleet, the *Legion* identifying a BR.20 bomber, which escaped interception in thick cloud. This plane was heard making a sighting report.

At 1255 hours the first of the expected air attacks was picked up by radar; two formations were reported coming in from the north and the east at thirty miles range. Fulmars intercepted and shot down one Cant shadower but at 1300 hours six BR.20 torpedo-bombers appeared low to port and carried out their attacks. Barrage fire from the battleships supplemented by the destroyers destroyed two of the torpedo-bombers at 1302 hours, but the others launched their missiles at the fleet, at about 5,000 yards range. Three of the torpedo-bombers attempted to penetrate the destroyer screen but were met by a fierce barrage and decided to attack the port wing ship, the *Lance*.

The three bombers dropped their torpedoes from a height of 300 feet at the *Lance* who had considerable difficulty in avoiding so many; two were very near misses, but she survived. Her next astern, *Isaac Sweers*, was also missed by a mere thirty yards and *Rodney* had to swing hard to port to avoid another torpedo, but no ship was hit. The destroyers managed to hit one of these three, which crashed in flames close to the *Lively*. The Fulmars meanwhile despatched another of a second group; so the Italians lost five out of twelve aircraft for no result, but one of the Fulmars flew into the barrage and was destroyed.

Another torpedo-bomber assault developed at 1327 hours, again in two groups of five or six planes each, this time from the starboard side of the convoy. Heavily engaged by the destroyer screen they pressed on through and three concentrated most bravely on the *Nelson*. The first dropped its torpedo a mere 450 yards from the battleship and scored a hit on the battleship's port bow. The huge vessel whipped as the explosion took place, but the Italian pilot did not survive to enjoy his success. Passing over the *Nelson* at 200 feet, he was immediately destroyed by the combined close-range fire of the *Prince of Wales* and *Sheffield*.

Laforey Class as designed

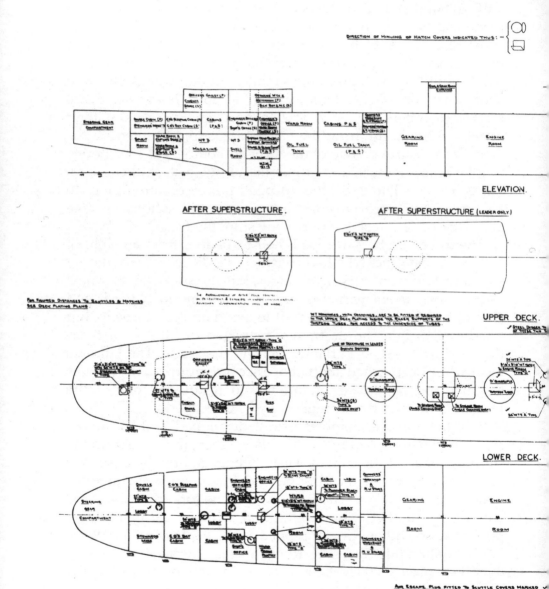

DIRECTION OF HINGING OF HATCH COVERS INDICATED THUS :-

ELEVATION.

AFTER SUPERSTRUCTURE.

AFTER SUPERSTRUCTURE (LEADER ONLY)

UPPER DECK.

LOWER DECK.

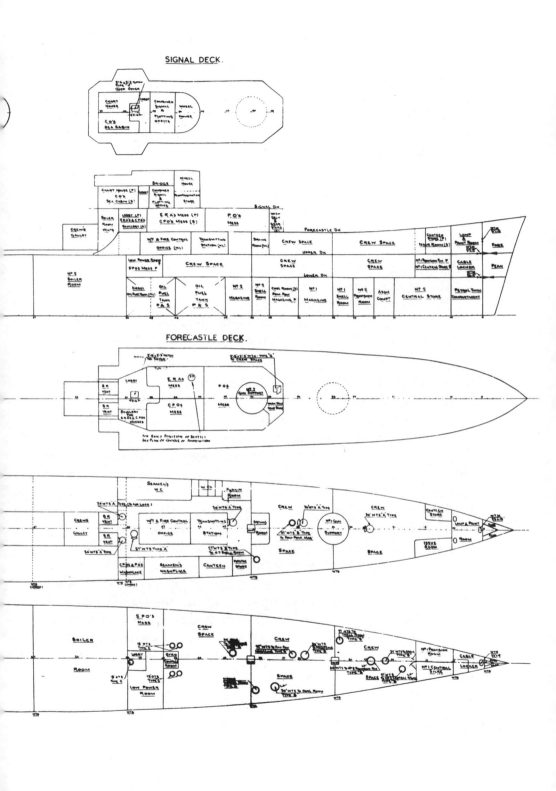

SIGNAL DECK.

FORECASTLE DECK.

Nelson's speed was reduced to 18 knots as a result of this hit but a second torpedo launched at 1,000 yards range was avoided. The third Italian BR.20 was meanwhile engaged by *Laforey* and shot down just ahead of the screen, the *Forester* picking up one survivor. Somerville wrote to his wife.

> As regards the torpedo attack we took our toll of them. There were some indescribable scenes. I saw one burst into the most enormous sheet of flame as she was hit and brought down by one of our destroyers. The one that hit us flashed by with tracer bullets going into him and disappeared with smoke coming from an engine, whilst another that flashed by was hit by one of our pom-poms and burst into three pieces in the air. About the same time a CR42 fighter that was machine-gunning one of the destroyers was brought down and crashed into the sea...

Another bomber was destroyed by the Fulmars and *Rodney* destroyed one of the Fleet Air Arm fighters; the remaining attacks were ineffectual.

Only a brief respite was given, for at 1345 hours a third attack developed from the south-east; about a dozen SM.79s were reported. Once again they split into two formations, the larger of which under fire from the destroyers on the starboard screen withdrew. Three others were equally frustrated and attacked the ships on the screen after finding it impossible to penetrate the barrage. This time it was the *Lightning* which was narrowly missed but again no hits were scored and another bomber went down to the fighters. Another three attacked on their own: one approached *Ark Royal* and was destroyed by her; and another attacked the damaged battleship but her missile was avoided. A CR42 fighter was seen performing acrobatics over the convoy at this time, presumably to divert attention from the torpedo-bombers. After a considerable expenditure of ammunition the destroyers hit him, and he dived into the sea.

While this attack had been taking place a report that the Italian battle fleet was at sea was received and the *Nelson, Rodney* and *Prince of Wales* with a screen of six destroyers turned to intercept. *Legion* was left to operate with the *Ark Royal*. The Italians actually had two battleships, five cruisers and fourteen destroyers at sea. *Nelson* had to drop out and was replaced by *Edinburgh* and *Sheffield* but the Italians turned back before contact could be made and no action resulted.

Laforey formed up as part of Force 'X', the close escort to take the convoy through to Malta, with the cruisers *Edinburgh*, *Sheffield*, *Euryalus* and *Hermione* and destroyers *Foresight*, *Forester* and *Fury* (which all had their mine sweeps streamed), *Cossack*, *Zulu*, *Oribi*, *Farndale* and *Heythrop*.

That evening the convoy with close escort went on toward the Sicilian 'Narrows' as usual and were subjected to scattered torpedo-bomber attacks, *Laforey* sighting two about two miles ahead in the gloom at 2010 hours. Several of these aircraft were shot down but managed to torpedo one of the merchant vessels, the *Imperial Star*, which later had to be sunk. The others arrived safely at Malta.

Meanwhile, the main fleet had turned back to the west at *Nelson*'s best speed of 14 knots. Just after midnight *Legion* reported an anti-submarine contact but this was not confirmed. The rest of 28 September passed quietly, although again *Legion* carried out an anti-submarine hunt after *Duncan* reported a contact, again without results, at 1942 hours. *Nelson* was sent back to Gibraltar that evening but the other two battleships and *Ark Royal* turned again to meet the returning cruisers and destroyers from Malta.

At 0555 hours the *Prince of Wales* picked up a radar contact ahead of the fleet, which carried out an emergency turn to port. Three minutes later the *Gurkha* sighted an approaching torpedo track. Almost immediately a second was seen, both travelling at 40 knots and too close to be avoided. The *Gurkha* could do nothing at all, but to their amazement and relief both torpedoes passed beneath the ship without exploding. The submarine had obviously meant them for the battleships and only the alertness of the radar plot in *Prince of Wales* had saved her. *Gurkha* immediately followed up the torpedo tracks and in company with *Isaac Sweers* carried out a hunt without success, returning to the screen at 0700 hours. The Ls were on their mettle now, and with their superior detection equipment and experience in the North Atlantic they were finding the conditions in the Mediterranean ideal. At 0810 hours *Gurkha* again made a positive contact nearly ahead and made a deliberate attack firing a fourteen-charge pattern at 0815 hours. Six minutes later a heavy underwater explosion was heard. *Gurkha* was still sniffing round the scene when ordered to rejoin at 0841 hours. This attack was not confirmed as a kill post-war however.[4]

Force 'X' joined at 1030 hours on 29 September and the combined force headed westward back to Gibraltar. They were still in submarine-infested waters, however, and at 1645 hours the *Lively* sighted what she took to be a ship's lifebelt with mast about 1,000 yards away. It was identified as a submarine periscope breaking surface and *Lively*, already under heel to conform with the zig-zag of the screen, increased speed to 24 knots. Two torpedo tracks were sighted as the destroyer closed and fired a fourteen-charge pattern set shallow. *Legion* joined the hunt and dropped a five-charge pattern. *Legion* then stationed *Lively* on the starboard beam and the two ships began a deliberate hunt.

At 1700 hours *Lively* attacked with a fourteen-charge pattern a definite contact. After firing contact was regained showing the target moving at one knot but despite this contact was again lost and not regained.[5] At 1930 hours *Laforey* and *Lightning* proceeded ahead into Gibraltar with *Prince of Wales* at high speed, leaving the *Rodney* to gain safety at her own best speed. The submarines were thick on the ground in the approaches to Gibraltar and at 0928 hours on the 30th the irrepressible *Gurkha* again obtained a contact which was confirmed as a submarine 2,000 yards ahead of the fleet.

She attacked at once in position 37° 10' N, 00° 56' E, and fired the standard fourteen-charge pattern set shallow at 0933 hours. A black circular buoy came to the surface as a result of this attack and a heavy underwater explosion was heard and felt at 0945 hours. Oil started to come to the surface but *Gurkha* lost contact. *Legion* was assigned to help and she picked up a contact and attacked with full pattern at 0955 hours and again at 1009 hours.

After this second attack wreckage and oil appeared. Among the pathetic remains fished out of the water were an Italian dictionary, a mattress, pieces of wood, one with part of a human scalp attached to it by a splinter of metal, a cork stamped with the word 'Chianti' and other oddments. *Legion*'s doctor was reported as being 'in his element' diagnosing parts of Italians. The Italians later admitted the destruction of the submarine *Adua*.

Let Captain Lentaigne of the *Gurkha* recount how this highly accurate and successful attack was carried out by his command.

Gurkha and *Lance* were fitted with the special anti-submarine equipment, *Gurkha* having slightly more sophisticated equipment installed than *Lance*. *Legion* and *Lively* were fitted with radar, as were most new destroyers, but although *Gurkha* was Senior Officer's ship of the 4-inch gunned division of the Ls she and *Lance* lacked radar except for a gunnery set to compensate for the extra anti-submarine apparatus. All four of these ships had the larger depth-charge pattern which was a great asset. On the other hand this pattern greatly increased the weight aft and raised the draught aft from a designed 15'3" to 17'6". This was a disadvantage as not only did it put up fuel consumption, but it increased the turning circle, a handicap when hunting submarines, or dodging dive-bombers.

To elaborate: *Gurkha* sank the Italian submarine *Adua* and she caused *Adua* to blow up within a few seconds of the pattern exploding. The Admiralty analysis showed at least one depth charge exploded in contact with the hull. You would think that *Gurkha* was a good hull for a submarine attacker. The real fact is that all the trumps fell into my hand. Conditions were good and the *Adua* was detected at near maximum range. She was going at near full submerged speed to fire at the line of ships we were screening. I think her target was *Ark Royal*. I was going at 17-knots, almost attacking speed, and the bearing was fine on the bow. So I did not alter revolutions and my two small alterations of course were made with only five degrees of wheel. So there was no change in underwater noises, and I think that *Adua*'s Captain thought he was undetected. He made no attempt to dodge. A brave man. From first detection to disintegration was about three minutes.

The senior officer of the starboard screen in *Cossack* signalled the Royal Netherlands destroyer *Isaac Sweers* to join me in subsequent search and attack. I did not receive this signal and to avoid a double gap had already ordered *Legion* to turn and join me. Before he arrived a round object that looked like a mine and other wreckage was on the surface. I was cautious as I knew that German submarines were deliberately sending wreckage up after an attack to distract attackers and to give them a chance of counter attack. On the other hand the detonation of the submarine was so great that it shook *Gurkha* and my engineers thought that we had been torpedoed.

Then *Legion* joined and dropped a pattern on a contact a little distance away and followed this contact to the eastward. My operators said he was after a shoal of fish so I returned to the scene of my attack. Wreckage was still coming to the surface and I lowered a boat to search and pick up what might be of interest. In the meantime my anti-submarine officer, Lieutenant E.A. Herring, asked permission to dive overboard to swim to the round object and investigate. I agreed but warned him not to approach it if any antennae wires were to be seen. He swam round finding none and dived to inspect it below water. He was back on the surface in a moment and instantly shouted, 'Look out'. Nothing happened. He then swam over to us and said that there was a thickish wire hanging below the object, and it came over towards him when he grasped it. On the bridge of the *Gurkha* we had all seen the thing tilt and realised that it was a buoy of some sort. It was hoisted in and taken to Gibraltar, where the Intelligence boys were very interested. It proved to be something new and unexpected. Also picked up were parts of a desk with correspondence and a book of codes.

No further excitement followed this series of attacks but the Italian submarine force had been forewarned of the arrival of the Ls in the Mediterranean in no uncertain way by this convoy. The *Lance* then went into dock at Gibraltar on 1st October for a refit, which lasted until the 12th. *Lively*, however, was sent to help escort convoy WS12 between the 8th and 9th.

Both *Laforey* and *Lightning* returned to Scapa Flow as part of the escort for Prince of Wales, arriving on 6 October. After a short refit at Rosyth *Lightning* and *Greenock* remained in Home waters until they were permanently allocated to Force 'H' in October, sailing on the 25th and reaching the Rock four days later.

Perhaps as a result of the mauling they had received the Italian submarines operating off Gibraltar were replaced by German U-boats during the following weeks. The difference was soon felt but it was first blood to the escorts when the trawler *Lady Shirley* sank the *U-111* off the Canary Islands in October. Her nine-man crew had rescued forty-four of the enemy and, as the victors' own total uninjured complement was just nine, it was felt they needed back-up and so *Lance* was sent to escort the victorious little vessel into Gibraltar. The German submarines soon began to hit back hard, however.

Gurkha had sailed for the UK on 14 November, for a refit and upgrade at Devonport Dockyard, which lasted until early December. Then on 9 December she was allocated as part of the escort for convoy WS14, along with *Nestor* and *Foxhound*. On 13 December she was relieved by the *Vanquisher*, and with *Croome*, these ships conducted a U-boat hunt.

When not putting their heads into the lion's mouth fighting through convoys to Malta, the destroyers of Force 'H' were not allowed to rest on their laurels. Among the many chores allocated to them was the escorting of convoys up from the Rock to Home waters where they reinforced the local screens for part of the journey. One such convoy was HG 75 which consisted of sixteen merchant vessels and the CAM ship *Ariguani* which was escorted by five small escorts. *Legion, Cossack, Duncan, Lamerton* and *Vidette* from Gibraltar were despatched to provide some more substantial aid to this convoy. However, when the U-boats struck the first victim was the famous *Cossack* herself, torpedoed by the *U-563* west of Cape Spartel. This famous ship was hit and the forward magazine blew up with an awesome explosion. Commander Jessel remembers the scene:

> The whole forecastle and superstructure before the bridge vanished and the ship was on fire. Most of the personnel on the bridge, including Captain Berthon, Captain (D), were killed. *Legion*, with the aid of a corvette, extinguished the fire and rescued survivors, a score of officers and men being injured, some seriously. Our wardroom was converted to a sickbay, where they were tended by our doctor for some ten days. The convoy itself suffered grievous loss, including the Commodore's flagship. During the next three nights, further though less serious losses were experienced, but the destroyer *Lamerton* sank a U-boat. *Legion* was then ordered to leave the convoy, refuel in the Azores, and thence sail north to meet the *Prince of Wales*, which had just sailed on her ill-fated voyage to Singapore. *Legion* stayed with her for four days during which the four destroyers on her screen took turns to oil in the Azores. We then parted company for our return to Gibraltar, there landing our wounded passengers, and found *Laforey* and *Lightning* had arrived to join our flotilla.

Notes

1 It is interesting to note that in the guise of fiction two of the Ls turn up in a bitter Gibraltar convoy battle in Nicholas Monsarrat's novel *The Cruel Sea* where he named them *Lancelot* and *Liberal*. It was obviously based on a true encounter.

2 The other destroyers were *Bedouin, Eskimo, Somali* and *Tartar* under the command of Captain C. Caslon, Captain (D) 6. The troops were commanded by Major A.R. Aslett. The naval force was codenamed *Rebel*. The destroyers refuelled from the tanker *War Pindari*. Guided into the approaches of Vestfjord by the submarine *Sunfish* the whole force arrived off their objective without being once sighted or reported by the German aircraft searches.

3 See also E. Gilroy's account, *Struck by Lightning* (Privately Published, Rochester, Kent) whose accounts and dates are not always totally reliable.

4 *Gurkha's* target was the submarine *Diaspro*, which was damaged.

5 *Legion* and *Lively* had attacked and damaged the submarine *Serpente*.

Chapter 6

Fighting Force 'K'

The arrival of these two ships offset the departure of the *Lance* and the *Lively*. It had become apparent that, with the departure of the bulk of the *Luftwaffe* for the Russian Front, it was again practicable to station surface forces at Valletta to back up the submarines based there in striking at Axis convoy routes to Libya. Accordingly, the two light cruisers *Aurora* and *Penelope* were sailed from Scapa Flow on 12 October and on passing Gibraltar the *Lance* and *Lively* joined them after embarking two 18-inch aerial torpedoes and 200 rounds of spare 4-inch ammunition, for an uneventful voyage to Malta. These vessels were the new striking force and were soon to earn themselves a formidable reputation as Force 'K'.

The force arrived at Malta on 21 October. It was to prove a brief but very rewarding association with the two small cruisers 'adopting' the two big destroyers, *Aurora*, the *Lance*, and *Penelope*, the *Lively*. So integrated did the ships become that signalling in action, always a tell-tale pointer, was reduced to a minimum, and the Italians were soon bewailing their efficiency. Two abortive sorties followed but on the night of 8/9 November Force 'K' made themselves felt in no small way.

A Maryland aircraft sighted six Italian merchant ships escorted by four destroyers some forty miles to the east of Cape Spartivento at 1400 hours that Saturday afternoon. The force left Malta to intercept but the aircraft lost contact and the ships altered course to return to Valletta. However, at forty minutes past midnight they ran straight into this convoy and caught them completely unawares. The British ships made no mistake.

The methods to be employed in attacking a convoy had often been discussed between the Captains of the four ships of Force 'K': after the first General Alarm Bearing, S.O.K. (Captain Agnew of *Aurora*) had only to make two more signals during the whole action – one to reduce speed, and one to warn against wasting ammunition. Everyone knew what to do, and it only remained for them to do it.[1]

The Italian convoy comprised the merchant vessels, seven in number, with a close escort of six destroyers, *Fulmine*, *Euro*, *Maestrale*, *Libeccio*, *Oriani* and *Grecale*. As further cover the Italians deployed two heavy cruisers (8-inch guns, 10,000 tons against the *Aurora*'s and *Penelope*'s main armaments of six 6-inch guns each), with a further four destroyers, but these lagged too far behind the convoy to be of any real assistance.

The ships of Force 'K' worked around the convoy to silhouette them against the moon and got within 6,000 yards range undetected. *Aurora* then opened fire on the nearest destroyer escort and *Penelope* engaged a second. *Aurora* then led the force round and passed up the eastern side of the convoy and the merchant ships were deliberately and in turn engaged by all four British ships.

> The ships seemed to make no effort to escape, and it was all too easy; they burst into flames as soon as we hit them. A large tanker was like a wall of flame, and an ammunition ship gave a superb display of fireworks before she blew up with a tremendous explosion. We could soon see about eight burning ships and a great pall of smoke where the ammunition ship had been.[2]

Both *Aurora* and *Lance* fired torpedoes to add to the holocaust and only one Italian fired back before being reduced to a shambles by *Penelope*. The *Lively* reported that two torpedoes passed astern of her but no British ship was hit. The final tally was that all the Italian convoy was sunk, including the destroyer *Fulmine*. The destroyers *Euro* and *Grecale* were damaged. In addition next morning the destroyer *Libeccio* busy picking up survivors was torpedoed by a British submarine and sank in tow. Not a good night for the *Duce*.

Penelope signalled *Aurora*: 'Congratulations to *Aurora* on her magnificent *Borealis'*.

Great claim was made by the Italian Air Force, of which Count Ciano the Italian Foreign Minister was himself sceptical, that they had attacked and hit one of Force 'K's' cruisers on their return to Malta. Vice-Admiral (Malta) sent Force 'K' the following message in connection with this totally false assumption.

> It is with great regret that I see in the Italian broadcast that one of the cruisers received two hits and a destroyer one hit during torpedo bombing. I can only think that in view of the lack of damage I saw to-day the Dockyard is more efficient than I thought or your camouflage excellent.

This brought forth the following from the Captain:

> There was an air-Wop from Taranto,
> Who set out for an exploit gallanto.
> He sinka da cruise
> And get into da nooze,
> To make up for da kick in da panto.

When Ciano received breathless confirmation from his air chiefs that their claims must be true because one of the British cruisers was anchored near the dry-dock in Valletta he cynically noted in his personal diary that this was like saying a man was slightly dead because he had gone to live near a cemetery! Anyway, whether believed or not Force 'K' was to demonstrably prove it was alive and kicking in the weeks which followed.

Meanwhile, for the remainder of the flotilla still based at Gibraltar things, while far from dull, had slowed down, and apart from the occasional sortie into the Western Basin to fly off aircraft reinforcements for Malta, the Ls found themselves on routine patrols in the Straits hoping to catch submarines trying to break in. The ancient aircraft carrier *Argus* arrived at Gibraltar from home at 2300 hours on 7 November, escorted by *Laforey* and *Lightning* with a cargo of Hurricane fighters, while the aircraft transport *Athene* with further disassembled fighters embarked, arrived the following day escorted by *Gurkha*, with the Dutch destroyer *Isaac Sweers* and *Zulu*.

On 10 November Force 'H', the battleship *Malaya*, the carriers *Ark Royal* and *Argus*, light cruiser *Hermione* and destroyers, *Laforey*, *Lightning*, *Legion*, *Gurkha*, *Sikh*, *Zulu* and *Isaac Sweers*, sailed from the Rock to carry out another aircraft ferry operation, *Perpetual*, which was successful. On the return home, however, the *U-81* torpedoed the famous *Ark Royal*.

Admiral Somerville's *Report of Proceedings* spelt out how this came about.

13 November

An underwater explosion observed by *Legion* in her wake at 0413, was also heard by several ships. *Legion* at this time was the starboard destroyer. This was probably a torpedo exploding at the end of its run, but the occurrence was not reported to me until daylight.

At 0817 I informed Force H that submarines had been reported in the vicinity and that great vigilance was necessary. Until 0900 course had been shaped to give the impression that it was intended to pass south of Alboran Island, but at this time a sharp alteration was made to 305° to pass to the northward, subsequently turning to 270° and approaching Gibraltar directly from the eastward, through the centre of the area.

On previous occasions Force H has usually returned to Gibraltar along either the Spanish or Moroccan coasts, making the final approach from the NE or SE. This was probably known to the enemy and it was thought that in consequence any U-boats in the vicinity were more likely to be in positions near the shore.

At 0955 *Laforey* reported investigating a contact to starboard, and an emergency turn away 90° was made. *Laforey* dropped two depth chargers, but contact was lost and the fleet turned back to 310° at 1008. At 1157, *Lighting* reported contact to starboard, and an emergency turn of 90° to port was made. The contact was immediately negatived and the mean course of 270° was resumed at 1201.

Ark Royal requested freedom of manoeuvring to carry out deck landing training at 1515, and I replied approving this, provided *Ark Royal* kept well inside the anti-submarine screen during flying operations. *Ark Royal* informed me at 1418 that she had fourteen aircraft to land on at 1515, and suggested she should do this from a position on *Malaya's* disengaged (port) quarter, as *Malaya* was expected to be firing at that time. I approved the proposal.... – 'Your 1418 approved, but keep well under the screen'.

Laforey reported a contact to port at 1518, and an emergency turn was made to starboard. *Ark Royal* altered course to 286° for flying at 1529, and flew off six Swordfish and two Fulmars. Five Swordfish were flown on, and at 1535 *Ark Royal* turned to port to regain her position in the line, altering course again to 286° at 1538 ready to fly on.

Legion, the starboard wing destroyer, turned to 250° at this time to cover *Ark Royal*, turning back to port when *Ark Royal* moved in to regain station. Just before turning to the course of the fleet, hydrophone effect (H/E) was reported on the starboard bow, but, as this coincided with the approximate bearing of *Gurkha*, the next ahead, and faded out when *Legion* turned to the course of the fleet, it was disregarded and not reported by *Legion*. The S.D. operator subsequently stated that H/E on this occasion was louder than any he had heard previously. This suggests that the H/E heard was in fact that of the torpedo fired at *Ark Royal*.

At 1540, the remainder of the Force turned to 290° in accordance with zig-zag No. 11 which had been ordered. At this time I instructed the commanding officer, *Malaya* (Captain Cuthbert Coppinger) to keep clear to port of *Ark Royal*, who was four cables on *Malaya's* starboard quarter, until she had completed flying on, as the course of the two ships converged slightly. At 1541....*Ark Royal*, who was bearing 077° four cables from *Malaya*, was struck by a torpedo on the starboard side.... *Malaya* altered course away to port, increased speed and eventually steadied on 240°. *Gurkha* and *Legion*, the rear destroyers on the starboard wing, at once turned outwards to search the area to the north and east of *Ark Royal*, i.e. the probable direction of the attack. Captain (D) 19th DF, in *Laforey*, ordered the remaining destroyers to form screening diagram No. 5 on *Malaya*.

At this time *Ark Royal* was still going ahead at considerable speed listing to starboard and apparently under port wheel. A number of aircraft were still circling overhead. At 1549 *Laforey* and *Lighting* were ordered to join *Ark Royal* who appeared to be easing down. Signals were made to VACNA to send tugs to assist *Ark Royal* and for the immediate despatch of all A/S craft and aircraft from North Front to patrol. *Hermione*, some six miles distant was ordered to join *Ark Royal*. At 1552 the remaining three destroyers, viz., *Sikh*, *Zulu* and *Isaac Sweers*, were ordered to form screening diagram No. 3 on *Malaya*.

Situation at 1610. *Ark Royal* was apparently stopped and listing heavily to starboard, but reported she had steam on her port engine. *Legion*, *Gurkha* and *Lightning* had closed and were circling *Ark Royal*. *Legion* was alongside *Ark Royal* and *Hermione* was closing. *Malaya*, now distant 4.5 miles from *Ark Royal*, was returning to Gibraltar at 18 knots, screened at first by three destroyers and subsequently by two destroyers, when, at 1615 I despatched *Zulu* to join *Ark Royal*. *Argus* was some distance astern but overhauling *Malaya*. *Argus* flew off two Swordfish for A/S patrol at 1615.

Somerville later wrote to his wife that:

The strange thing is that our ASDICs gave no warnings this time and no one saw the track of the torpedo. I can't understand how one torpedo should have caused the loss of this fine ship.

He also wrote to Admiral Cunningham:

> It was quite the worst inquiry I have ever attended...
> Forbes [Admiral of the Fleet Sir Charles Forbes, C-in-C
> Plymouth who was President of the subsequent Board of
> Enquiry] appeared to be convinced it was poor ASDIC
> conditions. I don't agree as I think the shot was fired just
> outside the A/S range. *Legion*...heard H/E but did not
> report it... Had she reported it I think we could have
> turned in time to make it miss ahead... The bad thing is
> that one torpedo should have caused so much damage. A
> M/L only 50 yards off when she capsized had an Aldis on
> her [an Aldis Signal Lamp as the carrier sank in darkness]
> and reported the hole as being 120–150 feet long and 30
> wide midway between the starboard bilge keel and the
> centre line of the ship. It now appears that the damage
> must have been far more extensive than it appeared to be
> at first.

Reverting to the viewpoint of the Ls at the time of torpedo hit,
the *Ark Royal* quickly took on an appreciable list to starboard
and the *Legion* was ordered alongside. Commander Jessel
recalled:

> As the *Ark*'s wireless masts were in the horizontal position,
> we had to go alongside well aft, and there, because of the
> list having brought her port screw nearer the surface, there
> was risk of it damaging our hull. 1,489 officers and men
> were embarked, and were landed at Gibraltar.

The First Lieutenant wryly recalls that after the survivors, ten
times *Legion*'s normal complement, were disembarked he
remembered looking woefully at the Wardroom fridge that
night. 'All the locusts had left us was one bad tomato!!' *Laforey*
immediately took *Legion*'s place alongside to provide power for
pumps and lighting until the *Ark Royal* managed to raise steam.
But it was all in vain for a small fire broke out and the carrier,
despite all further efforts, increased her list. She finally sank at
0600 on 11 November despite the presence of tugs.

Subsequent operations from Gibraltar were largely curtailed. On 16 November *Gurkha* and *Lightning*, along with *Sikh* and *Zulu*, escorted *Argus* and flew on aircraft from the North Front before returning to harbour. Later the same day *Laforey*, *Gurkha*, *Legion* and *Lightning*, along with *Sikh*, *Zulu* and *Isaac Sweers*, sailed as *Nelson* sailed to return home for repairs and a dummy convoy sailed to make a brief diversion to the eastward overnight in a vain attempt to draw Axis attention from a sortie by Cunningham's fleet. On 30 November the 19th Flotilla was conducting anti-submarine sweeps in the Straits, but to no avail. On 15 December, *Gurkha* was returning to the Rock from the UK in company with the destroyers *Nestor*, *Foxhound* and *Croome* when they found and sank the *U-127* off Cape St Vincent, an excellent result.

The remainder of the year continued in a fairly low-key manner at Gibraltar due to the lack of sufficient warships. *Lightning* was temporarily detached along with the destroyers *Harvester* and *Highlander*, as escort to the battleship *Duke of York*, which was taking the Prime Minister and his party to America to confer with President Roosevelt (the *Arcadia* Conference). Unfortunately, her commanding officer, Commander R. G. Stuart, was taken ill and her First Lieutenant had to take her to sea on 11 December. Weather conditions proved extreme and the three destroyers, after refuelling at Ponta Del Gardo in the neutral Portuguese Azores between the 15th and 17th, failed to rendezvous with the *Duke of York*. They finally reached Bermuda on 22 December and then sailed for Norfolk, Virginia, where they belatedly arrived on the 31st.

Lightning and her compatriots sailed to St John's Newfoundland from Norfolk on 12 January, arriving four days later to refuel and then left on the 18th for Greenock. They arrived on the 25th and a new captain, Commander H. G. Walters, joined the ship. Some weather repairs were undertaken after her punishing and fruitless perambulations and then she rejoined Force 'H' again heading for Gibraltar, arriving on 4 February having circumnavigated the North Atlantic.

Meanwhile, back at Gibraltar on 19 December *Laforey* and

Gurkha had been part of the screen during practice shoots by *Malaya* and also escorted *Argus* on exercises on 20 December. Two days later *Gurkha* sailed with the light cruiser *Dido* and destroyers *Arrow*, *Foxhound*, *Nestor* and *Zulu* for Malta and the eastern Mediterranean. Their voyage was uneventful save for the usual air attacks and *Gurkha* arrived at Alexandria on 29 December and joined the main Mediterranean Fleet. On 3 January, Admiral Somerville visited *Laforey* to say farewell as he later sailed for home aboard the *Hermione* on hauling down his flag and handing over command of Force 'H' to Vice-Admiral Sir E.N. Syfret.

On the 18 January *Laforey* was acting in support of Convoy SL97 along with the destroyer *Hesperus* and rewarded, after a succession of depth charge attacks, with an enemy U-boat being brought to the surface, where she was quickly taken under fire and finally sank. She proved to be the *U-93* from whom forty-one crew were rescued. In a similar manner *Laforey* and *Lightning*, with the destroyers *Active*, *Anthony*, *Blankney*, *Croome*, *Duncan* and *Firedrake* from Gibraltar, were sent to reinforce the escort of another big troop convoy, WS16, which they helped escort until the 21st when they escorted the carrier *Argus* from that group back into the Rock.

Another Hurricane flying-off operation was planned, *Spotter I*, with the carriers *Eagle* and *Argus*, the battleship *Malaya* and the light cruiser *Hermione* being escorted by the *Laforey*, *Lightning*, *Active*, *Anthony*, *Blankney*, *Croome*, *Exmoor*, *Whitehall* and *Wishart*. However, the operation had to be cancelled due to defects in the Hurricanes' fuel tanks. This flying off operation was finally successfully carried out by the same force between 6 and 8 March as *Spotter II*. While awaiting the next such operation the destroyers carried out intense anti-submarine patrols in the Straits area, and during one of these *Lightning* had her rudder damaged and had to be docked. No lessons had been learnt by the RAF, however, and another attempt to fly off aircraft, staged between 20 and 22 March as Operation *Picket I*, also had to be aborted for the self-same reasons. Once more the defects had to be rectified before the fighters could be flown off safely, which was done on the 27th.

We will have to revert back to earlier momentous events in the central Mediterranean and at Malta where *Lance* and *Lively* had continued to be well employed. The Force was carrying out a sweep during the afternoon of 24 November with the ships spread five miles apart. An attack by a Junkers Ju 88 on *Lively* resulted in near misses but no damage and half and hour later smoke was sighted to the north-west. This was a small fast convoy consisting of the oil tankers *Maritza* and *Procida*, escorted by the destroyers *Lupo* and *Cassiopea*. They had left the Greek port of Piraeus for Benghazi by the eastern route in the hope of avoiding Force 'K's' usual stamping ground of the Sicilian Channel but they were unlucky and were some 100 miles west of Crete when located.

Penelope was the nearest ship and proved capable of dealing with the entire action almost single-handed. The two Italian destroyers made smoke to protect their charges. 'However several straddles from the cruiser's main armament and the Italian boats ran past their charges and left them to their fate'.[3] A few more salvoes from *Penelope* and both were left on fire and eventually sank. The *Lance* and *Lively* had little to do but help fend off repeated air attacks on the return to Malta. *Lance* then went into dry-dock at Malta until 15 December.

Soon after this news was received on Japan's entry into the war. One result of this which was to affect the Ls was that the Australian destroyers operating with the main Mediterranean fleet at Alexandria were called home and it was decided that the 4th Flotilla should despatch four destroyers to make up for their loss. The ships selected were the *Sikh* (Commander Stokes), *Maori*, *Legion* and Dutch *Isaac Sweers*, and they duly sailed for Malta en route to Alexandria on 11 December.

It was known that the Sicilian Channel was mined, and they were ordered to keep inside the three-mile limit off the Tunisian coast. Meanwhile, after the chaos and heavy losses caused to their conventional convoys by Force 'K', the Italians had decided to run in essential supplies to Libya using their warships, and the two light cruisers *Alberto di Giussano* and *Alberico da Barbiano* with the destroyer *Cigno* had sailed accordingly from Palermo for Tripoli with a deck load of cased petrol urgently required by the Army in the desert. The British flotilla was sighted by Axis aircraft, but when the cruisers turned back to avoid them they instead ran straight into the British force.

Whilst rounding Cape Bon *Sikh* sighted the two cruisers and the British destroyers followed them round the cape for a few miles astern. Almost immediately afterward the Italians reversed course. Again Commander Jessel describes events as seen from *Legion*'s bridge that night:

> We were in an extremely fortunate position, with the Tunisian coast obliterating the horizon to the west and a bright, rising moon to the east, which clearly silhouetted the Italians at 1500 yards range. *Sikh* fired her four torpedoes at the leading cruiser and trained her guns on the second. *Legion* was the next in line. I had expected *Sikh* to have taken the second ship for his torpedo target, and so I also chose the leading ship for *Legion*. We turned to fire exactly in *Sikh*'s wake. As our second torpedo left its tube the target burst into flames as one of *Sikh*'s torpedoes went home. We checked fire, steadied, and then started a second swing, firing the remaining six torpedoes at the second cruiser, which was also hit. (This shift of target whilst firing an outfit of torpedoes is thought to be unique in torpedo history.) Meanwhile of course all four of us had opened up with the gunfire.

Both cruisers were sunk, although the destroyer accompanying them managed to escape. When the four destroyers steamed into Valletta harbour *Lance* and *Lively* manned ship and cheered in their sister who had so quickly adapted herself to the job they had until then assumed to be their own private preserve. One amusing anecdote arose from this action as Commander Jessel later recalled.

> When *Legion* sailed from Gibraltar to join the fleet at Alexandria she had embarked some passengers, mostly Army and RAF officers. But there was one civilian, the Assistant Director of Naval Stores, who was to enquire into

certain Store problems at Alexandria. Being a quite senior
Civil Servant, it was decided that he should occupy my
harbour cabin, a very fine apartment, except perhaps for
the 4-inch gun support that passed down through the
middle of it.

On the morning after our action with the two Italian
cruisers, we were steaming at full speed hoping to get
close enough to Malta to be under its fighter umbrella
before enemy bombers could find us. At about 0845, the
first two fighters appeared above us, and I ordered one
watch to breakfast (we had been at action stations all
night). In the wardroom, those officers off duty sat
themselves down, and started to eat in hungry silence.
Punctually at nine o'clock, into the Mess walked the
Assistant Director of Stores, all spruce and freshly shaved.
Sitting himself down, he turned to one of the officers and
asked, 'Did anything happen last night. I thought I heard
gunfire?'

After a few days the four destroyers left for Alexandria and
while on passage were ordered to join Admiral Vian's force,
which was fighting through the *Breconshire* to Malta from the
east. Force 'K' contributed the cruisers *Aurora* and *Penelope*,
and destroyers *Lance, Lively, Maori, Sikh, Zulu* and *Isaac Sweers*
as Force 'C' to this operation, M42. The Italian battle fleet was
out and made brief contact before drawing away again in a
scrambling encounter known later as the First Battle of Sirte
on 17 December. *Legion* was not allowed the opportunity to
repeat here her torpedo skills against the Italian surface ships,
but she was to get another chance before many days had
passed.

Their arrival at Alexandria was less fortunate. They entered
the gate on the night of the 18th and the following morning saw
the battleships *Queen Elizabeth* and *Valiant* and the tanker *Savona*
sinking at their moorings onto the harbour bottom after being
badly damaged in the audacious Italian frogmen attack. At the
subsequent enquiry evidence was given by a coxswain of the
gate patrol that he had seen some object 'moving on the water as

the second destroyer had passed through the gate'. That destroyer was the *Legion*!

She was able to exact a measure of revenge shortly after, however. The British Tobruk supply vessel *Volo* was sunk off Mersa Matruh on 28 December and a long hunt for her killer took place by the *Legion* and *Kipling* in the area, resulting in the sinking of the *U-75* in position 31° 50′ N 26° 40′ E.

Meanwhile, Force 'K', minus *Lance* for a short period, was going about its business. On 1 December they intercepted and quickly despatched the ammunition ship *Adriatico* off Benghazi. While returning from this sortie, another ship was sighted and the force diverted to catch her. She turned out to be the oil tanker *Mantovani* with a solitary destroyer escort, the *Alaiso da Mosto*. Force 'K' caught up with them off Tripoli after some very hard steaming. The Italian destroyer fought very gallantly to defend her charge. She was taken under fire by both British cruisers and after being hit by salvoes from both almost simultaneously, blew up and sank.

The *Lively* was employed in picking up a number of survivors from the tanker, which resulted in the following exchanges of signals:

Lively from *Penelope*: 'What was your bag?'

Penelope from *Lively*: 'One Army officer, one Merchant officer and nineteen seamen.'

Lively from *Penelope*: 'Are they Huns, Wops or assorted?'

Penelope from *Lively*: 'All Italians – they say there were no Germans on board. Lieutenant Rosso of Artillery was in charge of draft from First Artillery Regiment. A surly man.'

Penelope from *Lively*: 'I find it hard to understand their Italian and French owing to apparent differences in vocabulary!'

S.O.K. from *Lively*: 'Prisoners eat like wolves. Have shown Rosso the *Punch* cartoon of Musso, but no sign of a smile.'

Next morning after a stormy night passage:

> *Lively* from *Penelope*: 'I hope your guests had a pleasant night?'

> *Penelope* from *Lively*: 'They were sick all over my ship!'

The *Gurkha* was still operating on the convoy routes out into Gibraltar and participated in yet another successful anti-submarine sweep, when, in company with the *Nestor*, *Foxhound* and *Croome*, they located the *U-127* to the south-west of Cape St Vincent. After a hunt the submarine was finally destroyed on 15 December.

Force 'K' had proved itself so successful that it had been decided to reinforce it with ships from the Mediterranean Fleet, but on one of the first operations that the enlarged force took part in disaster struck. With the new additions of the cruiser *Neptune* and destroyers *Kandahar* and *Havock*, Force 'K' sailed from Malta at 1800 hours on 17 December to escort the naval supply ship *Breconshire* into Malta on the final leg of her supply run from Alexandria and took part in the brief First Battle of Sirte, when the Italian fleet withdrew after a short skirmish when the British destroyers threatened a torpedo attack. Force 'K' refuelled at Malta and immediately sailed again to intercept a reported convoy bound for Tripoli. Instead, some twenty miles from the coast, the whole force ran into an unreported minefield.

At 0100 hours on 19 December the *Neptune* struck two mines, which wrecked her propellers and steering gear. The other two cruisers immediately put their helms hard over but this failed to save them and both detonated further mines; the *Aurora* was badly damaged as a result. She was eventually brought back to Malta escorted by *Lance* and *Havock*. *Penelope* and *Lively* stood by and *Kandahar* went in to help the *Neptune*, which had drifted onto yet a third mine. The destroyer also struck and her stern was blown off. At 0400 hours *Neptune* struck yet another mine. This fourth blow proved too much and she capsized with the loss of her entire ship's company save one man. *Jaguar* was sent out from Malta and eventually found the drifting hulk of *Kandahar* and rescued her crew but the ship had to be sunk. Force 'K' was thus eliminated in a few brief hours.

This disaster also marked a turning point in the life of the Ls, for, from a highly successful and offensive role they were now to be forced very much on the defensive, and the period now to be considered was one of high losses for the flotilla with very little reward. They also took part in several supply runs to Tobruk (which had just been re-taken) and on one of these *Legion* co-operated with the *Kipling* in the sinking of the German submarine *U-75* on 28 December.

Legion continued to operate from Alexandria during December and January, by which time the destroyer screen for the Mediterranean fleet had been reduced to a mere ten vessels. With the loss of the battleship *Barham* in November and the damage to the *Queen Elizabeth* and *Valiant*, not a single Capital Ship remained on that station and with the Japanese running wild in the Pacific Ocean no carrier could be spared either. Therefore only the light cruisers of the 15th Cruiser Squadron and the few remaining destroyers were left to keep the eastern end of the Mediterranean Sea open. *Legion* was joined by her sister ship *Gurkha* at this time, and together *Lance* and *Lively*, with *Havock* and *Jaguar* co-operated in the passing through of the *Glengyle* to Malta and the bringing out of the *Breconshire* from 6 to 10 January, Operation *MF2*.

On 17 January *Lance*, *Lively*, *Jaguar*, *Sikh* and *Zulu* (escorting *Penelope*) met Convoy MW8B from Alexandria, escorted by *Gurkha*, *Legion*, *Maori* and *Isaac Sweers*, and took them into Malta, arriving on the 19th. Following that *Lance*, *Lively* and *Legion* with the destroyers *Maori* and *Zulu*, and light cruiser *Penelope* escorted the merchant ships *Glengyle* and *Rowallan Castle* from Malta as Convoy ME9, handing over to the Mediterranean Fleet on 26 January when *Kingston* joined Force 'K' and *Lance* transferred to the 22nd Destroyer Flotilla.

On 12 February *Lance* escorted the AA cruiser *Carlisle* along with the destroyers *Avonvale*, *Eridge* and *Heythrop* escorting Convoy MW9A, *Clan Campbell* and *Clan Chattan*, which later joined up with *Rowallan Castle*. Both groups were subjected to prolonged and heavy air attacks. *Lance* and *Legion* escorted *Penelope* with the sole remaining merchant ship, *Rowallan Castle*, which was badly damaged and being towed by the destroyer *Fury*, until, under threat of surface attack, she had to be sunk by *Lively*.

On another occasion Mr Hay, the Officer of the Watch aboard *Legion*, actually sighted a minute object on the horizon, which proved to be the conning tower of a U-boat some ten miles away. The evening mirage had elongated its image (not an unusual phenomenon in those waters). In company with the *Isaac Sweers*, the *Legion* closed and opened fire, causing the submarine to crash-dive. The two destroyers followed up with heavy depth-charge patterns but eventually lost contact. Two days later on 12 January this submarine, *U-374*, was sighted on the surface by the British submarine *Unbeaten* who torpedoed and sank her. One of her survivors later revealed that the depth charges dropped by *Legion* and *Isaac Sweers* had badly damaged her so that she could not dive, which accounted for her helpless state when *Unbeaten* found her.

It was during the January operation to Malta that the flotilla suffered its first loss. On the 17th, while proceeding off the Libyan coast at 17 knots the *Gurkha* was hit in the stern by a torpedo fired by *U-133*. The actual point of the explosion was in the vicinity of the wardroom and a hole about twenty feet by thirty was blown in which extended from one foot above the waterline to an undetermined depth. The damage was extensive abaft the engine room and the after superstructure collapsed. Immediate flooding took place and spread rapidly to most of the compartments abaft the engine room, which itself slowly flooded. The fire main was fractured and a fire, fed from the oil from the after tanks, enveloped the after end while the ready-use ammunition ignited and exploded. The after bank of torpedo tubes jammed and were out of action as were the after guns but A and B mountings remained operational. The switchboard was wrecked and the electrical supply failed.

Gurkha lay immobilised, listing heavily to port but the *Isaac Sweers* most gallantly closed the stricken vessel and towed her clear of the burning oil fuel, rescuing all but nine of her complement. The little destroyer finally turned over on her beam-ends, just one-and-a-half hours after being hit, and sank off Sidi Barrani. There was an aversion to this name, after the loss of a second ship of this name in so short a time (the Tribal destroyer of same name went down in April 1940), and it was not until the 1960s that another warship was so called.

Captain Lentaigne has provided the author with a graphic account of *Gurkha*'s last moments.

At dawn *Gurkha* reformed on the screen for the expected morning air attack. *Gurkha*'s position to be on the starboard bow of the *City of Calcutta* so that her powerful anti-aircraft armament would be of the best use. *Gurkha* was steaming to her new position thus, past bulk of the *City of Calcutta* and about half a cable to starboard of her, when two torpedoes hit her. One or more of the after magazines exploded and the ship came to a stop. She was badly on fire aft, both engine rooms and one boiler room were flooded and water was gaining in the forward boiler room.

The ship was surrounded by oil fuel which caught fire and this spread forward to near the bridge.

The ship's company had fallen out from action stations and were at cruising stations and so nearly all the officers were in the wardroom having breakfast when the torpedo struck. All save one were killed instantly. This one was sitting in an armchair. Although his legs were broken he paddled the armchair across the flooded wardroom and dived out of the hole on the starboard side. There was about a yard of clear water between the ship's side and the burning oil. A young New Zealand AB saw this officer and went over the side and dragged him forward when he was hoisted on deck – a very brave act for which the AB was awarded the BEM and he certainly saved the officer's life though unfortunately this officer lost one leg.

Legion assumed command and detached *Isaac Sweers* to stand by *Gurkha*. When she arrived *Gurkha* was surrounded by flames with frequent explosions of ammunition and depth charges. There was a gentle breeze blowing and the ship was making slight leeway, also an emergency radio transmitter was working. So *Isaac Sweers* was called and told to come as close as possible to windward. A six-inch manilla rope was buoyed and slowly paid out to windward, *Isaac Sweers* found the rope and slowly towed *Gurkha* free from the flames.

Non-swimmers and wounded were then transferred to the Dutch destroyer in whalers and rafts – the other boats were badly burnt and useless. Just before the ship capsized the remainder of the ship's company swam over to the *Isaac Sweers*. I thought that the ship would last a few moments longer than she did and was still on board directing the swimmers when she dived – rather foolish of me.

One man I remember, whom I had remanded under arrest on a serious charge before leaving harbour. When the ship was hit I ordered his release and he was brought up on the bridge and I told him he was free for the time being. Some time later when I had ordered everyone on deck so that no one would be trapped below, he appeared with a mug of tea and a plate of cornflakes. He handed them to me saying, 'They say you have not had time to eat anything, Sir'.

The *Legion* meanwhile proceeded into Malta to form a truncated Force 'K' with the *Penelope* while *Lance* sailed to Alexandria having exchanged places with *Kingston*. Commander Jessel again recalls the situation at Malta during these difficult days when the *Luftwaffe* assault on Malta was working up to a peak, which it reached in March and April 1942:

During our two months in Malta, the situation steadily deteriorated as enemy bombing attacks were progressively increased. *Legion*'s eight High Angle guns were constantly in action, as we lay at our moorings in Grand Harbour. Who, before the war, could have visualised that ever happening?

As these attacks grew so did the losses and any chance of Force 'K' resuming the previously successful actions was drastically curtailed. In February the *Maori*, which had been sent to join them, was hit, and sank, in a heavy night attack on the harbour, and *Legion*'s boats rescued some of the survivors. One survivor, Victor Vine, found himself drafted aboard the *Legion* as a replacement. *Legion* herself was attacked by bombers on 26 January and a near miss caused minor structural damage and the ASDIC was put out of action for a time. On completion of her repairs *Legion* was assigned to the 22nd Destroyer Flotilla.

Lively still continued to operate from Alexandria and sailed with the light cruisers *Naiad*, *Dido* and *Euryalus*, and destroyers *Hasty*, *Hero*, *Kelvin*, *Kipling*, *Jervis*, *Sikh* and *Zulu* on a sweep for a reported damaged Italian ship. The force was repeatedly attacked by aircraft and on 11 March, Admiral Vian's flagship, the light cruiser *Naiad*, was torpedoed and sunk, going down very quickly with heavy loss of life off Mersa Matruh. *Lively* joined *Jervis* and *Kipling* in rescuing the 533 survivors, including the Admiral himself.

The relief of Malta proved the overriding object in the early months of 1942. Convoy MW9 run in mid-February, as we have seen, had not been a success. The four empty store ships from Malta got through to Alexandria but all the three full ones bound for Malta were sunk and so by March the situation was serious. A renewed attempt was bound to be made to get four ships through to the island, and this was codenamed Convoy MW 10.

The convoy itself consisted of the much-tried Naval Auxiliary *Breconshire* and the store ships *Clan Campbell*, *Pampas* and the Norwegian *Talabot*. For the close escort right through to Malta were the anti-aircraft cruiser *Carlisle* and six Hunt Class destroyers, *Beaufort*, *Dulverton*, *Avonvale*, *Hurworth*, *Heythrop* and *Eridge*. These latter carried out a pre-operation sweep against U-boats but were far from successful, the *Heythrop* being torpedoed and sunk on 19 March. The remainder refuelled at Tobruk and joined the convoy at dawn on the 21st.

The 'Main Escort' consisted of the cruisers *Cleopatra*, *Dido* and *Euryalus*; the destroyers *Sikh*, *Zulu*, *Lively*, *Hero*, *Havock* and *Hasty* of the 22nd Flotilla and *Jervis, Kipling, Kelvin* and *Kingston* of the 14th Flotilla. *Penelope,* and *Legion, Decoy* and *Fortune,* from Malta, sailed with MW9 under Operation *MF4* to meet these forces at 0800 hours on the 22nd. They were sighted by both submarines and aircraft and air attacks started early on the 22nd and continued all day. *Decoy* and *Fortune* exchanged places with *Lance,* which again rejoined Force 'K'. Worse was to come for the Italian battle fleet was also at sea steering to intercept with the battleship *Littorio* and cruisers and destroyer support.[4] Neither *Penelope* nor *Legion* had details of Admiral Vian's fighting plan but both adapted to a degree that was outstanding.

At 1410 hours the *Euryalus* reported smoke, which first sighted the Italian fleet, and by 1434 hours this had been confirmed. The *Legion* was stationed on the inner AA screen about one and a half miles on the starboard beam of the rear ship of the convoy with *Lively* in a corresponding position to port. They, together with the Hunts, had been providing a barrage fire, which had so far protected the convoy from any casualties during the constant and increasing scale of air attack.

At 1426 hours Petty Officer F.C. Bernard sighted the enemy, bearing 010 degrees, and this was reported to Admiral Vian, by light and W/T, from the *Legion.* The contact was made with four ships and the range was twelve miles. Although forewarned by a British submarine, this meeting was much earlier than anticipated. Admiral Vian at once put into effect his tactical plan and the *Carlisle* and the Hunts were left as anti-aircraft and anti-submarine escorts with the convoy while the remaining warships turned towards the enemy, forming as they did so, into five divisions, on a northerly course. When between the convoy and the Italian cruiser force (for such it turned out to be), they began laying a thick smokescreen.

The *Legion* joined the *Dido* and *Penelope* to form a second division of the Striking Force and joined in the smoke laying but after half an hour and some exchange of gunfire the cruisers, including *Penelope,* were ordered to concentrate and the *Legion* 'tacked herself on' the rear of the 14th Flotilla and placed herself under the orders of Captain (D) 14. The *Lively* was the second ship of the 5th Division astern of the *Sikh* with *Hero* and *Havock* behind while *Legion* and the 14th Destroyer Flotilla formed the 1st Division. Although most of the ships were masked by the thick smoke during the first phase of the engagement *Legion* twice came under fire when to the windward of the screen.

'Being at the tail of the line our stern frequently projected from the smoke and the enemy had a good attempt at knocking it off,' remembers one eyewitness.

The gun action had commenced at 1436 hours and by 1444 it had become clear that this first Italian force consisted of cruisers and not, as was first thought, battleships. Some three-quarters of an hour after firing commenced these vessels turned away and were lost in the smoke. There was a brief lull but worse was to follow. At 1637 hours four enemy ships were sighted, followed three minutes later by three more, and this time the British got their first sight of the mighty *Littorio*'s nine 15-inch guns. They recommenced the smoke screen and the cruisers engaged targets as they appeared with their puny 6-inch and 5.25-inch guns. The enemy replied, all the time trying to work around the smoke of which they were obviously not too keen on penetrating. The *Cleopatra* was hit on the bridge but *Dido* claimed to have scored a hit on a heavy cruiser in return.

While the cruisers were thus occupied the *Littorio* worked around into a favourable position. All that stood between them and the convoy as the cruisers hurried up from the rear, were the four destroyers of the 5th Division. These four little ships sighted what was thought to be two destroyers at 1640 hours and engaged them, the enemy turning away, but at 1740 hours two cruisers and the *Littorio* herself came into view. She was sighted at 16,000 yards range, bearing 330 degrees, by the *Sikh* at the head of the line and for forty minutes the *Sikh* engaged her with her 4.7-inch guns. The *Havock* had been damaged ten minutes before by a heavy shell and had been detached to join the convoy, therefore the brunt of fending off the Italian main force rested for this period on the *Sikh*, *Hasty* and *Lively*, but both the latter two ships had their firing arcs masked by *Sikh*'s smoke, as did the other British divisions. The gallant holding action by the three destroyers was relieved at 1820 hours when the cruisers came up in support and *Cleopatra* fired torpedoes. The 5th Division's turn came at 1832 hours when Captain (D) 14 led round the smoke to attack. The *Littorio* and two cruisers were sighted bearing 290 degrees, at six miles range, heading south. The flotilla was doing a reverse 'S' turn to the north when *Legion* received the W/T order 'Blue 270'. Commander Jessel was therefore convinced that the intention was a line of bearing attack and it appeared to him that the destroyers were too bunched so he opened out, steering first 250 degrees and then 230 degrees. While the other destroyers commenced firing at the enemy Leviathan at about 10,000 yards range *Legion* was forced to steer toward the battleship passively for a while.

At 1839 hours with the enemy battleship bearing 280 degrees course 180 degrees, the *Legion*'s little 4-inch guns opened fire at 8,000 yards using radar to range. Several hits were scored and the *Littorio* replied with her main armament. The battleship's three triple 15-inch turrets divided their fire each on a separate target, three gun salvoes being fired. The 15-inch shell splashes were accompanied by smaller ones and it appeared that the secondary armament was under main armament control. *Legion* was the beneficiary of *Littorio*'s 'A' turret.

The first salvo fired at *Legion* was well over and wrong for line so Commander Jessel held his course. The second was about 300 yards over and nearly right for line so *Legion* 'turned toward the enemy'. The third salvo was very close to the destroyer's port bow, several splinters coming inboard. However, when the huge splashes came they swamped the bridge and put all the binoculars out of action as a result of which the signal to turn to fire torpedoes given by Captain (D) 14 was missed. The 14th Flotilla turned, at a range of 6,000 yards, to starboard, the *Kingston* being hit as she did so.

However, the *Legion* continued to close her mighty antagonist at 30 knots and it was not until the range was down to a point-blank 4,400 yards that Commander Jessel turned his ship to port at 1844 hours and Lieutenant B.G. O'Neill fired a full eight-torpedo outfit. The main armament continued to fire but a cryptic note on Commander Jessel's report of this action regretted that 'unfortunately the pom-pom was loaded with self-destroying ammunition and was therefore not used'.

The *Littorio* began to turn away following this audacious assault and *Legion* continued to make smoke while retiring on an easterly course. The Italian battleship was again sighted at 1847 hours and 'fired a parting shot at us'. *Legion* then rejoined the *Penelope*.

Meanwhile, *Lively* had come back into the fray and at 1850 hours the *Sikh* observed a torpedo hit aboard the *Littorio* and five minutes later the three ships of this division also turned to fire but due to the smoke only the *Lively* actually did so, loosening an eight torpedo outfit without an observed result. She was subjected to the same treatment as her sister and at 1852 hours a salvo of 15-inch shells burst close alongside to port. The brass plate of one of these projectiles holed the side plates forward. Controlled flooding took place in the two forward mess decks and maximum speed was reduced to 20 knots. Fortunately, the Italians had had enough and were retiring rapidly to the northward and no further contact was made with them.

Fighting a modern battleship armed with nine 15-inch guns at point-blank range with eight twin 4-inch popguns was not something that even the Ls came to accept as routine. Here are two eyewitness accounts, one an executive officer and the other an ordinary AB at the gun, aboard the *Legion* as she made her audacious turn under the muzzles of the *Littorio*. First AB Vine:

> We sailed at about eight p.m. with *Penelope* and again I think we all realised that big events were portending. We spent a quiet night, though one of preparedness, and met the convoy and the Alexandria escort about eight the next morning. We had, during the night, received a submarine's report that several heavy ships had been heard leaving Taranto and that a destroyer screen had been sighted.
>
> The recce plane found us at about nine a.m. and we had one or two half-hearted torpedo bombing and bombing attacks but they seemed to be concentrating on the

warships rather than the convoy and again I felt that we were likely to see surface ships before the day was out. We had met the Wops before just prior to Christmas and had outwitted them with smoke and the fading light but quite frankly I didn't relish the idea of contacting battleships with our light forces in full daylight and with a comparatively slow convoy. You see we couldn't run away like the Italians.

During one bombing attack about 1330 the *Euryalus* sighted smoke. We all thought it might have been a blind round fired by *Lively*. I think we really knew it wasn't but we tried to persuade ourselves that it was! About 1415 we sighted four heavy ships on the horizon and I went off to my action stations. Our four cruisers and about twelve destroyers, including ourselves, went out to meet the foe. We put up a most impressive smoke screen – we were following *Dido* and *Penelope*. The cruisers were firing hard and every now and again splashes would fall quite close but nothing very frightening. We then learnt that the enemy consisted of four cruisers and that they were retreating to the northward. How pleased we felt that we had driven them off. All the while we were being subjected to mild air attack. After we had driven the enemy off we returned to the convoy.

About 1615, ships were again sighted but this time they included a battleship. Various reports were received concerning the strength of the enemy which actually consisted of one *Littorio*, two 8-inch cruisers, four 6-inch cruisers and some destroyers, truly a formidable force. They were only twelve miles away with a speed of thirty knots and four hours of daylight remaining. I ate a biscuit.

Again we made smoke, we had by this time joined up with the 14th Flotilla *Jervis*, *Kipling*, *Kingston* and *Kelvin* – with ourselves on the tail – the trouble was, with the wind astern, our stern protruded from the smoke. O'Neill rather aptly compared it to having one's head and shoulders in an air raid shelter with one's bottom sticking out and the

enemy cruisers certainly had a crack at that stern of ours –
Crack, whistle-splash, splash, splash – we were straddled
many times and it was a beastly feeling. I didn't duck as
Reg Hay and I had only got a canvas screen to duck behind
and our common sense helped.

We were definitely delaying the enemy with smoke but
he was gradually getting closer to the convoy and his aircraft
were all round, bombing and spotting and the time simply
crawled. We still had about two hours of daylight left.

About 1815, our division was told to attack with
torpedoes. I had rather dreaded this order but once it was
made I think one had a feeling of exhilaration. In we went
to attack the enemy obscured to us by smoke. We were in
line abreast, Captain D and the other three Ks on the right,
about three cables apart, and ourselves, well clear, to the
left – the direction in which the enemy was travelling. We
came through the smoke and sighted the enemy about
eight thousand yards away and the Ks did some very
pretty concentration and I could see they were hitting the
battleship with their 4.7s. The *Littorio* was a magnificent
sight. She must have been going at thirty knots but in spite
of the heavy sea was hardly putting up any spray. She was
dividing her fire. I only saw one full broadside. Her 15-
inch shells made a great mushroom of flame but her 6-inch
secondary armament one could not see because of their
flashless propellant. The splashes from the 15-inch seemed
immense, their ranging appeared good but the spread was
bad. About two miles astern of the battle-wagon and
putting up clouds of spray were two cruisers which I think
must have been 8-inch gunned 'Trentos'. The forward
funnel of the leading one was very prominent. We opened
fire with our 4-inch at 6,000 yards – we had not done so
before for fear of interfering with the K's concentration –
and it was about this time that the *Kingston* was hit by a 15-
inch shell. An ugly fire could be seen flaming through a
hole about her pom-pom platform and I was afraid she
was finished.

The enemy then appeared to shift his fire from *Kingston* to us. The first salvo was well over, the next nearer and the third impressively close, most unpleasantly so. We altered toward this one in the approved style. I wondered when on earth we were going to fire torpedoes. We seemed, at 4,400 yards, to be almost within pistol shot. Eventually we turned and fired, Chief putting up a nice drop of smoke. We were fired at three more times and one 15-inch brick fell alongside – most unpleasant and it smashed up a Carley float. After that the enemy turned for home and we were not bothered by the Wop fleet any more. We joined *Penelope* and then found the convoy after nightfall. We passed a quiet but alert night, the weather was rather foul and we were drenched but our tails were right up and I've never tasted anything so delicious as the rather sodden cheese and biscuits and hot cocoa.

Commander Cartwright's tale makes an interesting comparison with AB Vine's aboard the same ship.

I was a survivor from the *Maori*, Tribal Class destroyer [sunk in an air raid on Malta harbour], and with a few other ratings joined the *Legion*. It was grand to be back aboard another destroyer. When I looked around the boat I felt safe as she had eight 4-inch high-level guns against air attack. We were soon made welcome by our new shipmates but all we had in the way of clothing was a pair of blue jeans, one pair each of vest and pants and a pair of plimsoles, so the First Lieutenant bought us new suits. We were taken on to quarterdeck and met Commander Jessel who told us the way the boat was run. It was a happy ship.

A few days later we escorted empty merchant ships from Malta to meet Admiral Vian with his convoy from Alex. Later we went out with *Penelope* and met his force once more turning back with them to help escort in several full merchant ships. There were four or five ships and I was lookout at this time.

When aircraft were spotted on the starboard side a message came through that there were unidentified ships in that direction and the aircraft started dropping flares. A large shell burst behind one of the merchant ships in the convoy. I saw an H Class destroyer turn to investigate and she found it was the Italian battle fleet.

The next thing we hear is that *Havock* had been hit in the starboard magazine. Luckily the magazine was empty. Another Italian cruiser almost managed to finish her off but one of *Havock*'s single 4.7s fired a shot and he veered off. We were told to go in and leave the merchant ships to get to Malta with the 'Hunts' as escort. I was still lookout and there was a smoke screen right ahead of us. You could see our destroyers all in line abreast moving out. As they reared up and down you could see flashes of their guns. Shells from the enemy were coming between our ships. We then went in to 5,000 yards or even closer, then the destroyers turned to starboard and went to line ahead, all close in front of the *Legion*.

I was relieved from lookout and reported on 'A' gun, my battle station. While this was going on we had been through the smoke screen and by then I was loading on 'A' gun. We were going a fair speed, the sea was coming over the bows and around 'A' gun all we had to keep it out was the splinter shield. When the sea came over the water stayed in the 'A' gun area so we were fighting the enemy *and* paddling.

We were firing semi-armour-piercing (SAP); the sea was getting rougher and rougher. After six SAP in these conditions when I picked up a couple of anti-personnel shells, I was not going to put them down so we loaded them and off they went. We were bouncing around and at times firing at aircraft, also at a low angle, when they crossed our sights.

I was relieved again and went back on lookout. I will never forget the sight of the smokescreen. As I looked up the smoke was going past the mast and you knew you were still alright – for the old White Ensign and the Battle Flag were blowing out as we scudded along. We stayed in the area till dusk and then slipped away.

Despite a lot of post-war excuses from *Supermarina* and British apologists it is not too difficult to sum up this action objectively. It is true that the wind and weather were of help to the British forces, but even so the Italian battleship and cruisers should have benefitted more from the rising gale than the smaller and therefore less seaworthy British vessels. In addition Vian was hampered by the need to keep between the Italians and his convoy and all the air activity was on the Axis side. Finally of course Vian was completely outclassed in weight of armament. In theory the defence of the convoy was impossible, in practice the fact that time and time again the British destroyers were able to close the *Littorio* to within point-blank range, says much for the training and courage of their crews and very little for the determination and efficiency of the Italian battle fleet.

It was yet another example of how the policy of arming British destroyers with powerful torpedo armaments, as against heavy gun armaments, paid handsome dividends. However, this was more in fear than execution as, apparently unbeknown to the Axis, most of the British boats had landed half their torpedo outfits to ship an extra AA gun and therefore the threat was only half that expected. It was enough. The mere threat of torpedo damage to heavy capital ships from the always aggressive British destroyer forces was one of the key factors in the otherwise almost inexplicable and timid attitudes of many of the Axis naval commanders of the Second World War. Post-war it was cramping instructions imposed by long-dead leaders that became the universal excuse but it is hard to see how anything other than the examples set early in the war could be the real influence. The self-sacrifice of destroyers like the *Glowworm*, *Acasta*, *Ardent* and *Hardy* had made a lasting impression on the Germans and was transmitted to their allies at sea. This impression was constantly reinforced by the automatic response of British destroyer commanders on sighting a superior enemy force, as typified by Commander Jessel's terse phrase in his report, 'I turned *towards* the enemy'.

Unhappily, the fruits of this famous victory were very short lived for, although they had outfaced the Italian battle fleet, the *Luftwaffe* was to wreak vengeance for this humiliation. The air attacks, always heavy, intensified as the convoy and the damaged warships struggled toward Malta. The convoy itself was dispersed at 1900 hours on 22 March, the bulk of Vian's force returning to Alexandria. Both groups were heavily attacked from the air. Heavy weather on the night of the 22nd/23rd forced the cruisers and destroyers to face day-long attacks on the latter date and the *Lively* had to drop back to repair damage. Her speed was reduced for an hour to enable this to be done and the fleet marked time at low speed to enable her to catch up. However, she was still isolated when subjected to a severe dive-bombing attack by six Ju 87s who, ignoring the main force, concentrated on the cripple. *Lively*, the official report read later, 'had to act the part.'

She escaped, however, any further damage but at 2248 hours she reported that she was unable to maintain more than 17 knots and she was therefore detached to Tobruk where it was considered she could effect sufficient repairs to enable her to continue to Alexandria later.

Legion and the others heading for Malta fared much worse. She, together with the cruiser *Carlisle* and the Hunts, endeavoured to shield their charges into Malta with the *Penelope*, while the damaged *Havock* and *Kingston* also sought shelter there to repair. In fact, what appeared to be shelter was to turn into a death trap for the majority of these ships. At dawn on the 23rd heavy air attacks took place, which brushed aside the covering Spitfires to score a hit on the *Breconshire*. The two cruisers made attempts at towing but in vain. *Talabot* and *Pampas* reached Malta intact but *Clan Campbell* lagged behind and only had the *Eridge* for escort when attacked by bombers, hit and ultimately sunk.

Legion after a peaceful night found herself in a heavy offshore mist close in to the island, but despite this the *Luftwaffe* made several attacks; lone aircraft dived through the cloud to drop their bombs and climb away before the guns could track them. At 0900 hours she was told to retrace her steps and locate and aid the *Eridge* and *Clan Campbell* but before she had gone far another quick attack by a lone Ju 88 took place. There was little or no warning and the four-bomb stick fell across the ship, three bombs falling over while the last was a very near miss amidships on the starboard side. This severely damaged the ship's side abreast the engine room, and split the forward bulkhead to the engine room. Controlled flooding took place in the engine and after boiler rooms. The starboard HP turbine feet were fractured and speed was reduced to 20 knots. The flooding was only just within the capacity of the pumps to cope with.

Legion was still some twenty miles from Grand Harbour and Lieutenant-Commander Sayer, the Engineering Officer, considered that she might not get there before the boilers primed, so *Legion* shaped, on one engine, course for Marsaxlokk Bay. Here they stayed for two days during which time work was done on the feed system to risk steaming, still on a single engine, round the island to the dockyard. They were joined in the bay by the *Breconshire*, also damaged, and during the operation to get her in another destroyer, the *Southwold*, was mined and sunk. Nor was this by any means the end of the disaster for *Breconshire* herself was again attacked, hit again by bombs and sunk before she could reach Valletta.

Meanwhile, the *Luftwaffe* had mounted a furious assault on the two ships that had got through and both were soon hit and set on fire, sinking with only 5,000 tons of the convoy's total cargo of 25,900 tons unloaded. *Legion*, under constant air attack, also limped into Grand Harbour and joined the other cripples refitting there – *Lance, Kingston, AvonVale* and the cruiser *Aurora*. Such was the fury of the bombing raids on the dockyard that it was feared that all the ships there would quickly become losses and so great attempts were made in between air raids to get the ships away to sea and safety. For many it was too late. The *Carlisle, Hurworth, Dulverton, Eridge* and *Beaufort* sailed for Alexandria on 25 March and got through, but few of the others shared their good fortune.

That same evening *Legion* secured inboard of *Penelope* and *Lance* at the Boiler-House wharf together with a submarine. A severe air attack took place without damage and after it was over one commentator recalled they all trooped aboard the *Lance* and enjoyed themselves drinking beer and shooting terrific *lines*.

Commander Jessel remembers this period well.

Amongst the many inconveniences of being stationed at
Malta in 1942 was the infrequency of the arrival of mail
from home. It had to be flown from England to Sierra
Leone, thence across Africa to Alexandria, and then over
the Eastern Mediterranean to Malta. Day after day, the
postman would return aboard empty-handed, and the
poor 'Postie' was getting fed up with the abuse that was so
undeservedly bestowed upon him.

Postie's action station was trainer of the Gun-Director
tower. One day while at sea, warning was given of enemy
aircraft approaching and soon some Ju.87s were sighted;
the Director and the guns were trained onto the
appropriate bearing, and, soon, Postie spotted the enemy
in his powerful glasses. He trained the Director dead on,
and then started to give a running commentary, much in
the style of the BBC's Richard Dimbleby. 'Here she comes
– straight towards us. She's gone into a dive. Bomb has
been released. Here it comes. Ruddy great thing the size of
a hammock. It's painted bright red. Like a pillar box. Here
comes your!!! Air Mail.'

The next forenoon was fairly quiet – the bombers came in about
1130 hours and it was during this raid that *Talabot* and *Pampas*
were both hit. A fire party from the *Aurora* dealt with the *Pampas*
and a similar party from *Penelope* went out to deal with *Talabot* in
the tug *Ancient*. About 1400 hours the *Ancient* was near-missed
and a frantic signal was made to *Penelope* asking for a tow as the
ammunition in the merchant ship was liable to blow up at any
time. The little tug *West Cocker* was alongside the *Legion*, slightly
holed, and a party of volunteers under *Legion*'s Executive Officer
towed the *Ancient* and two barges clear from this danger. About
1615 hours another series of heavy raids began and all guns were
manned in the warships. The first wave came in and the
warships in the group at the wharf was obviously their target,
there were several near misses.

Another wave was followed by a third and these raids by Ju
88s were capped by a concentrated attack by Ju 87 *Stukas* (the
inverted gull-wing dive-bombers), twenty of which took part.

As a result of this devastating pounding *Legion* was hit.

The *Stukas* released their bombs from between two and three thousand feet and an eyewitness who followed the flight of the bombs described them as 'large', but they were probably only 500 kg. Two, or possibly three, of these were direct hits on the forecastle and 'B' gun deck and it is thought that these bombs passed through to the lower messdecks before they exploded with a very large impact. A fourth bomb exploded on the jetty, to port, close alongside. The ship was split open forward and went down rapidly by the bow, turning over on her port side and sinking in five minutes. The order to abandon ship did not reach 'Y' gun crews who remained firing until they had to swim for it.

Thus a great little ship was lost and with her went twelve of her crew. A year later, prior to the invasion of Sicily, divers cut her wreck in half; the halves were raised, towed out to sea and let go in deep water. One of the divers had retrieved a wardroom entrée dish and many years later this dish, suitable inscribed, was presented to Commander Jessel by surviving members of the ship's company at the first of many reunion dinners. Commander Jessel also retained the ship's bell.

And then there were six!

She was not long survived by her sister *Lance*. She had sustained damage from the same attack that had sunk the *Legion* when the latter's forward magazine, fortunately half empty, blew up and *Lance* was therefore condemned to stay at Malta as the air attacks grew in intensity, while the more fortunate ships like *Penelope* got away to safety. *Kingston*, in a similar state, was wrecked in dry-dock and on 4 April came *Lance*'s turn. She was hit twice in one attack and although one bomb fortunately failed to explode she was severely damaged, although still seaworthy. Lieutenant Commander Style recalls this attack.

> During the constant bombing we in Force 'K' had to undergo the *Lance* suffered a great many near misses. These, over a period of time, caused strain in the hull riveting, the rivet heads began to split and this necessitated docking. The affected rivets had to be drilled

HMS *Laforey*. (From a watercolour by Bernard Gribble, RBC, SMA)

HMS *Legion* as first completed for Western Approaches Command.

HMS *Laforey* on completion. August 1941. Note pendant numbers are painted up incorrectly, as this is never done for Leaders.

HMS *Laforey* at Scapa working up. Pendant painted out, and weather damage evident on her new paint already.

HMS *Lightning* on completion, 8 September 1941.

HMS *Lance* as first completed.

The Lofoten Raid, 4 March 1941.

Commander Jessel and Lieutenant Cartwright on *Legion*'s bridge.

A Norwegian fishing boat alongside *Legion*'s port quarter. Note pom-pom, searchlight, depth charge throwers and Carley rafts.

HMS *Lively* at full speed.

HMS *Lightning* early in 1942.

HMS *Gurkha* as first completed.

Gurkha with *Legion* in the background, on patrol in Western Mediterranean, mid-1941.

The sinking of *Ark Royal*, November 1941. *Legion* approaching the carrier's quarter to pick up survivors.

Legion secured alongside the stricken carrier.

While *Legion* embarks survivors *Laforey* (left) and *Lightning* (photo taken from) provide A/S Patrol.

Force K. *Penelope* and *Lance* at Valetta, December 1941.

Force K. An Italian tanker is sunk. *Lively* stands by to pick up survivors.

HMS *Lively* at Valetta, late 1941.

Lance heads *Breconshire* into Malta harbour after another supply run.

Legion enters Valetta harbour after Battle of Cape Bon.

The victorious destroyers enter Valetta harbour after sinking two Italian cruisers in a brief night action. Note Force *K* cruisers *Aurora* and *Penelope* on right and *Lance* on the left.

Legion turning through smokescreen to fire torpedoes during the 2nd Battle of Sirte. *Legion* approached the *Littorio* to within point-blank range and engaged her with her 4-inch guns.

Lance bombed several times in dock at Malta finally abandoned. Note huge hole in hull, 'A' and 'B' guns apparently undamaged.

Lively at full speed after being hit and near missed by a stick of bombs in the Central Mediterranean, 11 May 1942. She sank soon afterwards.

Laforey in northern waters.

HMS *Lookout* on 28 October 1942, en route to the North African landings from Scapa.

Lightning approaching St Helena to refuel. She is on her way back from Diego Suarez operation to take part in Malta Convoy Pedestal, August 1942.

HMS *Lookout*. Early appearance.

HMS *Loyal* on 30 October 1942. Note 20mm guns on quarterdeck, and in bridge wings. Also peculiar funnel band markings with white at top starboard and black to port and alternative at bottom.

HMS *Loyal*, November 1942. Flotilla markings now correctly painted.

Lightning with dazzle scheme for Atlantic.

HMS *Lookout* in home waters, 1942.

Lookout on patrol in North African waters, early 1943.

Laforey at full speed during the bombardment of Pantellaria, 8 June 1943.

Lookout astern of *Eskimo* off Sicily, 11 July 1943.

Lookout laying a smokescreen off Salerno beachhead. Note both sets of tubes are shipped.

(Below left) *Lookout* off Naples early in 1945.

(Below right) The forward gunhouse of HMS *Lookout*, Malta 1945.

A cheerful crowd aboard *Lookout* in Valetta dockyard, 1945.

HMS *Loyal* alongside the floating dock at Valetta, 10 May 1948. Note that both these ships retain the tripod mast and have not shipped a lattice despite several 'expert' claims to the contrary.

HMS *Lookout* in reserve at Devonport, 10 November 1945.

out and replaced over a large area of the hull and *Lance* was dry-docked in Number Two dock at Valletta for this long and laborious job to be undertaken, and thus we missed the Second Battle of Sirte.

Unfortunately during this period of immobilisation the German air attacks on Valletta harbour reached their peak and we had to just sit and 'take it'. To avoid unnecessary loss of life half the ship's company were always at rest at Ghain Tuffieha on the other side of the island. It was always the rule when dry-docked for the ship to be de-ammunition and thus *Lance* could only man her .05s and her pom-pom to protect herself against the rising crescendo of air attack. We were fortunate in that our pom-pom was manned gallantly by a young gunner, A.B. Popple. During the time we became so accustomed to the bombing that we could judge whether a particular raid was to be directed at us personally or at ships in adjoining creeks perhaps only three hundred yards away.

In the first raid in which *Lance* was hit, I remember we three officers aboard had just rushed to see whether we could send aid to the submarine moored next to us which had been hit and was sinking. As we reached the deck we could at once tell that we were for it and almost immediately the bombs struck.

It was 1430 in the afternoon when we were hit and after the concussion I can remember little other than falling to the deck and seeing my left arm severed below the elbow in front of me. I also had splinters through my thigh and chest. Lieutenant Peter Dallas-Smith had his leg badly shattered and eventually amputated and Chief Engineer King was wounded in the seat.

It was a rule aboard *Lance* at this time that every officer carried morphine and we were given a shot through our clothing immediately. Unfortunately in the aftermath of the attack we were only given half a dose, but a full dose was indicated on the label. Our shots therefore soon wore off but we were not able to receive any additions until the time for the full dose had passed. We were eventually evacuated to 45 Field Hospital where we were very well looked after. Fortunately we three officers were the only casualties from this particular attack.

Before she could be patched up enough for a dash to safety a further raid took place on 5 April, which resulted in another near miss while she was still in Number Two dock. *Lance* was blown off the stocks and partially submerged in the dock. Repairs were spasmodically got underway between the air raids but on 9 April *Lance* was the object of yet another attack while still under repair. Several heavy bombs were near misses and she was left badly damaged with her stern submerged in the dock. She was nearly upright and had her topsides amidships and the forecastle above the waterline but was plainly a write-off although 'A' and `B' mountings were themselves undamaged. These guns and other workable fittings were eventually removed and stripped and she was listed as beyond repair and laid up.

Like *Legion* she lay at Malta rusting until there was time to remove her to safety and it was not until August 1943 that she was towed to Gibraltar and then to Chatham, where she arrived in September. Her broken hull then lay 'under survey' at Chatham until June 1944 when it was finally decided she was not worth repair and that same month her hull was towed to Ward's shipbreaking yard at Grays in Essex.

And then there were five.

Notes

1 Eyewitness account from *Our Penelope*, Guild Books, 1943.

2 *Our Penelope*, Guild Books.

3 *Our Penelope*, Guild Books.

4 Actual composition of the Italian force was battleship: *Littorio*; cruisers *Garza* and *Trento* (8-inch), *Giovanni Della Bande Nere* (6-inch); destroyers *Alpino, Fuciliere, Bersagliere, Lanciere, Aaiere, Grecale, Ascarf, Geniere, Scirocco* and *Oriani*.

Chapter 7

Sweeping the Med

*L*aforey and *Lightning* had been living a comparatively quieter life, for following the sinking of *Ark Royal* in November 1941 Force 'H', as we have recounted earlier, was largely limited to flying off reinforcements for Malta from the carriers *Eagle*, *Argus* or *Furious*. At the beginning of April, however, the force was called further afield. With the Japanese raid against Ceylon earlier in the year there was great concern lest the Vichy Government allow them to occupy Madagascar as they had Indo-China, and thus outflank our limited forces in the Middle East and the Indian sub-continent. With the Mediterranean closed to our shipping, the threat to the remaining life-line round the Cape was very great. Accordingly, Operation *Ironclad* was prepared against this island to forestall any such move. Troops were embarked in the United Kingdom but the only naval force of any strength which could be diverted to support it was Force 'H' reinforced by Home Fleet vessels. The initial assault was to be made on Diego Suarez, a Vichy French bastion vocal in its support for Pétain and Laval.

Accordingly, *Laforey* and *Lightning*, as the most powerful British destroyers still afloat, were joined by their new sister *Lookout* fresh from the builders. She had run her trials and had commissioned into the 19th Flotilla at the end of January, and among her new equipment was FH3 RDF. After working up at Scapa Flow she had helped to screen the Home Fleet covering the outward Russia Convoy PQ12 to the Kola Inlet and the returning QP8 to Iceland, along with the battleships *King George*

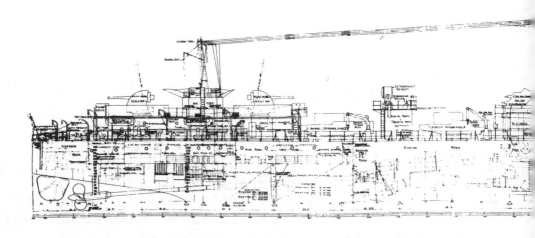

4.-inch gunned *Lance* as completed

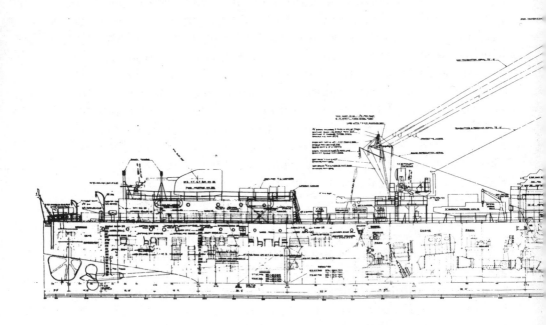

4.7-inch gunned *Laforey* as completed

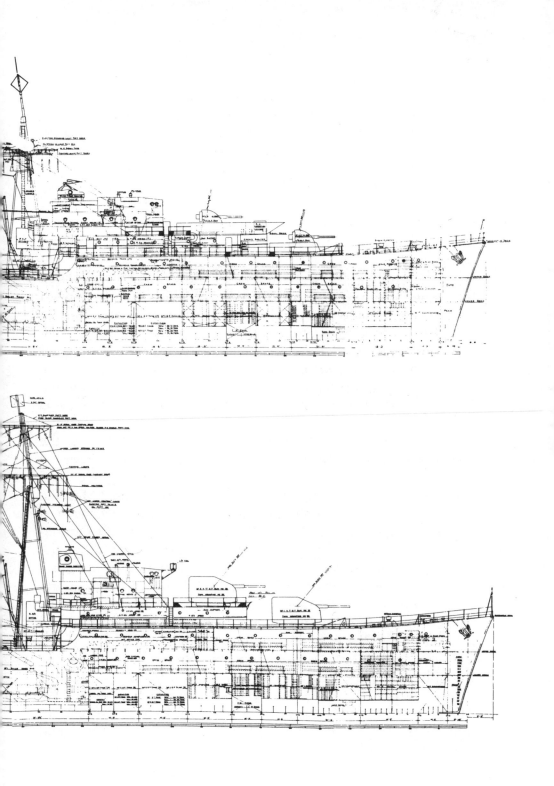

V and *Duke of York*, battle-cruiser *Renown*, carrier *Victorious*, heavy cruiser *Berwick*, light cruiser *Kenya* and destroyers *Ashanti*, *Bedouin*, *Echo*, *Eclipse*, *Faulknor*, *Fury*, *Grove*, *Inconstant*, *Icarus*, *Intrepid*, *Javelin*, *Ledbury*, *Onslow*, *Punjabi*, *Tartar*, *Verdun*, and *Woolston* and ex-American four-stackers *Lancaster* and *Wells*.

When the German battleship *Tirpitz* made a brief foray *Lookout* was one of the destroyers assigned to escort the *Victorious*, which hunted and launched an air strike against her, but unfortunately it failed to score any hits at all and the enemy escaped.

Along with the destroyers *Aldenham* and *Grove*, *Lookout* joined the escort of the assault convoy WS 17, which left the United Kingdom and made its way via Gibraltar, Freetown and Durban into the Indian Ocean. The naval force was mainly a Force 'H' affair, with the battleship *Malaya*, light cruiser *Hermione* and destroyers *Active*, *Anthony*, *Inconstant*, *Javelin*, and *Pakenham* escorting the troopships of WS17A to Freetown and on the Durban where they arrived on 22 April via Freetown, St Helena and Cape Town.

The three L Class destroyers left Durban on 22 April with the fast part of the force (Z) for the assault, sailing from Durban on 28 April with the aircraft carrier *Illustrious* and light cruiser *Hermione* after conducting bombardment exercises on 2 May. On 4 May they made landfall and early next morning *Laforey* and *Lightning*, together with the *Anthony*, went ahead and marked and buoyed the swept channel to Courier Bay after the minesweepers had done their job, and led the landing ship *Royal Ulsterman* in guiding her with their searchlight, and later giving gunfire support to the touch-down. *Lookout* was screening the carrier *Indomitable* and heavy cruiser *Devonshire* at this period and later helped with bombardments of Vichy positions.

Vichy resistance was overcome by bombardments by the battleship *Ramillies*, which *Lookout* and *Lightning* screened during a report that Japanese surface ships were in the vicinity. These turned out to be the Armed Merchant Riders *Aikoku Maru* and *Hokoku Maru*, which had sailed from Penang on 5 May and successfully eluded the British Eastern Fleet. Somerville wrote in his diary '...two Jap raiders off Durban to eastward. 20-knot ships, well armed. What I've been expecting.' But he signally failed to locate them or stop their work. He also noted '...at least four U-boats [sic] operating in Mozambique channel.' On 9 May the two Japanese ships captured the 7,987-ton Dutch tanker *Genota* in 17° 40′ S, 72° 20′ E. On both 10 and 15 May they refuelled the Japanese submarines including the *I-10* carrying midget submarines to attack the *Ironclad* fleet. On 5 June they made another kill to the south of the Mozambique Strait, where they found and sank the British freighter *Elysia* with British troops on board in 27° 19′ S, 37° 01′ E. The two raiders rendezvoused with the Japanese SubRon 8s *Ko* detachment before going on the hunt again. They final success did not take place until 12 July when they captured the 7,113-ton New Zealand freighter *Hauraki* in 17° 36′ S, 80° 27′ S. They both returned safely to Singapore Naval Base on 10 August.

Laforey also gave support to the audacious assault by Royal Marines landed by the *Anthony* in the rear of the French defence works on the Antisirana Peninsula. As usual the French forces put up only token rearguard actions from strong-point to strong-point and *Lightning* was, on 6 May, called upon to bombard machine-gun nests while the next day the *Lightning*'s 4.7-inch guns were again utilised to soften up resistance on the Oronjia Peninsula.

The *Laforey*'s captain, Captain (D) 19 'Tubby' Hutton, was his usual quiet but efficient self during this operation and an example of his attention to detail and how it affected the campaign is given by his First Lieutenant.

> During the invasion of Madagascar we were treated to a smart piece of navigation by Captain Hutton. *Laforey* led the fleet into the invasion beach – a large, sheltered, but unpopulated harbour on the north-west coast – through a narrow, rocky channel, using only the mountains silhouetted by the rising moon as a guide.
>
> This was a marvellous bit of pilotage by Captain Hutton and our navigator. Dimly lit marker buoys were dropped on the way in and all the convoy and escort reached the

anchorage safely, undetected and on time.

The buoys were 'Dan-buoys' with battery-operated magazine lamps attached to the tops of their staves and were prepared in Durban for us before sailing. Captain Hutton took the ship to sea for a trial lay before we sailed in earnest and his precautions were absolutely justified, for, on this trial, the buoys proved top-heavy and ineffective. They were modified with the success later seen.

With as much of Madagascar in British hands as necessary to prevent the Vichy government handing it over to the Japanese as they had done in Indo-China the year before, the three L Class destroyers together with *Active* and *Duncan*, were released from further *Ironclad* commitments on 27 May and on their way to join the Eastern Fleet at Colombo in Ceylon (now known Sri Lanka). However, when a Japanese midget submarine damaged the battleship *Ramillies* at Diego Suarez, the latter two destroyers were sent back there (a classic case of closing the stable door!) and only the Ls continued east. The trio refuelled at the Seychelles Islands on the 31st of the month and next joined took station with the rest of the East Indies fleet, under their old Force 'H' commander James Somerville, on 1 June. Here they screened the aircraft carriers *Formidable* and *Illustrious* and light cruiser *Gambia* in an exercise before reaching Colombo itself on 5 June where they found the flagship, the battleship *Warspite* at anchor.

These ships, known as Force 'A', the fast portion of Somerville's ageing fleet of ships, carried out an 'offensive' sweep between 12 and 18 June toward the Chagos Islands, refuelling at Addu Atoll. However, on 21 June Somerville was noting again 'Signal from Admiralty that *Indomitable* is to fill up with Sea Hurricanes and to be at Freetown by 29 July. *Nelson* and *Rodney* to remain there also. Looks like another W Med convoy...' Indeed it was and the carrier along with the two battleships which had been on their way to reinforce the Eastern Fleet, were to be part of the escort and so promptly turned round and sailed back again. And to escort them and also take part in that great operation went the *Laforey*, *Lightning* and *Lookout*.

The three destroyers again refuelled at the Seychelles on 28

June and arrived at Mombasa on the coast of Kenya on 1 July
and left escorting *Indomitable* on 9 July. They refuelled at Pointe
Noire in the Belgian Congo being joined by the light cruiser
Phoebe, also destined for the convoy operation and the whole
force reached Freetown on 28 July. They sailed again on 1
August and on the 5th rendezvoused with the carriers *Argus*,
Eagle and *Victorious*, the cruisers *Charybdis* and *Sirius* and
destroyers *Vansittart*, *Westcott* and *Wrestler* to carry out
Operation *Berserk*, a three-day training period for the carriers in
readiness for the convoy to Malta, Operation *Pedestal*. We will
describe that battle later.

Meanwhile back in the hard testing ground of the
Mediterranean the last surviving 4-inch L of the quartet, the
Lively, had gone the way of her sisters. It will be remembered
that she limped into Tobruk after being damaged by a shell
casing during the Sirte battle. During April and May this
damage was made good and by the beginning of the latter
month *Lively* was a fully combat-worthy unit once more. At this
time the whole scope of all British naval operations in the
Mediterranean were at their lowest ebb. The projected aerial
assault by the Axis to capture Malta had, it is true, been called
off but this was not known and the island was now in desperate
straits. Rommel had flung the Eighth Army out of Tobruk once
more and was pressing hard on their defence works at the
Egyptian border. With Malta neutralised, at least for the time
being, supply convoys were running almost unhindered from
Italy into Libya bringing the German general oil, troops and
supplies to bolster his offensive.[1]

Thus it was that for *Lively* and her companions in the 14th
Destroyer Flotilla their supreme hour of trial was at hand. A
report was received on 10 May that an Axis convoy consisting of
three merchant vessels escorted by three destroyers was sailing
from Italy to Benghazi. It was therefore decided at the highest
level to attempt an interception of this force around dawn on the
12th, when, it was estimated, the convoy should be off Benghazi
harbour. *Lively* was an old hand at this game but this time the
odds were far from in her favour.

It was therefore decided to attempt the interception with the four most modern and powerful destroyers left to the Mediterranean Fleet, the ships of the 14th Flotilla, and at 2000 hours on 10 May these vessels, *Jervis* (Captain A.L. Poland – Capt. D14), *Jackal*, *Kipling* and *Lively*, slipped their cables and slid quietly out into the Eastern Mediterranean.

Aboard the destroyers Captain Poland and his fellow commanders can have been under no illusions as to their probable fate for they were experienced destroyer skippers. Poland had undergone the effects of prolonged dive-bombing off Norway earlier in the war and knew that small ships stood very little chance unsupported. As Captain Poland's flotilla would obviously be putting its head into the lion's mouth it was felt that if the ships were sighted the Italians would merely reverse course until the danger had passed. To avoid this if possible the flotilla was routed mid-way between Cyrenaica and Crete – right, in fact, into the heart of 'Bomb-Alley'.[2] Furthermore, in view of the absolute need to keep the destroyers' presence secret it had been felt that any form of standing air patrol over the flotilla on the 11th would have to be abandoned for fear that such a group of aircraft would quickly be plotted on the Axis radar networks and pinpointed. Instead plans were made for the Beaufighters of 272 Squadron to be held at instant readiness on the 11th so that they could be scrambled to go to the ships' assistance should the destroyers be picked up by enemy reconnaissance aircraft.

On the 12th it was planned that fighter protection would be given to two Beaufighters from 0800 to 1000 hours; by four Beaufighters until 1630 and by Kittyhawks from 1630 hours until dusk. The operational range of the Beaufighters was stated to be 230 miles from Tobruk. By this time of course the expected annihilation of the Italian convoy would have hopefully taken place thus doing away with any further attempts at secrecy.

Air reconnaissance was arranged for by ASV aircraft during the nights of 10th/11th and 11th/12th and also during daylight on the 11th. Pre-emptive strikes against known Axis bomber bases were out of the question; there were fifteen such bases within range of Benghazi and the RAF only had two squadrons of aircraft suitably equipped for such a mission. Strong fighter sweeps were to be made over forward air bases in Cyrenaica but this would be the only deterrent.

In order to assist the Beaufighters, should they have to be called upon, primitive forms of fighter-direction were installed in *Jervis* and *Lively*, but at this stage of the war the system, as we have seen earlier, was by no means perfected and was found often to be 'patchy' in the extreme. Captain Poland was instructed that the operation was to be abandoned and his force was to return at once to Alexandria if he should be sighted during daylight on the 11th, or should he find himself unable to reach a position some ninety miles north-west of Benghazi by 0600 hours on the 12th. In naval circles at Alexandria it was estimated, unofficially of course, that their chances in either case were about ten to one against.

At first all seemed well and at high speed the four ships with their sterns tucked well down, hurried through the friendly darkness. Dawn on the 11th revealed an empty sky and the bustling flotilla sped on ever deeper into hostile waters. By noon they were midway between Tobruk and Crete, but here their luck, until then incredibly good, finally ran out.

The Germans maintained almost non-stop reconnaissance flights over this area and at 1405 hours a Heinkel 111 passed directly overhead on a northerly course, followed half an hour later by a second. Neither aircraft was detected by the ships' radar sets until they had already passed over the force. The enemy aircraft were not heard reporting the force either, which at 1405 hours was in position 33° 41' N, 25° 33' E, but at 1553 hours a message came in from the monitoring services at Alexandria stating that the flotilla had in fact been sighted by the enemy on three occasions between 1000 and 1400 hours!

In accordance with his orders Captain Poland signalled the flotilla to reverse course and broadcast an immediate emergency request for assistance to the RAF in Egypt. The destroyers had at that time notification of a possible enemy submarine contact and Captain Poland felt that as they were now being shadowed there was little point in increasing his speed above the normal hunting maximum of 17 knots. Thus the four lithe vessels came about on course 130 degrees and in line abreast commenced an anti-submarine sweep.

With all guns cleared for action and at full elevation there was little the destroyers could do but keep a tense watch on the hostile sky for the first signs of the promised fighter cover. Several hours passed without either this or the approach of German units and it was not until 1620 hours, in anticipation of air attacks which could not now be long in coming, that the flotilla formed in loose diamond formation and increased speed.

Again the radar made no sighting but at 1630 hours the news that two Beaufighters of 272 Squadron were in radio contact was passed down to the thankful crews. Four minutes later the aircraft were in sight but less than a minute after that their relief was abruptly terminated with the arrival, again unheralded, of the first five Junkers Ju 88s. These were from 1/L.G.I, a unit based at Heraklion in Crete and commanded by *Hauptmann* Joachim Helbig; it consisted of eight Ju 88A-4s which had only recently undergone an intensive anti-shipping course. The two RAF Beaufighters had just established communication with *Jervis* and *Lively* when this group located them. There was no time for the fighters to make any interceptions before the attack commenced.

Helbig led the attack from out of the sun, the bombers diving from 3–4,000 feet down to 2,500 feet. Twisting and turning at over 30 knots the flotilla took violent avoiding action, all their guns firing frantically, switching from one target to another as the bombers swept over them at full throttle. All the ships had narrow escapes and it was soon obvious that the Germans had fielded their first eleven. But it was *Lively*, with her superior anti-aircraft armament, which bore the brunt of the first attack.

Two salvoes of bombs hit or near-missed her, causing her to sink within three minutes. Three or four bombs were direct hits on or about the waterline abreast 'A' gun; one penetrating the bulkhead separating the watch keepers' and stokers' messes. The stricken destroyer listed to starboard well down by the bow as a second salvo of bombs fell a cable's length away to starboard, abreast the after torpedo tubes.

This double blow proved too much for the little ship and she immediately began to heel to starboard and in a few seconds was on her beam ends. Only a single Carley float was released in time and the ship's company abandoned her over the high side, relying on their lifebelts and keeping together as much as possible until they could be picked up. A minute later the *Lively* was rent asunder by an explosion forward and went down in position 33° 23′ N, 25°39′ E, by the stern.

Between 1647 and 1748 hours the other destroyers took the opportunity of a lull in the attacks to return and pick up her survivors, *Jervis* rescuing seventy-six officers and men and *Kipling* 117, while the *Jackal* carried out an anti-submarine sweep around them. Unfortunately, *Lively*'s captain, Lieutenant-Commander Hussey, DSO, died on board *Jervis* after being rescued.

On completion of their rescue mission the remaining three destroyers steered course 130 degrees at 28 knots. The Beaufighters had continued to patrol overhead while this was being done but the delay was to cost the flotilla dear. Strangely enough the fact that they had sunk one of the ships was unknown to the German pilots and although they had suffered no casualties they headed back to their base convinced that they had failed.

However, in subsequent attacks mounted throughout the afternoon both the *Kipling* and the *Jackal* were hit and ultimately sank with heavy loss of life, and from this ill-fated sortie the *Jervis* alone returned laden with survivors from her three sister ships, entering harbour at Alexandria at 1330 hours on the 12th. Thus in one brief day's action and with trivial loss to themselves (one Heinkel 111 claimed shot down), the *Luftwaffe* had crippled the offensive capacity of the 14th Flotilla and destroyed three of its finest ships. It was a cruel blow. The final tally of killed or missing from *Lively* was forty officers and men. When the facts were later released the German pilots concerned earned themselves a considerable reputation, while at home and the fleet there was much anger that such a hopeless mission should have been forced upon the Mediterranean fleet at this time. For Captain Poland it had been a bitter introduction to his leadership of the 14th Flotilla. For the Ls it meant the loss of half of their ships; for now, there were only four.

Lookout was the newest of the Ls to commission, joining the fleet in February 1942 and the 19th Flotilla at Gibraltar in April. She had joined her two sisters during their sojourn in the Indian Ocean but while they were there bigger events were stirring in the Mediterranean. Two convoys for Malta had been mounted in June soon after *Lively's* loss, one from the eastern basin and one from the western end. Both had suffered similar fates and after heavy losses only two ships had got through from both convoys. It was becoming very clear indeed that the island would fall unless more substantial relief was forthcoming very soon. Thus it was that throughout July planning was taking place the other side of the world from the resting Ls which was to involve them ultimately in the toughest and most hard-fought of all the Malta convoy operations, *Pedestal*.

Accordingly, very strong naval forces were assembled from the United Kingdom, Gibraltar, the Eastern Fleet and from Force 'H' itself. No fewer than two battleships, *Nelson* and *Rodney*, four carriers, *Victorious*, *Indomitable*, *Eagle* and *Furious* (with Spitfires for Malta), seven cruisers and thirty-two destroyers were brought together to fight through fourteen fast merchant ships including the large oil tanker *Ohio*. The *Indomitable* was, as we have seen, escorted up from the South Atlantic by *Laforey*, *Lightning* and *Lookout* to meet with the other fighting carriers to exercise their aircraft as a team before convoy and escort entered the Mediterranean to take on the *Luftwaffe*, the *Regia Aeronautica* and the Italian Navy. On the passage north to the Straits of Gibraltar the *Lightning* picked up survivors from the sunken Norwegian ship *Tank Express*, and during refuelling movements at the Rock opportunity was taken to land them there.

Rendezvous was made for Operation *Berserk*, the aircraft exercise, on 5 August 1942, and during this much trouble was experienced in oiling from tankers with largely untrained crews.

The *Lightning* could not be secured correctly due to lack of proper hawsers and it took three-quarters of an hour before she was in position; but almost at once both hawsers parted. A second attempt also ended with the same result and nightfall ended a third try.

During the exercises a fighter ditched from *Victorious* and although *Laforey* and *Fury* made a long search for the pilot he was not recovered. At dusk on 8 August the *Indomitable* and the three Ls were sent in to refuel at Gibraltar itself, rejoining the escort on the mid-morning of the 10th. The whole force entered the Straits on the night of 10/11 August and were picked up by an Italian submarine in the small hours and unsuccessfully attacked. However, the Axis were fully alerted and the very strong counter-measures that they had been preparing were put into effect.

Against *Pedestal* the Germans and Italians could range almost five hundred aircraft, two cruiser squadrons, two destroyer flotillas, twenty submarines and twenty-three motor torpedo boats in addition to the many minefields laid around Malta's approaches: it promised to be a tough fight and so it proved.

At midday the *Furious* moved out to the port quarter of the convoy to commence her flying-off operations of Spitfires for Malta and as her anti-submarine screen she took the *Lightning* and *Lookout*. At 1229 hours the first flight of eight was flown off but the second despatch was interrupted when, at 1315 hours, the carrier *Eagle* was hit by four torpedoes fired by the German submarine *U-73* and rolled over and sank. So quick was this disaster that it stunned the senses. Aboard the *Lightning* J. Hall remembers how:

> I had just got to my off-period (having done the Forenoon watch), resting place, I should say between 1245–1315. I heard four explosions and as the *Eagle* was abreast of where I was I first looked across towards her and whipped up my camera and in minutes it was all over. We swung round to search and dropped depth charges but to no avail.
>
> Unfortunately these photographs, taken from a distance, were all lost together with most of my personal effects, when *Lightning* was sunk a few months later.

Immediately the *Laforey* and *Lookout* were ordered to stand by the stricken vessel and *Lookout* joined with the cruiser *Charybdis* in making a depth charge attack on the possible position of the U-boat but with little effect. Together with the rescue tug *Jaunty* the two destroyers finally picked up sixty-seven officers and 862 ratings from the *Eagle* and these they transferred to other destroyers which were returning to Gibraltar with the *Furious* that night on completion of her mission.

During the whole day the destroyers took turns in replenishing from the oiler *Brown Ranger* but this was suspended just before dusk when air attack, condition Red, was sounded throughout the force on the approach of a large formation of Junkers Ju 88s.

Captain Hutton, as the Senior Destroyer Officer, had just exchanged the following 'cheerful' news with the tanker's skipper as the bombers came into sight:

Laforey to *Brown Ranger*: 'How many destroyers have completed fuelling today?'

Brown Ranger to *Laforey*: 'You are the thirteenth!'

Fortunately this attack was driven off without loss to the convoy and six of the bombers were claimed destroyed. Nightfall brought a brief respite but all knew that the bombers would come in greater numbers by far the next day, that U-boats would be gathering and at dusk came reports of the Italian Fleet putting to sea.

And so it turned out. The first raid by aircraft was at 0907 hours and was followed almost continuously by ever larger formations, both Italian and German. These were fought off by a terrific barrage and by determined work by the few Fleet Air Arm pilots from the remaining two carriers. The submarines were also very active. At 0920 hours *Laforey* in her position as 'Guide of the Fleet' obtained a contact and made an attack which drove the submarine, the Italian *Brin*, down. Further attacks by the *Fury* and *Foresight*, discouraged the *Brin* from making an attack.

As the air attacks grew in intensity losses were inevitable but up until dusk only one merchantman, the *Deucalion*, had been damaged. In return the *Ithuriel* sank by ramming the submarine *Cobalto*. At 1637 hours *Lookout* joined *Tartar* in attacks on another, the *Emo*, again driving her away from an attacking position. Just before 1800 hours the day's heaviest aerial attack took place with all forms of aircraft taking part. The destroyer *Foresight* was hit by an aerial torpedo and later had to be sunk but none of the merchantmen was hit.

At the climax of this attack twelve Junkers Ju 87s carried out a text-book dive-bombing attack on the carrier *Indomitable* hitting her with two heavy bombs and scoring three near misses. The carrier was very badly damaged with large fires issuing from her and the *Lookout*, *Lightning* and *Somali* were detached to assist her. At 1914 hours *Lookout* closed the stricken ship to help her in fire-fighting. Despite the dangers of blazing aircraft fuel cascading from the flight deck Lieutenant-Commander Forman ran his little ship alongside and manned hoses. By 1930 hours the situation aboard the *Indomitable*, although bad, was under control and she was able to steam under her own power.

Soon after this the bulk of the heavy escorting ships, Force 'Z', turned back from the Sicilian Narrows as was normal practice leaving the convoy with their close escort, Force 'X', to penetrate through to Malta that night. All the Ls were retained with the main force and did not participate in the night and day battle which followed.

Attacks by submarines and E-boats massacred the merchant ships and the escorts during the night, but happily the Italian cruiser squadrons were withdrawn, on Mussolini's personal orders as it happened, when almost within striking range. This saved the convoy from almost certain annihilation and thus it was that five of the vital merchant ships survived, despite renewed air assaults, to reach Malta and so lift the siege.[3] It was a famous battle.

The Ls returned to Gibraltar with the rest of Force 'Z' on 15 August and the survivors for Force 'X' joined them there a few days later. Malta was never to be so isolated again as she had been in those desperate months between February and August 1942 although not until November of that year did a further large convoy get through to them.

Between 16 and 18 August *Laforey*, *Lightning* and *Lookout*, along with *Antelope*, *Keppel*, *Malcolm* and *Wishart*, escorted the

Furious who carried out a second flying-off sortie to complement *Bellows*, Operation *Baritone*, thus giving the lie to the Italian claim (both at the time and on American internet sites since) that their submarines had damaged the carrier and forced her to return to dock. The gallant old veteran was totally unscathed and completed this second replenishment unharmed and the ships were back at Gibraltar on the evening of the 18th.

After this operation the *Laforey* spent a little time at Gibraltar on anti-submarine patrols and on 3 September she and *Lookout* escorted the troopship *Leinster* into that harbour from WS22. On the 12th *Laforey* left the Rock for Southampton to carry out a full refit in a commercial yard which lasted right through to 20 November, when she undertook trials and went to Scapa Flow to work up again. *Lightning* and *Lookout* also returned home for refits during this period, the former at Chatham and the latter on the Clyde. On completion of the refit *Lightning* joined *Laforey* at Scapa on 23 November and then escorted the troopship *Duchess of Atholl* from Liverpool to join convoy KMF5 reaching Gibraltar once more on 20 December. Meanwhile, the last, much delayed sister, the *Loyal*, finally commissioned for service on 21 October. The whole quartet was thus ready for service at the end of November 1942. *Lookout* actually sailed as part of the escort for the battleship *Rodney* on 23 October and the other two joined the ships of Force 'H' for the first of the great amphibious operations, Operation *Torch*. This was the occupation of Vichy-held North Africa and Force 'H' with a strong force of battleships, carriers and cruisers was there to prevent any intervention by the Italian fleet, but none was forthcoming. *Laforey* and *Lightning* left Scapa Flow on 7 December for the Clyde and joined convoy KMF5 bound for Algiers at Greenock, both destroyers arriving at Gibraltar on the 21st.

The only sign of opposition was the attacks of German submarines on the convoys and in one of these, Convoy KMF 5, the liner *Strathallan* was torpedoed by *U-654* in the approaches to Oran on 21 November. The *Lightning* went alongside the burning vessel and embarked no fewer than one thousand American troops and nurses and put them ashore at newly occupied Oran. The *Laforey* then took the blazing liner in tow but the fires so damaged her that she sank while still in tow, the next day.

Meanwhile, the *Loyal* had been working up and in December the whole four Ls were allocated again to Force 'H' and arrived at Gibraltar at the end of the month. January 1943 found them all based on Bone which was the forward Allied base and the Ls operated in the Sicilian Channel against German and Italian convoys bringing in supplies and later against the small ships desperately trying to evacuate the remnants of the *Afrika Korps* from Tunisia. Known as Force 'Q' this force comprised the light cruisers *Ajax, Aurora, Penelope* and *Sirius* with destroyers *Laforey, Lightning, Lookout* and *Loyal*. The *Luftwaffe* reacted violently to the advance of the Allied armies and Bone was subjected to repeated and severe air attacks at this time, *Ajax* being damaged. In one of these vicious air raids the oil tanker *Empire Metal* was hit and set ablaze and had to be put under by *Laforey* as she was a hazard to other shipping. On 3 January another attack set afire the tanker *Empire Morn* and damaged the minesweeper *Alarm* which had to be beached. During manoeuvres during this attack *Lightning* was in collision with the destroyer *Lamerton*, but not seriously damaged. On the 6th the supply ship *St Merriel* was bombed and *Lightning*'s crew helped fight her fires.

The *Loyal* had her baptism of fire while anchored in Bone Harbour, and on the night of the 16/17 January was firing her main armament to supplement the port's barrage in heavy attacks. The Ls with other destroyers and from time to time with cruiser support also had some successes against the Axis convoy routes. On the night of the 17/18 January, for example, the *Lightning* and *Loyal* were engaged on an anti-shipping sweep in the Gulf of Gabes and in the early hours of the 18th came upon and quickly sank the supply ship *Favor* (1,320 tons) and the Italian naval tanker *Tanaro* (1,339 tons), without damage to themselves.

The *Lookout* was engaged in convoy operations from Gibraltar at this time and was on hand to rescue survivors from the Canadian corvette *Louisburg* when she was torpedoed and sunk off Oran on 16 February, rescuing fifty survivors. The *Lightning* had also been engaging enemy aircraft at Bone earlier and on the night of 1/2 January had landed a fire party which boarded the blazing merchant vessel *Daihanna* which had been hit during this attack and succeeded in putting out the fire. On the nights of 14th to 17th inclusive she engaged enemy aircraft off Bone.

Also in January *Lightning* and *Loyal* had made a sweep south of Cagliari and destroyed the Italian naval oiler *Tanaro* of some 3,000 tons which was seen to blow up with a heavy explosion. *Lightning* had shot down one bomber off Bone on 12 January but thereafter the attacks died away. On 30 January *Lightning* was part of the escort for the fast minelayer *Abdiel* on an operation off the Skerki Bank, but this was abandoned due to E-boat activity. In February *Lightning* underwent a refit at Algiers, rejoining Force 'Q' at the end of month, but on 1 March another heavy air attack on Bone caused some damage, and twelve casualties, two of them fatal.

The *Abdiel*'s Skerki Bank mine lay finally took place on 5/6 March, with *Lightning*, *Loyal*, *Pakenham* and *Paladin* providing cover for her. This was followed by escort duties between Bone and Algiers with *Loyal* guarding the Infantry Landing Ships *Royal Scotsman* and *Royal Ulsterman* and on the 11th *Lightning* herself took aboard 120 medical staff of the RAMC for Bone.

During March with some light cruisers the Ls joined Force 'Q' in sweeps in Sicilian Channel. On 12 March the *Lightning* and *Loyal* were operating with the cruisers *Aurora* and *Sirius* off Bizerta. The whole force was engaged during the day by a force of twelve German torpedo-bombers, but suffered no damage and the *Lightning* shot down one aircraft for certain. The attack lasted from 1851 to 1930 hours and died away with the coming of darkness. However, the force continued its patrol and while off Galita Island and proceeding at 28 knots the *Lightning* was hit by a torpedo from the E-boat *S.55*. This torpedo struck the ship right forward and the engines were ordered to stop to prevent further damage to the ship's bows. After the *Lightning* had lost steerage way voices were heard shouting in German and almost immediately a second torpedo struck her approximately abreast the fore end of the engine room. The ship broke in two and settled in the water. Within a very short time the *Lightning* was abandoned and the bow and stern sections became vertical and sank rapidly in position 37° 53′ N, 09° 50′ E. The *Loyal* managed to rescue 183 survivors, including her Commanding Officer, from her complement of 227.

And then there were three.

The *Lightning* it is interesting to record was replaced in Force 'Q' by the Polish destroyer *Blyskawica* (Lightning). *Laforey* joined this vessel in bombardments of Axis positions west of Bizerta on 27 March. The sweeps continued. On the night of 20/21 April the *Loyal* was in action again during a sweep off Cape Guardia when she sank some small vessels south of Marittimo. The *Laforey* and *Tartar* were on a similar mission on the night of 28/29 April when they ran into another large E-boat concentration in position 37° 46′ N, 01° 33′ E which were apparently escorting a surface submarine, again in the central Mediterranean south of Marittimo. Only prompt action by the two destroyers prevented a repetition of the *Lightning* tragedy. The *Laforey* rammed and sank one of the E-boats which she cut in two. The destroyer's stem was buckled and the forepeak and cable locker flooded. Speed was reduced to 19 knots, but despite this the other E-boats did not press home any attack. The conclusion of the British report on this short sharp action was that 'we were lucky'.

At the beginning of May the Axis in North Africa were obviously defeated and the Ls took part Operation *Retribution*, the blockade of the Cape Bon peninsula following Admiral Cunningham's execution to 'Sink, Burn, Destroy. Let nothing pass.' Very little did. On 8 May the *Laforey*, *Loyal*, *Tartar*, *Bicester*, *Oakley* and *Zetland* sortied from Bone to comply with this order. On the same night the three Fleets came upon an evacuation convoy and quickly sank two small supply ships, *KT5* and *KT21*, off Cape Bon itself. The following morning the two Ls were engaged with German shore batteries off Sidi Davd. The batteries included mobile 88-mm guns which proved very hard targets to neutralise.

The *Laforey* was steaming at 25 knots during this

bombardment but despite this was hit in the engine room by a shell from one of these guns.

This shell struck about six feet forward from the fore bulkhead and a foot above the waterline and made a hole in the side plating about eight inches in diameter. It detonated just inboard of plating and severe damage was caused by splinters. The main feed tank was holed and minor controlled flooding took place in the engine room through the shell hole. But this one hit and the splinters resulting from it demonstrated the frailty of destroyers. Many steam pipes were cut and the engine room filled with steam, although the *Laforey* was still able to steam on one engine.

The firing circuits and communication circuits were cut resulting in the gun elevation, training and director firing being rendered non-operational, as were the communications to 'X' gun, and from the bridge to the engine room, pom-pom mounting and quarter deck for a time. Speed was reduced to 15 knots, but later increased to 20 after some repairs and 'X' gun was made operational in local control only. In this condition she limped into Malta for repairs on the 10 May.

She was soon back into the fray, however, and on 15 May she picked up twenty-three German soldiers off Plane island. *Lookout* had made a similar catch of a round dozen soldiers from a small boat off the island. However, this German attempt at a 'Dunkirk' was a very small-scale affair and the greater bulk of their forces in Tunisia surrendered with the result that a quarter of a million men went into captivity and Axis hopes of dominating the Mediterranean went with them. On the 23rd *Laforey* and *Lookout* were still patrolling the central Mediterranean and sank a small supply ship, the *Stella Marlis*, which they caught between Trapani and Pantellaria. She was probably trying to run in supplies to the latter island which was now under siege; in fact the island was next on the list of targets for the Allies.

The Italians had described this rock in the middle of the Sicilian Straits as a fortress, and indeed it was well fortified. Accordingly, a sizeable task group of cruisers (*Aurora, Euryalus, Newfoundland, Orion* and *Penelope*), and destroyers (*Laforey, Lookout, Loyal, Jervis, Nubian, Tartar, Troubridge* and *Whaddon*) were assigned to soften up its defence preparatory to an invasion, Operation *Corkscrew*. On 8 June and again on the 11th the *Laforey*, *Lookout* and *Loyal* were part of this naval force which subjected the unhappy garrison to intense bombardments, but the follow-up landings were not necessary as the signal that the garrison wished to surrender, 'through lack of water', was received. The *Lookout* actually received the official surrender of the neighbouring island of Lampedusa the same day and with the fall of these islands the dangerous straits were finally cleared. The willingness of the Italian garrison to surrender was not followed by the Germans in Sicily and the *Lookout* was subjected to a total of twenty-five dive-bombing attacks during the evening but survived without damage.

With these lesser fortresses cleared out of the way the next major operation was the assault on Sicily itself, Operation *Husky*. Throughout June preparations were being made and convoys and troops were assembled to initiate this breaching of the 'Soft Underbelly' of Europe. Meanwhile, the siege of Malta was finally lifted and so much had the atmosphere changed from one year earlier that in June His Majesty King George VI visited the island, embarked in the famous cruiser *Aurora* of Force 'K' fame. The Ls were ever linked with the Malta story and it is good that at this moment of triumph one of the class was represented as the *Lookout* was part of the destroyer escort on 19/20 June for His Majesty.

Early in July *Lookout* and *Loyal* participated in the preliminary exercises for the Sicilian landings and were allocated as part of the screen for Support Force East, comprising the light cruisers *Mauritius*, *Newfoundland*, *Orion* and *Uganda*, who were to give gunfire support to the planned British assault to the east of Syracuse by XXX Corps.

On 10 July Operation *Husky* was finally mounted. Again, although Force 'H' was on hand with a brave show of strength, the Italian fleet did not put to sea in defence of their homeland. The only inconveniences suffered were attacks by German bombers and Italian and German submarines. *Laforey* operated off *Bark* beachhead in the British landing sector and later also joined the Support East force contributing her quota of shells to the defending enemy's discomfiture. On 15 July she welcomed aboard General Alexander and his staff and took him to the port of Augusta, then with the destroyer *Nubian* she joined the cruisers *Orion* and *Uganda* from Mata to conduct further bombardment duties on the eastern coast of Sicily. *Laforey*, *Lookout* and *Loyal* escorted troop convoy KMF36 for these landings.

Shore bombardments were frequent, *Lookout* being so engaged against artillery positions near Catania on 18/19/20 July along with the light cruiser *Newfoundland* and destroyer *Blankney*. Later the three Ls were screening *Newfoundland* back to Malta when she was attacked by two Axis submarines, the *U-407* and the *Ascianghi*, but escaped unharmed.

The *Laforey* also had the satisfaction of dealing positively with this undersea Axis threat when, on 23 July she attacked and quickly sank the Italian submarine *Ascianghi* off the southern coast of Sicily with the destroyer *Eclipse* of the 8th Flotilla. Damage was inflicted on Force 'H' but no large vessels were sunk and the island of Sicily itself fell with lightning speed and resulted in the fall from power of Mussolini himself. The *Lookout* had carried out bombardment duties during the landings while the *Loyal* was attached to the 17th Flotilla.

Notes

1 Obviously no surface vessels could operate from Malta at this time and even the submarine and torpedo-bomber attacks had been severely curtailed by the blitz of March and April which reached a climax in May. Force 'H' was largely otherwise engaged and the Mediterranean Fleet had been reduced to four light cruisers and ten destroyers. Even their main base at Alexandria was under threat from the thrust of Rommel's Panzers.

2 The author has given the full account of the last sortie by the 14th Flotilla in an article in *Warship International* (June, 1971), which has been more recently reproduced in his anthology *Destroyer Action*, (Kimber, 1974). This account is merely an outline of that version.

3 For the full account of this convoy battle the reader is invited to turn to *Pedestal* by the author published by Crecy (UK) and Miller (Malta), while both *Destroyer Captain* (Kimber, 1975) and *Two Small Ships* (Hutchinsons, 1957) give two destroyer captains' accurate eyewitness accounts of the action.

Chapter 8

The Final Actions

Preparations now went ahead for the crossing of the Straits of Messina and the occupation of Italy proper. *Loyal*, with the destroyers *Offa* and Polish *Piorun*, gave fire support near Pessaro and also on 2 and 3 September, *Lookout* carried out bombardments in the Straits and at Reggio Calabria during Operation *Baytown*. It was hoped that with these landings the weaker member of the Axis would collapse and indeed the Armistice did follow; however the Germans were prepared in advance for the event and responded with their usual vigour and efficiency with the result that the hoped-for walk-over in Italy turned out to be a long slow slogging match ashore.

Meanwhile, the Ls were to spend the remainder of their brief lives in support of the Army ashore in this bitter and protracted struggle. On 21 August *Laforey* led five destroyers in a sweep around the toe of Italy passing at times within five miles of the shore but without flushing any worthwhile targets. The Calabrian side of the straits were heavily guarded with mobile gun batteries but the destroyers on this occasion escaped unscathed.

In September came the Allied landings at Salerno, Operation *Avalanche*, and all the Ls were actively engaged in covering bombardments for the army attempting to establish itself ashore. *Lookout* joined the Northern Attack Force, Task Force 85, with the light cruisers *Mauritius*, *Orion* and *Uganda* and AA cruiser *Delhi* for the first landings. The *Loyal* had performed a similar function on 3 September during the Calabrian landings and her duty was to become a familiar chore for the other two boats over the next few months. *Loyal* had bombarded the Cape Armis Reggio at this time but joined her two sisters off the Salerno beaches on the 8th. As usual German reaction was prompt and the destroyers found themselves called upon frequently in an attempt to silence the infuriating mobile 88-mm guns which the Germans were so adept at using. These proved to be elusive targets and the Ls suffered heavily at their hands on 9 September due entirely to the selfless way they closed these guns to take the heat off the troops ashore.

The *Loyal* took one direct hit from a three-inch shell which fortunately did not detonate. The ship was hit on the starboard side of the forward boiler room, about three feet above the waterline. This shell perforated the *Loyal*'s side and the bulkhead between the boiler rooms and finally came to rest in the tubes of Number Two boiler. It blew a hole some 32 inches wide and the tear it made in the bulkhead was ten inches long. This shell cut eight low-power multicore cables. 'X' gunhouse was operational in local control only. She limped away to Malta and finally completed repairs at Palermo during the next days.

Laforey was even more hard hit this day and she took no fewer than five direct hits by 88-mm shells, two of which were delayed action, one burst instantly and two others failed to explode. An 88-mm gun was shelling the beaches and causing severe casualties among the troops. Without hesitation 'Tubby' Hutton took his ship in to point-blank range, all guns firing. They soon destroyed the gun itself, and its ammunition dump, but not before *Laforey* had been hit in return by several shells. The first struck the after end of the forecastle just above the upper deck level and detonated four feet inboard, but caused only minor structural damage to the bulkheads and surrounding structure. The second hit on the waterline abreast the forward boiler room, detonating on impact and blowing in a hole some three feet by 1½ feet. The resulting splinters damaged the boiler tubes, oil fuel transfer pipe and ring main, and the power to 'B' and 'X' gunhouses; the main lighting circuits were lost for a short while.

As the *Laforey* heeled to turn away from the coast, water

flooded into the forward boiler room. The third shell struck the coaming of the forward boiler room air casing and detonated in the boiler uptake. Splinters damaged the uptakes and air casing of both boilers, the steam drum of Number One boiler, the main steam pipe, the fire main, boiler tubes, ring main and the bulkhead between boiler rooms. The fourth hit was on the depth-charge rack under the after torpedo tubes; it was deflected through the base of the firework trunk and passed overboard without exploding. The fifth and final shell went through the searchlight platform and also passed overboard without exploding. Even so it caused minor damage to the emergency conning position.

After these hits the *Laforey* had the forward room out of action and the efficiency of the after boiler room impaired by the temporary loss of air pressure. But she was soon repaired. Her casualties were one man killed and two wounded. The 88-mm gun was quite the most efficient Axis land weapon of war the Ls had to contend with at this stage of their lives although a new and vastly more potent air weapon made an unwelcome appearance during this campaign. The *Loyal* had a patch slapped over her damage and was back in action on 12 September at Volturno along with *Lookout* and the Dutch gunboat *Flores* and the next day she was near-missed by a FX 1400 radio-controlled glider-bomb. These weapons had wrecked considerable havoc amongst the crowded anchorages off the beachheads and many fine ships were to be sunk or damaged over the next few months. *Lookout* was also near-missed by one of these weapons on 16 September, suffering some damage which was repaired at Malta.

At Salerno the *Loyal* fired some 1,714 rounds at the enemy and her Commanding Officer was awarded the bar to his DSC, the Sub-Lieutenant H.E. Howard the DSC and two ratings the DSM for *Loyal*'s work in leading in the minesweepers for the approach to the beachhead. Once the beaches were established the flotilla found itself transferred during October to the Adriatic where it found itself on constant call from the Eighth Army who were pushing their way slowly up the eastern coast of Italy. Again progress was slow and German resistance great. *Laforey* and *Lookout* both provided gun support when the Germans made a determined counter-attack on the beachhead on the 13th.

Laforey and *Lookout*, along with the gunboat *Flores*, were in close support when the Army made the crossing of the Volturno river on 4 October and on the 13th. On the latter date the two ships were proceeding at 13 knots when they were attacked by twelve bombers. *Laforey* received two near misses by small (250-kg) bombs and *Lookout* was near-missed by another which again only caused minor damage. At the end of October they returned to Malta to refit and their place was taken by *Loyal* and *Quilliam*. *Lookout* was deemed in need of a major repair and machinery refit and this was commenced at Taranto naval base on 13 October. This proved far more protracted than expected and *Lookout* did not rejoin the 14th Flotilla at Mata again for a considerable period.

On 1 November *Laforey* escorted a pair of freighters from Malta to Naples and another convoy back to Augusta where she assisted a US merchant ship that had gone aground in a gale in that harbour before returning once more to Malta. During November and early December these two destroyers carried out patrol and bombardment duties in support of the Eighth Army. On the 19th, while off Pescara, they sank a German F-fighter in a brief engagement. The *Loyal* received a direct hit from a 3-inch calibre shell during the action when shore batteries opened fire as the British destroyers descended on the German convoy. The shell hit the port side forward, abreast the port side at upper deck level, which caused a hole in the side plating two feet by one foot round but did not impair her fighting efficiency.

Laforey intercepted two E-boats approaching Allied shipping in Naples Bay on Christmas Day 1943 and engaged them with radar-directed fire from her fore turrets, but these elusive targets managed to get away. Also on 25 November *Loyal* shelled Civita Nuova and, again, on 2 December bombarded positions at San Benedeto and Ancona and sank three small schooners to the north of the port of Pescara and damaged two others in a brief and one-sided action. On the night of 29/30 December destroyers *Laforey*, *Loyal* and *Faulknor* with the Dutch gunboat *Flores*, escorted No. 9 Commando in a raid on the Tyrrhenian coast two miles north of the mouth of the Gangliano river. The raid was a success. On 30 December Gaeta was shelled. After this the Ls returned to Naples re-ammunition ship, and rejoined the 19th Flotilla operating with the revival Force 'K' for a brief period.

The *Lookout* was also in this force but in February came the Anzio landings, Operation *Shingle*, and all three ships were earmarked to support this further operation. Ronald Sired aboard the *Laforey* reminds us that much of this work of patrol and bombardment in the Mediterranean winter was not all honey and death-defying bravado.[1]

At action stations, as an acting Control Rating, 1st class, I was to be in the director as Rate Officer. At defence-stations I was in charge of the director's crew, consisting of the layer, trainer and range-taker; I was also in charge of the main armament as far as opening fire was concerned.

At 1800 I closed up at the director for the last dog watch. We passed through the Straits of Messina and slowly the dusk closed in over the sea. At 1930 the ship's company went to action stations and the armament state was reported to the Captain. All instruments were lined up, circuits were closed and checked and then we settled down on the alert. I found the director was equipped with a gunnery surface set of radar, operated by training the director around its axis. This was my duty, to operate this radar set when necessary, mostly at night. The small radar box was situated on my left side; its screen was about eight inches square, and, when switched on, showed a pale-green light, called a scan. Little green flashes of light flickered at odd intervals and by placing a narrow movable range-scale across the scan to one of the tiny green flashes (or pips), I was able to measure the range of a vessel or low-flying aircraft. Each little pip denoted the presence of a surface object. The director was not very large, shared with four other men, and there was little room in which to move about. In fact, there was no room, one was able only to sit and wriggle on one's small padded seat with many instruments in front and to each side.

The rest of the night and early morning was spent at action stations and by 0400 I was feeling cramp. As the director was only a small armoured box with steel seats, one could hardly be blamed for wanting to stretch one's legs. I had just enough room to turn round and even then sharp metal corners dug me in the ribs or took a piece of flesh from my neck. A destroyer's director was one of the more fiendish inventions of the 'Backroom boys' and I often wished I could have met some of them. When seated normally my feet usually kicked the trainer in the neck whenever I moved, and the Control Officer always managed to wake me with a sharp elbow as I snatched a quick doze. Constantly, the director had to be trained round, first one way then the other, in order to keep an all-round radar and visual watch. The dull greenish light from the screen lit the inside of the director with a pale sickly glow. It was amazing how the cold wind whistled through chinks in the badly fitting metal plates. In really wet weather, water oozed through the rubber-lined window flaps, and trickling down the inside of the tiny compartment, formed pools on the metal deck.

On 1 November she had sailed as escort for two fast merchant ships bound for Naples which arrived on the 2nd. This type of routine work was to fill in the next two weary months. On 3 November she sailed with a nineteen-ship convoy and arrived at Augusta on the 4th. The same evening she left for a night patrol and at 0400 hours was diverted to the aid of an American merchant ship aground to the north of Augusta. *Laforey* arrived an hour later and pulled the stranded ship off and then sailed to Malta to refuel. On the 6th she left for Sliema carrying out anti-submarine exercises on the way. She arrived at Naples on 23

December and spent most of Christmas Day on anti-E-boat patrol in the Gulf of Naples. She obtained a radar contact at 2350 hours and opened fire but the two E-boats escaped.

Again let Ronald Sired describe winter weather conditions in the Bay of Naples that do not quite conjure up a picture of sunny Mediterranean holidays.

A gale warning was received early in the afternoon and by 1600 *Laforey* was rolling in a heavy ground swell that swirled its way into the Bay, driven by strong gusts of wind. As I was duty Petty Officer, I had to detail duty men to keep watch on the fo'c'sle as anchor watch-men and I frequently paid visits there myself to view the cable. Steam was raised at 6 p.m. ready to shift berth should occasion demand. It was a swine of a night; powerful gusts of wind made the destroyer wallow heavily. As we were at single anchor, we did not roll or pitch freely as at sea, but with a stilted, restricted movement that seemed to penetrate one's stomach.

On the fo'c'sle the cable creaked and groaned but held safely. Loose metal links of the port cable screeched as they rubbed together and the wind-driven rain whipped into my face as I staggered aft on the weather side of the upper deck to examine the whaler and other deck fittings. Amidst the gale-driven rain squalls, I watched the angry glare of Vesuvius flare up and die down as banks of thick cloud obscured its 3,800-foot peak. By midnight I was dead tired and, as soon as I was relieved by the middle-watch Petty Officer, I went into the mess, had a quick shower, and before I turned in, a couple of tots of rum which I had saved for such a night as this. In all I spent a very unpleasant New Year's Eve.

By daylight on New Year's Day the gale was spent and, although the bay was still rough, we were not jerking about so much. Shipping began to move about the harbour and at 5 o'clock that evening *Laforey* sailed from Naples bound for Maddalena, a former Italian naval base between Corsica and Sardinia.

As soon as we put our bows outside the bay, I knew we were in for a rough trip and we were. The hands staggered to action stations at 7 p.m. and by 11 o'clock we were doing eighteen knots and meeting close-set waves head-on. Heavy seas continually broke over our bows with a crash and a flurry of wind-driven spray. At times *Laforey* shuddered as she rolled crabwise over a great wave, pitching into its trough with a bone-shaking jar.

No one was allowed to move about the upper deck so that the ship's company was forced to remain at action-stations all night. A very uncomfortable night it was, too. Even though I was well wrapped-up in a clammy coat, with an oilskin draped over me, I still felt the icy wind as it found chinks in the tightly closed director's doors. The rain drove in and spattered over the five men. We were a wet and miserable crowd. An occasional look through the narrow windows showed the bows of the destroyers buried by rough seas and, as water hurled itself over the bridge and director, one instinctively ducked as it smashed against the thick glass windows.

I sustained a number of bruises by being knocked about inside the director and the muttered curses from the crew turned the air blue. The wind, direct from the Alps, found its way into every nook and cranny with unerring accuracy. On one occasion, a tremendous wave broke on 'A' turret with a colossal crash and I felt *Laforey* tremble violently as her bows broke through a succession of large waves and masses of sea-water spilled over the forepart of the ship like a cataract. I later spoke to a member of 'A' turret about this; he had the impression that the entire turret was about to be swept away.

So much for DNC's theory of a true 'Weatherproof turret'. Bombardment duties in company with the *Faulknor*, *Loyal* and Dutch gunboat *Flores* followed on the 29th at Gaeta which they hit on the 30th, returning to Naples to refuel and re-ammunition. Another patrol in the Gulf followed. On the night of 5 January while on a similar patrol she was ordered to sink an abandoned Liberty ship which she did with gun and torpedo. Further bombardments of the Gaeta area took place on 18 January in company with *Spartan, Orion, Faulknor, Jervis* and *Janus*. After refuelling at Naples she sailed to meet a convoy of eight ships bound for the Anzio landings and at 1245 hours met the *Jervis, Loyal* and landing ships.

The actual landings took place on the 22nd and the *Laforey* and *Loyal* led in, opening fire in support of the troops going ashore. The two Ls were later sent to reconnoitre the coast toward Rome. Both remained off the beaches with the cruisers of the 15th Cruiser Squadron and destroyers of the 8th, 14th and 19th Flotillas on hand for the numerous bombarding duties required. Again the German reaction was violent and radio-controlled bombs again made their marks on the warships. On the 23rd *Janus* was hit by one and when *Laforey* went to her aid she herself was near-missed. On the 27th they refuelled at Naples but were back off the beaches on the 29th when the light cruiser *Spartan* was hit by one such bomb and sunk. The destroyers picked up survivors and then went back on patrol off 'Peter' beach.

These duties continued as the Germans made desperate attempts to throw the Allies back into the sea. In the event the beachhead held but again there was no quick descent on Rome and the stalemate continued. On 9 February the *Loyal* again fell victim to a mobile 88-mm gun while acting in a bombarding role.

The shell detonated aft on the upper deck starboard, above the after end of the engine room, about six feet in from the ship's side and punched a hole some 18-inches in diameter. The forced lubrication system of the starboard engine was pierced by five splinters. The electric leads to the torpedo tubes and to one of the steering motors, as well as all minor circuits, were cut. The fire mains were fractured causing temporary loss of cooling water to 'X' turret and the high power air line to this gunhouse was also severed. The torpedo tubes were damaged and their roller paths were distorted, reducing their training arc. The starboard main engine and one steering motor were put out of action but the ship was able to proceed at 20 knots. Repairs were effected at Taranto but took six weeks by unenthusiastic Italian labour. On 30 March she left for Malta ready to resume operations again at Anzio.

After conducting a bombardment of Formica and again replenishing, *Laforey* sailed from Naples on another routine anti-E-boat hunt with the fellow veteran Flotilla Leader *Faulknor* on 25 February, but was detached to the aid of the Tank Landing Ship *LST.422* which had been mined and had run aground at Sabaudia. *Laforey* was unable to help and the *LST* became a total loss. After rejoining the *Faulknor* a submarine contact was made at 1940 hours. This was the start of a very long hunt which lasted for several days and nights. The few remaining German U-boats in the Mediterranean were proving to be elusive foes and the two destroyers were still hunting at 1200 hours the next day when they were joined by the Hunts *Lamerton* and *Hambledon*. The long game continued until at 2145 hours an acoustic torpedo exploded close in *Laforey*'s wake as the U-boat's Captain tried to drive his relentless pursuers away. All through the following day the search went on without success and two further destroyers joined. However, on the 28th the hunt was finally called off, *Laforey* returning to Naples, oiled and re-ammunitioned and after embarking survivors from the *Inglefield*, which had fallen foul of a radio-controlled bomb of Anzio, took them to Malta.

She returned to the beachhead herself and alternated between there and Naples and carried out further patrols. On the night of 23/24 March while on a night patrol with the *Grenville* she opened radar-directed fire on E-boats but without a positive result.

On 29 March she sailed from Naples to join the *Tumult*, *Tuscan*, *Ulster*, *Urchin*, *Blencathra* and *Hambledon* who were engaged on another long hunt after picking up a contact to the north-east of Palermo. They were still searching in the evening of 30 March when at 1900 *Laforey* picked up a surface radar contact. The submarine had finally been forced to surface and hoped to escape in the darkness. *Laforey* opened fire and turned to the attack, when she was struck by three torpedoes. These hit her abreast the forward boiler room. The resulting explosions broke her back and she quickly settled amidships. Her bow and stern rose quickly and within two minutes of the explosions both halves disappeared. The U-boat, the *U-223*, was immediately pounced upon by the other destroyers and sunk but in the resulting confusion the loss of *Laforey* was not noticed.

Thus it was that when *Tumult* and *Tuscan* returned at dawn only sixty-five survivors were picked up. Ten officers and 172 men went down with *Laforey* and Captain 'Beaky' Armstrong was not among the survivors. This was the greatest loss of life associated with the L Class destroyers.

And then there were two.

Loyal continued operations in the Anzio area and on the night of 9/10 May was straddled by heavy bombs while lying in the anchorage, fortunately without severe damage. However, this, coupled with continuing bombardment duties led to the need for a refit and throughout the period April to early June 1944, she was in dock refitting and so was *Lookout*, at Taranto. On completion of these they both continued to go their separate ways.

Loyal returned to Malta after completing her repairs on 18 August and was assigned to the east coast of Italy in the Adriatic working from Ancona with the destroyers *Kimberley*, *Undine*, *Urchin* and the gunboats *Aphis* and *Scarab*. On 20 and 30 August she bombarded German gun positions and transport near Pescara on 4 September, with the destroyer *Urchin*. On the 7th with the gunboat *Scarab* she bombarded the Rimini area, which task she again repeated on the 18th. On 24 September she fired 434 rounds at gun positions some seven miles north of Rimini.

At this period the Americans had insisted on following up the Allied landings in the Normandy invasion with similar enterprises in southern France. They named it Operation *Dragoon*, but Churchill felt, in view of the unnecessary waste involved for no worthwhile objective, it should have been called Dragooned! The refurbished *Lookout* was assigned to this operation as part of the *Sitka* Fire Support Group (Task Force 86) under an American admiral. On 12 August this group, the US heavy cruiser *Augusta*, light cruiser *Dido*, and American destroyers *Gleaves* and *Somers*, left Naples for the bombardment area.

On 14/15 August *Lookout* was engaged in providing gun support when the Germans counter-attacked these landings at Levant Island and Port Cros. On 25 August she bombarded forts in the St Mandrier area in company with the light cruiser *Aurora* and the US destroyer *Kendrick*. On the successful conclusion of this operation against sparse opposition she sailed to take *Loyal*'s place in the Adriatic.

Between 10 and 25 September *Lookout* joined her sister in repeated gun duels around the Rimini area. On 12 October they bombarded batteries near Cesenatico. Much of their work was dull routine as always, although as David Braybrook remembers here they tried to enliven it when they had a run ashore.

Our duties had been mainly patrol in the Bay of Genoa and the southern French coastline, calling at Leghorn, Ajaccio, Toulon, Juan-les-Pins and other welcome spots. Malta was rather dull by comparison. This made up for an earlier dispiriting period when, having been refitted at Taranto in 1944 (where I joined her in May), *Lookout* finished her trials and took part in the South of France landings. Perhaps by reason of Italian sabotage or inefficiency *Lookout* broke down well within range of the shore batteries and black balls were solemnly hoisted and smoke was hastily laid!

While at Taranto earlier the First Lieutenant organised outings for swimming and rifle shooting. A 'commandeered' Army lorry was used and the No. 1 took the opportunity of these outings to search for new specimens with his butterfly net. On returning to the ship however he unfortunately took the wheel of the truck and backed into the harbour. First to appear from the murky depths was his hat, followed shortly afterwards by No. 1

but without the lorry. For obvious reasons it was never salvaged.

A rather pragmatic Surgeon Commander took a dim view of Sick Parade and prescribed TB injections for *all* minor ailments. He thus reduced attendances to the sick bay quite sensationally. An Italian docker hit by a falling spanner still got his jab before any other treatment!

It was while returning from one bombardment in the Rimini area at 20 knots that *Loyal* set off a ground mine laid in some 7½ fathoms. The explosion occurred some ten yards off the starboard side of the ship abreast the engine and gearing rooms and inflicted extensive damage. The ship's structure was strained and the bulkheads buckled over an area extending from the forward boiler room to the stern, mainly on the starboard side. The hull plating was corrugated to a maximum depth of eight inches and the side framing was set, inboard. Many rivets pulled through the hull causing leaks in the engine and gearing rooms. The upper deck lifted slightly abreast the centre of the damage.

Such was the enormous effect of this explosion that the structure of the starboard after fuel tank was split and this allowed oil to leak into the gearing rooms, gland and plummer block spaces and also into 'X' magazine. This resulted in a list to port of seven degrees, but this flooding was controlled in the engine and gearing rooms; however, 'X' magazine had to be closed down. All the main and auxiliary machinery, electrical and radar equipment and gun armament were extensively damaged by the shock and all steam and electrical power failed. Essential services were maintained by diesels. The *Loyal* lay completely immobilised and had to be taken in tow by *Lookout*. The main engines, after torpedo tubes and radar were out of action as was 'X' turret, while the others were in local control only. The effects of underwater concussion were devastating in this instance and much greater than expected pre-war.

Loyal was towed to Ancona by *Lookout* but such was the extent of the damage that she was soon paid off and regarded as a constructive total loss. The skilled manpower was not available to repair this almost brand-new and powerful destroyer, nor was there any longer the outstanding need for her as newer, albeit smaller and less powerfully armed destroyers, were being commissioned in dozens at this period of the war. She finally paid off at Taranto in February 1945, was towed to Malta and used there as a base ship. Here she lingered, with the hulks and memories of her sisters of Force 'K', performing this lowly role until late in 1947. In February 1948, she was finally written off and reduced to category C, the lowest grade, in preparation for scrapping. On 15 July 1948 she was towed home by the tug *Earnest* arriving at the breakers' yard in Milford Haven on the 31st. Here she was unceremoniously stripped and broken up.

And then there was one.

The 'Last of the Ls' as *Lookout* now became called in the Mediterranean Fleet, continued to give good service. In January 1945, she joined the 3rd Destroyer Flotilla, which contained some of her big half-sisters of the M Class, only five of which remained afloat. This most powerful group of warships operated out of Naples and patrolled and bombarded the north-west Italian coast. On 6 January she was bombarding the Massa, south-east of Spezia, area with the American destroyer *Woolsey* and, by many accounts, *Lookout* was outranging the 5-inch guns of that ship comfortably.

On the night of 17/18 March came her big moment. The Germans were using a number of destroyers they had taken over from the Italians and manned, and on several occasions the 3rd Flotilla had attempted to intercept them and bring them to action. This night the *Lookout* and *Meteor* were patrolling north of Corsica and had the 'assistance' of two French destroyers, the *Tempete* and the *Basque*.

Following a coastal radar report of enemy surface units being out the *Lookout* closed and located three destroyers by radar. She immediately opened a controlled fire on these targets, which were the German-operated *TA.24* (ex-*Arturo*), *TA.29* (ex-*Eridano*) and the *TA.32* (ex-*Premuda*). The *Meteor* joined in the battle and after some solid shooting by both British destroyers the *Lookout* fired six torpedoes at her two targets. In the light of a star shell the *TA.32* was seen to have been hit hard and was slowing down while the *TA.29* was stopping. *Lookout* fired her two remaining torpedoes but these missed and being cursed with no re-loads the *Lookout* steered to join the *Meteor* who was busily engaged finishing off the *TA.24*. Thus two German destroyers were sunk but the *TA.32* eluded the two French destroyers with ease and escaped in smoke through a minefield.

Commander Hetherington of the *Lookout* was a keen bridge player and was delighted to receive a signal from Malta congratulating him of his 'Small Slam'.

The routine continued much the same after this incident until the end of the war in Europe soon afterwards. On 23 and 25 April, for example, *Lookout* was once more engaged in bombarding German positions on the Italian Riviera in company with the French cruisers *Duguay Trouin* and *Montcalm* and she continued shoots in support of the 5th Army up to the date of the Armistice. When it came in May her job was done, and the last of the Ls joined the burnt-out wrecks and abandoned hulks of her once proud sisters at Malta. Here she remained for some months operating with the Mediterranean Fleet.

In October she left Malta for the last time and after calling at Gibraltar she arrived at Devonport in fighting trim, although of course she had been de-stored and had a much reduced complement. Here she was anchored in the Reserve Fleet with so many other famous destroyers. Here she lay idle for two years. It was to be expected that the very many over-age ships of her type should go to the breakers in the post-war cut down of the fleet, but it was still something of a shock when it was announced that *Lookout* was among the destroyers to be scrapped in October 1947, for she was barely four years old and still one of the most powerful destroyers in the fleet. It was however so, and she was not to enjoy the reprieve that the outbreak of the Korean War gave her M Class half-sisters, nor the subsequent re-birth that their purchase, modernisation and service in the Turkish Navy was to give them through to the late 1960s.

On 23 February 1948, the C-in-C, Plymouth, signalled to the Admiralty at Bath:

> Condition of *Lookout* is satisfactory for towing at sea but her seaworthiness would be much improved if the two in number oil fuel tanks (Nos. 3 & 4), immediately forward of the boiler room were pressured full with water ballast.

A hastily scribbled note in pencil by an uncaring hand was her only epitaph:

> 'Tow to Newport for scrapping.'

She was sold by John Cashmore and arrived at the breakers on 29 February 1948.

The last of the magnificent Laforeys had gone.

Notes

1 *Enemy Engaged*, William Kimber.

Appendix 1

The Original Weapons System

The L Class destroyers' 4.7-inch mounting. Data from the CB.1467 (BR.916) *Handbook for 4.7-inch Mark XI gun on the twin mark XX mounting*. Issued April, 1942.

The 4.7 inch Mark XX mounting was designed to accommodate two 4.7-inch Mark XI guns which fired heavy (62-lb) shells in an enclosed gunhouse in which the ammunition supply arrangements were also contained.

Weights

	Tons	Cwt	Gms	Lbs
Two guns and mechanisms unloaded	7	2	–	–
Sighting gear	–	12	3	6
Gun shield	6	7	2	18
Base and fittings	2	1	3	12
Remainder of mounting	21	8	3	11
Weight of mounting	37	8	3	11
Deck fittings	–	8	–	18
Hoist (B gun)	5	14	1	–
Hand operating gear for hoist	–	10	–	24
Hydraulic installation complete with oil cooler (B mount) on fixed structure	3	19	1	–
Air blast gear on fixed structure	–	11	–	7
Total weight of equipment	48	16	–	12
Recoiling mass	3	13	2	5
Elevating mass	7	1	–	–
Training mass	35	11	1	7
Training mass, including men and ammunition	37	7	1	–

Ballistics

Nominal muzzle velocity:		2,543 ft/sec
Range table muzzle velocity:	Max	2,575 ft/sec
	Min	2,400 ft/sec

Range table muzzle velocity with reduced charge:	Max	1,900 ft/sec
	Min	1,800 ft/sec
Weight of projectile:		62 lbs
Weight of charge:		12.8 lbs
Weight of cartridge (case & charge):		32.6 lbs.
Position of centre of gravity of gun (from breech face):		70.31-in (unloaded)
Of mounting including guns:		2-in. below trunnions and 4-in. forward of pivot

Of complete equipment: including hoists

	A	B	C
Above deck ring	24-in.	5-in.	24-in.
Forward of pivot	5¼in.	5¼-in.	2½-in.
To starboard	4-in.	–	2-in.
To port	–	4-in.	–

Forces of firing

Maximum force recoil (of each gun):	23 tons
Upward lift:	15 tons
Downward blow:	37½ tons

Limits of elevations

10 degrees depression:	50 degrees elevation

Distance between guns

Distance between guns:	96-in.

Air blast gear

Pressure in air bottles:	4,000 lb/in.
Air blast pressure:	500 lb/in.
Setting in relief valve:	600 lb/in.
Pressure at which safety disc bursts:	780 lb/in.
Broady reducing valve:	
(a) Reduced pressure from 4,000 lb/in. to 780 lb/in.	
(b) Reduced pressure from 4,000 lb/in. to 500 lb./in.	

Safety firing gear

Limits of operation:
10 degrees depression to 40 degrees elevation.
Type of mark of interceptor Mark IV*
Lag in elevation and training between angle at which interceptor fails and angle at which it could not be held up far enough to make contact
        3 degrees elevation
        0.5 degrees training (approx)

Training base and rollers

Holding-down bolts, 875 dia.	42 screws on 132.3-in. P.C.D.
	42 bolts on 121.5-in P.C.D.
Clip clearance:	0-02-in.
Number of rollers:	48
Flange clearance of rollers:	0.01-in.

Recoil and run-out

(A)	Working recoil:	26.5-in.
	Metal to metal recoil:	28-in.
	Force of recoil:	23 tons (each gun)
(B)	Initial pressure in recuperator:	750 lb/in.
	Final pressure in recuperator:	3,000 lb/in.
Packed back pressure:		1,200 lb/in.
Test pressure:		3,000 lb/in.
Charging pressure at working recoil for slip test:		1,250 lb/in.
(C)	Time of recoil and run-out:	0.75 sec. horizontal
		1.00 sec. at 50 degrees
(D)	Percentage of energy of recoil absorbed on the recuperators:	30% horizontal,
		24% at 50 degrees
(E)	Capacity of recoil buffer:	Cylinder and tank 20 pints, (692 cut-in)
Liquid in tanks:		8½ pints (294 cut-in)
(F)	Composition of buffer liquid	One part glycerine in one part lime water
	Test pressure on buffer:	7,000 lb/in
(G)	Intensifier charging pressure:	750 lb/in.
	Intensifier test pressure:	3,000 lb/in.
	Intensifier liquid:	1 part potash and soft soap to two parts heavy Torpoyl

Position of trunnions

Height:	84-in. above deck ring
Distance from centre pivot:	3-in. behind centre pivot

Cradle

Clearance of gun in cradle:	0.012-in. + .008-in.
	max. 0.05-in − .000-in. min.

Semi-automatic gear

Clearances	
Nominal normal full opening of breech without buffer action:	7.925-in.
Limits within which normal full opening	

could be adjusted under slow semi-automatic actions:	H. 7.94-in. L. 7.875-in.
Nominal maximum opening of breech including buffer action:	8.2-in.
Minimum clearance obtained between roller and semi automatic cam at nominal maximum opening of breech:	0.045-in.
Minimum recoil which allowed roller to clear end of the cam:	13.6-in.

Hauling back gear

Amount of haul back:	14.75-in.
Weight of gear:	94-lb

Hydraulic units

Electric motor	
Revs per min:	1,500
Type:	Self-ventilated
Direction of rotation:	Clockwise at commutator end
Volts:	220
HP	rms 45; peak 102

Pump

Revs per min:	275
Type:	V.S.G. size 24, Mark I 11, 'A' end, variable delivery auto-pump
Direction of rotation:	Looking at coupling – clockwise
Number of cylinders:	11
Stroke of piston:	1.85 in. maximum
Capacity:	32,000 cub in./men

Cooler capacity pressures	
Pressure in system (working):	850/1,000 lbs/sq in.
Test pressure:	2,000-lbs/sq in
Weight of pump unit ('A' end):	2,800-lbs
Weight of electric motor:	1,060-lbs
Weight of oil cooler complete with motor and pump:	750-lbs

Capacities	
Amount of oil in the system:	160 gallons

| Capacity of oil tank: | 75 gallons |
| Reduction gear ratios between motor and pump: | 5.5/1 |

Elevating gear

Max elevation and depression:	50 degrees E to 10 degrees D
Speed of elevating; depression per rev of handles:	2½ degrees
Elevating effort:	Average 22 lbs
Housing angle:	5-degree elevation
Type of elevation receiver:	'E' Mark IV
Rendering torque of friction plates:	10-in.

Training gear

Maximum angle of training	
'A':	145-degrees R and G
'B':	145-degrees R and G
'X':	173.5-degrees R and G
Speed of training, degrees per sec.:	.10 (power)
Degrees per rev of handles:	0.73 (hand)
Training effort (hand):	18 to 20-lb
Type of training receiver:	'D' Mark IV+
Rendering torque of friction plates:	.55-in tons (pinion torque)

Loading tray	
Weight of round:	94.6-lb shell and case
Pressure at rammer:	850-lb/sq in.
Stroke of ram:	25.6-in
Time taken to ram:	1 second
Time taken to withdraw:	1 second
A gag 0.25 in. diameter is fitted	

Sights

Ratios: gun to telescope:	1/1
Telescope to range dial:	80/7
Telescope to range handwheel:	0.5 degrees per rev
Telescope to deflection dial:	30/1
Telescope to deflection handwheel:	1 degree per rev
Tangent elevation:	30 degrees
Tangent elevation on range dial:	342 degrees .857
Deflection:	4-degrees 30-minutes R and L
Drift:	1 degree 26 minutes 36 seconds
Deflection and drift in deflection dial:	5-degrees 56 minutes 36 seconds

Automatic drift correction:	Adjustable 100 to 200
Max angle of elevation and depression:	50-degree elevation
For which sight ports were cut	10-degree depression
	(11½ degree wooded angle)

Shield

Thickness and material:	0.25 in. mild steel, PS 26
Maximum working radius:	10 foot 4 in.
Number, position and purpose of portable plates, including vent plates:	One vent plate in roof through which hoist gear was removed. One access plate at front for pipes receivers etc. Two access plates at rear for withdrawal of guns for loading trays. Four access plates in roof for lifting gear Five bottom plates or chutes for access to base.

Ventilation

Number of fans:	One
Type and size:	One 7½ pressure fan

Hoists

Shell hoists:	3
Rate of delivery:	10 rounds per min.
Stroke of ram:	36-in.
Amount of over-run between fixed and moving pawls:	3-in.
Number of shell in hoists (lifting):	11 in A and X mountings, 14 in B mounting
Cordite hoists:	3
Rate of delivery:	10 rounds per min.
Stroke of ram:	46-in.
Amount of over-run between fixed and moving pawls:	2.9373-in. in A and X, 2.49 in B.
Number of cases in hoists (lifting):	8 in A and X, 10 in B

Due to the central hoist arrangement the amount of handling of ammunition required had been greatly reduced compared with the previous destroyer designs and this enabled the heavier shell to be more easily used.

To provide more effective anti-aircraft fire the guns were given an elevation of

50 degrees compared with the more usual figure of 40 degrees and mechanical fuze setters were supplied.

The lengths of the trunks of the mountings varied with the position in the ship occupied by the mountings.

General notes

The mounting was arranged to accommodate two 4.7-inch Mark XI, Q.F. guns in separate cradles. Hydraulic power was used for training, ramming and operating the shell and cordite hoists. It was supplied from a pump situated on the fixed structure of the ship. The turret crew with the exception of the two breech workers were accommodated between the guns: the two gunlayers and the trainer at the front of the gunhouse; the sight-setter and fuze-follower behind the trainer; the two fuze setting numbers at the fuze setting machines; the four ammunition supply numbers at the centre and the two tray workers at the rear of the gunhouse.

A platform was provided for each of the breech workers on the outside of each gun and also a collapsible platform at the rear for access to the officers' look-out windows in the hood on the roof of the shield. The shield was made of steel and formed the gunhouse which enclosed the mounting. An access door was provided at the rear. The shield was bolted to a box section turntable. This turntable was supported by a number of rollers on a lower roller path, which was bolted to the deck ring, the upper roller path being screwed to the underside of the turntable.

During the firing the turntable was prevented from lifting by clips, the lateral thrust being taken by the roller flanges. Separate build-up carriages were secured to the turntables. The gunhouse and turntables were identical for all turrets and rotated about the hoists, which were fixed.

Pump room

The pumping room compartment of the ship housed an electric motor, a hydraulic VSG pump, oil tank and strainer.

Hoist casing

The hoist casings were secured to the ship's structure and connected the gunhouse with the magazine and shell rooms. The length of the casing for each turret depended on the turret's position in the ship. Two shell hoists and two cordite hoists were provided. Hand-elevating gear only was fitted. Each gun was elevated separately.

Both power and hand training gear were fitted and were operated by a handwheel and by crank handles respectively. Automatic training cut-off gear was provided to cut-off the power at the limits of training. A fuze-setting machine and tilting tray were fitted at the inboard trunnion of each gun.

The fuze receiver was mechanically connected by bevel gearing to both fuze and setting machines.

Ammunition supply

Shells were delivered to the gunhouse by the R and L shell hoists. Cordite was delivered by R and L cordite hoists. Shells and cordite were transferred by hand from the hoists to the tilting tray of the fuze setting machine. When the fuze had been set the, shells and cordite were launched from the tilting trays into gun loading trays on the cradles. The gun-loading tray was carried on a bracket which was arranged to swing on a tubular shaft projecting from the rear of each cradle. The loading trays were fitted with power and hand rammers.

Firing gear

The mounting was fitted for electric firing only. The guns could be fired by director, by the gunlayer's pedal-operated switch or by the breech-worker's push; for the two latter the source of electricity supply could be either LP mains or local battery. Safety firing gear was fitted which opened the interceptors in danger zones. The gear was controlled by cam plates situated on the deck beneath the turntable. The cam plates operated the interceptors by a system of links and levers.

Sighting gear

The mounting was fitted with sighting gear supported by columns which were secured to the top of the turntable at the front of the mounting. Each layer's telescope was controlled for laying from its own gun, being operated by gearing from the elevating arc. The trainer's telescope was controlled from the left gunlayer's telescope.

The trainer's and left gunlayer's telescope could be disconnected from the left gun and controlled together by hand, as a free trainer's sight. The sight in this condition could be operated by either the trainer or the left gunlayer. A safety trainer's sight was also fitted at the lookout hood in the gun shield for use of the OOT. Sight ports were fitted with glass windows and were provided for the use of the outside wipers which were operated from the inside of the shield. A black-out curtain immediately behind the sight setter excluded the light from inside the gunhouse from the sight-port windows.

Chutes for ejected cylinders

Chutes for the ejection of empty cylinders were provided at the rear of the turntable and chopper doors were fitted for closing the chutes when not in use. Racks were provided at the rear of the gunhouse for stowing shells when it was desired to empty the hoists.

No vent plate was fitted to the 'A' mounting owing to the risk of damage by blast from 'B' mount and venting was achieved through the chute doors.

4.7-inch Mark XI guns

The length of bore was 50 calibres, i.e. 19 ft 7 in. Polygroove system of rifling with 38 grooves having a uniform twist of 30 calibres. Probable life of barrel was 675 full-charge rounds. The breech block was reversible for right and left guns. Rounds-fired counters were attached to the upper supporting beam of both guns.

Ammunition supply

The two shell hoists were of the 'pusher' type. The number of shells in each full hoist was twelve in 'A' and 'X' and fifteen in 'B'.

Mark M 2-pdr quadruple pom-pom
This cut-down version of the 8-barrelled 'Chicago Piano' fitted in Capital Ships was first mounted as a destroyer weapon in the Tribal Class boats, and subsequently in the Js. The mounting was power driven and had a total weight of twelve tons.

Other details were:

Crew:	Six
Maximum elevation:	80 degrees
Depression:	10 degrees
Training arc:	710 degrees
Training speed:	25 degrees/second
Rate of fire:	100 rounds per gun
Maximum range:	3,800 yards
Feed system:	Stacked belts each holding 14 rounds
Total per gun:	112 rounds

Provision was made in the design for pom-pom directors to be fitted but this was in fact never done. This weapon was standard close-range armament in the first four years of the war but was ultimately replaced in the AA role by the 40-mm Bofors. As an anti-E-boat weapon, however, it was in great demand.

21-inch quadruple torpedo tube mountings
The 21-inch Mk IX torpedo remained the standard torpedo throughout the war and had a range of 11,000 yards at 40 knots. Pentad mounts had been fitted to the Js but the Laforeys were fitted with power-worked quadruple mountings. The after set was fitted with a cupola for local control in the 4.7-inch Ls but the fore set only had a spray shield. The 4-inch Ls carried a different mounting as will be related. In common with all other British destroyers, and in strict contrast to the Japanese flotillas, the Ls carried no torpedo re-loads.

The 4.7-inch Ls initially completed to mount a 4-inch HA gun in place of after tubes. The 4-inch Ls completed with both sets of tubes in place. British torpedoes were always pre-set for depth and speed before firing, and the ship itself was swung to give the torpedo spread during the firing. (The *Legion* made an attack which was the exception to this rule as related.)

There was an allocation of five Lewis guns to each flotilla which were kept at base during peacetime. These were probably not mounted in the Ls at all as by the time these vessels commissioned they had already been shown as useless for any function other than exploding drifting mines.

The only anti-submarine weapons carried on the original design were the usual rack and thrower arrangements of depth charges operated in conjunction with the ASDIC dome which were by this stage standard fittings. Subsequent experience saw the completion of the Ls with a much modified outfit as will be listed later.

No radar was of course planned for the original design but by the time the flotilla neared completion this had been shown to be indispensable, although limited supply had in the main restricted it to larger vessels. It is thought that *Legion* was the first destroyer to actually commission with radar equipment embarked and functioning.

No TSDS or minelaying was ever envisaged for this class of destroyer, and the practice of fitting alternate flotillas for either one or the other of these duties had been dropped with the growing awareness of the air menace which overrode other considerations at the time of completion.

In fire control equipment the Laforeys were in the van and were the first class to mount a combined Destroyer DCT and rangefinder. A full description of this is herewith included (see Appendix 2).

Appendix 2

The Fire Control System

Data from G.04114/38-Issued June, 1938.

1. Fore bridge
Target Bearing Indicator, centre line in destroyers, sided in Leader, Evershed Bearing Transmitter with Control Key, transmitted the bearing to (a) D.C.T. (b) Searchlight sights (c) Pom-pom mounting. The Gun Range and Deflection Receiver from the TS each side at IO's position. The Rangefinder range receiver (counter driven), from rangefinder in DCT with cut lamp.

2. Combined H.9/LA director control tower
Personnel comprised one Illumination Officer (IO) on bridge, one Control Officer and five ratings in DCT Director Sight Type P (HA/LA). Gyron roll unit stabilised both telescopes. Angular velocity of roll receiver operated time interval corrector adjusting firing contact to compensate velocity of roll. $^1/_4$ HP DC motor driving oil unit for stabilisation of sight.

3. Range and height finder
12-ft UKIV on AV mounting. Stabilised by B oil motor unit driven by $^1/_4$-HP DC motor controlled from Type P sight by mechanical shafting. Dial sight: No. 7 Mk 11* Spotting glasses for CO stabilised by B oil motor for range finder. Training engine was fitted to the tower. Range: Combined Range and Reflection Receiver from TS Range finder range transmitter (50 yard steps), to receivers in TS on bridge and local repeats (counterdram). Clock range (AA) receiver motor differentially with working head-set range finder from transmitter in fuze-keeping-clock in TS. Range takers cut – push foot-operated to cut lamp at TS range receivers and bridge.

4. Elevation
Direction setting unit contained: (i) Direction Setting Transmitter LA M type 3-ft steps to AFC Clock and Elevation repeater receiver in TS with local repeat, (ii) Direction Setting Transmitter HA M-type 6-ft steps to FKC with local repeats. N.B. Tilt was added in director setting unit to outgoing transmissions. Angle of sight transmitter on Type P sight, M-type 12-ft steps to FKC.

5. Deflection
Combined range and deflection receiver from TS

6. Bearing
Evershed OFI from TBI on bridge
Relative Bearing Indicator to show bearing of DCT (mechanical)
Line of Sight Training hunter to AFCC
Recentring motor from transmitter in AFCC
    Line of sight training transmitter to dial in AFCC.
    Line of sight Repeat from transmitter in AFCC.

7. Inclination
Target course HA
Angle of Presentation transmitter on drive to CO's glasses to screen of AA
Deflection Calculator dial and mechanism of Fuze Keeping Clock and to local repeat
Fall of shot rattler from TS
Fall of shot push to TS HA fall of shot instrument

General
Director change over pistol and firing circuits with pedal firing gear to 4.7-inch guns
Cross levelling gear with gun range receiver motor and hunter and Recentring motor controlling unit in TA via HA/LA C.OS
Gun ready lamp box-6 lamps
Fire Buzzer from A FCC or FKC
Night sight and illumination circuit
Cease-fire bell
Director Test push on cease-fire bell circuit with isolating switch in TS Kents
Clear-view screens for telescopes (from HP supply)
Switch for operating visible lamp at clock
Datum angle sight transmitter to clock and local repeat
80 cm rangefinder mounted on bracket of datum single sight transmitter for PIL

Transmitting Station	HA Control
Personnel	Fuze reader
LA Control	Range turning and rate operator
Clock worker	Target course and speed operator
Range spotting operator	Change of range operator
PIL worker	TE and APV operator
Deflection worker	Communications number
W/T operator	Deflection operator

Communications Number
Details of mechanism of the AFCC 1 or FKC are not dealt with.

Range

Range receivers from rangefinder. 2 in parallel.
(i) LA Counterdrum convenient to AFCC
(ii) HA Dial at FKC
Rangetakers cut lamps (2) at receiver from R/F
Gun range transmission components of FCC to:
(i)   Each 4.7-inch gun
(ii)   DCT for CO and for cross levelling
(iii)   Fore Bridge (2)
(iv)   Local repeat

Clock Range (AA) Transmitter component of FKC to R/F.

Elevation
(i) LA from DCT to AFCC and elevation repeat receiver in 3-ft steps
(ii) AA from DCT to AA Deflection Calculator (2 motors) in 6 ft steps

Gun Elevation Synchronous Units (bulkhead) operated via COS from either:

(i) LA Hunter in AFCC
(ii) AA Hunter in AA Deflection Calculator and drivers
Gun Elevation Transmitter to recentre hunter, receivers at 4.7-inch gun and local repeat.

Angle of sight
Power follow-up unit (20-volt motor) in FKC operated by a hunter controlled by Angle of Sight receiver motor.
(i) (Relays and Switch in FKC) set calculating mechanism
(ii) Angle of Sight receivers motor set pointers on checking dial of FKC Angle of Sight receiver motor

(i) and (ii) controlled by transmitting on type P sight in DCT (M type 12-ft steps).

Deflection
Gun deflector transmitter components of AFCC to:

(i)   Each 4.7-inch gun
(ii) DCT and Compass Platform
(iii) Local repeat

Datum reflection from transmitters to AFCC to receiver at W/T position AA Deflection Hunter of FKC(OC) recentred by M type motor-controlled AA Deflection/Cross levelling follow-up unit of AFCC via HA/LA.

AA Deflection/ Cross Levelling follow up unit.
Component of AFCC via COS from either:

(i) LA Hunter in DCT
(ii) HA Hunter in AA Deflection Calculator added Cross Levelling Correction or AA lateral deflection differentially to gun training transmitters components of AFCC
Transmitter component of Cross Levelling follow up unit to recentre hunter in either DCT or AA deflection calculator.

Bearing
Line of sight motor of AFC controlled from hunter in DCT
Line of sight transmitter in AFCC to recentre hunters and repeat in DCT
Line of sight receiver component of AFCC from transmitter in DCT
(NB This receiver was not used in AA Control)
Compass Control Motor from hunter and gyro compass receiver motor sets AFCC
Gun Training Transmitter component of AFCC to receivers at 4.7-inch gun mounts, local repeats and receiver in FKC
PIL: Datum Angle receivers component of AFCC from transmitter in DCT

Fuze AA
Fuze Keeping Clock contains constant speed motor at 22 volts
Fuze Transmitter on bulkhead to receivers in FS machine at 4.7-inch guns and local receiver.
Own Speed Indicator from Log.

Timing
Fall of shot instruments (LA or HA)

Appendix 3

General Fittings and Complements

On 7 April 1938 in the extracts from the Board Minutes, entry number 3544 read: 'The Board approved the Legend and Drawings for the "L" Class Destroyers and Leader of the 1937 Programme.'

In addition to the Legend as submitted the following details were specified as final. Firstly E-in-C requested that measurement trials should be carried out in the *Larne* and *Lookout*. *Lookout* and *Loyal* were to be fitted out as Flotilla Medical Office ships (FMOs). *Laforey* and *Lookout* were to be weighted and inclined.

The *sheering* stresses as compared with earlier destroyers were worked out as follows:

Ships	Hogging		Sagging	
	SF	(Tons/sq. in.)	SF (Tons)	(Tons/sq. in.)
G Class	228	2.47	196	2.13
Tribal Class	300	2.91	397	3.85
J Class	299	3.04	335	3.4
L Class	322	3.28	329	3.34

The metacentric height comparison was:

| J Class | 2.7 deep | 2.7 light |
| L Class | 3.0 deep | 3.1 light |

The machinery equipment to develop 48,000 SHP was listed as:

Boilers
Two in number, each of 24,000 SHP, arranged one in each of two boiler rooms. Working pressure 300 lbs/sq.in. Steam superheated to 660 degrees F. Working pressure at turbines 250 lbs/sq. in. Boilers were standard Admiralty type, 3-drum. In this boiler the first two rows of tubes next to the furnaces on each side were of $1^{3}/_{4}$-inch external diameter while the remainder were of 1-inch and $1^{1}/_{8}$-inch external diameter. The superheater was fitted in the space between the fourth and fifth rows of tubes in each bank. The feed water was usually supplied by a turbine-

driven feed-pump which discharged the feed-water through a float-controlled feed regulator and thence through the internal feed-pipes. These were situated in the lower part of the steam drums. A slotted internal steam pipe was fitted, through which the steam passed to the super-heater and thence through the stop-valve to the main steam pipes.

The air was supplied to the boiler by forced draught fans which delivered air to the boiler rooms and thence by trunking (this was partially incorporated within the structure), round the boiler casing to the burners. The boilers were arranged back to back, the uptakes being led to the single funnel.

Turbines
Two-shafted arrangement, each shaft being driven by a HP and LP turbine through a single reduction helical gearing situated in a separate gearing room abaft the main engine room. Parsons geared turbines.

Revs of props: 350 per min.
Dia. of props: 10 ft 8 inches.
Total SHP (2,400 each shaft): 48,000
Total power to be developed with the cruising stages in use was about 3,000 SHP. These turbines were, as already stated, supplied by the Parsons Steam Turbine Company of Wallsend.

Original Design (1938)
General fitments
Boats: One 25 ft fast motor boat, one 25 ft general service motor boat, one 27 ft whaler, one 16 ft dinghy, six N pattern 20 Carley Floats. (Seven in Leader.)
Anchors: Two 36 cwt stockless, one 5 cwt kedge.
Capstan: Double-headed combined capstan and cable holder.
Torpedo hoisting winch: One electrically operated – for use as boat hoisting winch.
Electrical power: Two 200 kW turbo generators, two 60 kW diesel generators.
Steering gear: Electro-hydraulic system employing two single acting rams operating on a tiller. A hand pump was installed for emergency use.
Searchlights: One 44-inch projector on platform between torpedo tubes – remote-controlled from bridge. Two 20-inch signal projectors on sponsons either side of bridge. Two 6-inch signal lanterns.

Wireless Telegraphy:

Destroyer:	Type 49A
	60B as alternative as fire control set
Leader:	49A (Main office)
	60B as alternative 2nd Office
	60B as alternative fire control
	D/F outfit
Provisions:	Three months supply.

The following Provisional Scheme of Complements was given on 14 April 1938.

Flotilla Leader	Peace	War
Captain	1	1
Lieutenant Commander or Lieutenant RN	1	1
Lieutenant-Commander (G) or Lieutenant RN (G)	1	1 (Flotilla duty)
Lieutenant-Commander (T) or Lieutenant RN (T)	1	1 (Flotilla duty)
Lieutenant-Commander (S) or Lieutenant RN (S)	1	1 (Flotilla duty)
Lieutenant-Commander (A/S) or Lieutenant RN (A/S)	1	1 (Flotilla duty)
Lieutenant-Commander (N) or Lieutenant RN (N)	1	1 (Flotilla duty)
Sub-Lieutenant	1	1
Midshipman	–	1
Commander Gunner (DF) or Gunner (DF)	1	1 (Flotilla duty)
Commander Gunner (T) or Gunner (T)	1	1 (Flotilla duty)
Commander Boatswaine (A/S) or Boatswaine (A/S)	1	1 (Flotilla duty)
Chief Petty Officer	1	1
Petty Officers	7	7
Leading Seamen	8	9
AB or OD	77	79
Chief Yeoman of Signals	1	1
Yeomen of Signals	2	2
Leading Signalmen	4	4
Signalmen	7	7
Commander or W/T Telegraphist	1	1 (Flotilla duty)
Chief Petty Officer Telegraphist	1	1
Leading Telegraphists	4	4
Telegraphists	9	9
Engineering Commander or W T Engineer	1	1 (Flotilla duty)
Commander or W T Engineer	1	1
Chief ERAs	2	2
ERAs	4	4
Chief Stoker	1	1
Stoker Petty Officers	5	5
Leading Stokers	11	11
Stokers	20	20

Destroyers		War
Commander or Lieutenant-Commander	1	1
Lieutenant-Commander or Lieutenant RN	2	2
Sub-Lieutenant	1	1
Midshipman	–	1
Commander Gunner (T) or Gunner (T)	1	1
Chief Petty Officers	1	1
Petty Officers	7	7
Leading Seamen	8	9
AB or OD	85	87
Leading Telegraphist	1	1
Telegraphists	3	3
Leading Signalman	1	1
Signalmen	3	3
Engineering Lieutenant or Lieutenant-Commander (E)	1	1
Chief ERA	1	1
ERA	4	4
Chief Stoker	1	1
Stoker Petty Officers	5	5
Leading Stokers	11	11
Stokers	19	19

4-inch gunned ships (1940)

Torpedo tubes:	Q R Mk X
Deep displacements:	2,630 tons
Light displacements:	1,947 tons
Draught:	10 ft ½ in.
Trim by stern:	26½ ft
VCG:	15.4
G M:	3.35
Max G Z:	1.27
Range:	60 degrees

Stowage of depth charges

18 on rails
24 in RU racks
8 on throwers
12 in carriers on upper deck
33 in warhead room
15 in upper deck stores

Equipment

W/T	Type 49 MR
	Type 4J as emergency fire control.
	D/F outfit Type FA1 in main office.

Proposed Complement

Commanding Officer	1
Lieutenant-Commander or Lieutenant RN.:	2
Sub-Lieutenant	1
Commander Gunner (T)	1
Chief Petty Officer	1
Petty Officers	10
Leading Seamen	12
AB or OD	112
Chief (E) or Lieutenant (E)	1
Chief Engine Room Artificer	1
Engine Room Artificer	4
Chief Stoker	1
Stoker Petty Officers	5
Leading Stokers	11
Stokers	19
Total (Peace)	201

For war to be added:

Midshipman	1
AB or OD	2
Stoker Petty Officer	1
Leading Seaman	1
Stokers	4
Electrical Artificer	1
Sick Berth Rating	1
Total (War)	212

Appendix 4

Ships' Badges, Battle Honours and Commanding Officers

Laforey
Flotilla Leader. Named after Sir Francis Laforey (1767–1835) who commanded
the *Spartiate* at the battle of Trafalgar 1805.
Second ship of the name.

Field: Per fess wavy white and blue
Badge: A lion's gamb gold grasping a torch
inflamed proper
Motto: Fero facem (I bear the torch)
Battle Honours: Heligoland 1914, Dogger Bank
1915, Dardanelles 1915–16, Atlantic 1942, Malta
Convoys 1941–42, Diego Suarez 1942, Sicily
1943, Salerno 1943, Mediterranean 1943–44,
Anzio 1944
Job Number: J 1819
Builder: Yarrow & Co. Ltd, Scotstoun
Laid down: 1 March 1939
Launched: 15 February 1941
Completed: 28 August 1941
Contract: £461,947.50
Pendant number: F 99. G 99
Adopted by: Northampton
Commanding Officers: Captain R.M.J. Hutton appointed March 1941,
Captain H.T. Armstrong appointed August 1943

Gurkha (originally *Larne*)
Launched as *Gurkha*. After the Tribal Class
destroyer *Gurkha* had been sunk off Norway in
1940 the men of the Gurkha Regiments
subscribed a day's pay per man to replace her
and *Larne* was thus renamed in their honour and
actually *launched* as *Gurkha*, despite what is
claimed in many 'reference books'. Third ship of
the name.

Field: Blue
Badge: Two crossed Kukris proper
Battle honours: Dover Patrol 1914–17, Norway
1940, North Sea 1940, Atlantic 1941,
Mediterranean 1941, Malta Convoys 1941–42
Job number: J 1113
Builder: Cammell Laird & Co. Ltd, Birkenhead
Laid down: 18 October 1938
Launched: 8 July 1940
Completed: 18 February 1941
Contract: £458,132
Pendant numbers: F63. G63
Adopted by: The Gurkha Regiment
Commanding Officer: Commander C.N. Lentaigne appointed October 1940

Lance
Second ship of the name.

Field: Barry wavy of four white and blue
Badge: Issuant from base a Lance red
Battle honours: Heligoland 1914, Belgian Coast
1917, Mediterranean 1941, Malta Convoys
1941–42
Job number: J 1820
Builder: Yarrow & Co. Ltd, Scotstoun
Laid down: 1 March 1939
Launched: 28 November 1940
Completed: 13 May 1941
Contract: £456,467.50
Pendant number: F 87. G 87
Adopted by: Bexley & Welling, Kent
Commanding Officer: Lieutenant-Commander
R.W.F. Northcott appointed February 1941

Legion
Second ship of the name.

Field: Blue
Badge: An eagle displaced upon a perch gold
Battle honours: Heligoland 1914, Dogger Bank
1915, Cape Bon 1941, Norway 1941, Atlantic
1941, Mediterranean 1941, Libya 1941–42, Malta
Convoys 1941–42, Sirte 1942
Job number: J 4051
Builder: Parsons (hull sub-contracted to
Hawthorn Leslie, Hebburn)
Laid down: 1 November 1938
Launched: 26 December 1939
Completed: 19 December 1940
Contract: £457,240
Pendant number: F 74. G 74
Adopted by: Cheltenham, Gloucestershire
Commanding Officer: Commander R.F. Jessel appointed November 1940

Lightning
Tenth ship of the name.

Field: Black
Badge: Three rays of lightning in band gold
Battle honours: Barfleur 1692, Vigo 1702, Velez
Malaga 1704, Louisburg 1758, Baltic 1854–55,
Diego Suarez 1942, Malta Convoys 1941–42
Job number: J 4052
Builder: Parsons (hull sub-contracted to
Hawthorn Leslie, Hebburn)
Laid down: 15 November 1938
Launched: 22 April 1940
Completed: 28 May 1941
Contract: £457,415
Pendant numbers: F 55. G 55
Adopted by: Doncaster
Commanding Officers: Commander R.G. Stewart
appointed April 1941
Commander H.G. Walters appointed December 1941

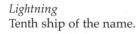

Lively
Twenty-second ship of the name.

Field: Barry wavy of four white and blue
Badge: An ankh (crux ansata) gold
Battle Honours: La Guayra 1743, Ushant 1778, St
Vincent 1797, Baltic 1855, Atlantic 1941,
Mediterranean 1941, Malta Convoys 1941–42,
Sirte 1942, Libya 1942
Job number: J 1114
Builder: Cammell Laird & Co. Ltd, Birkenhead
Laid down: 20 December 1938
Launched: 28 January 1941
Completed: 20 July 1941
Contract: £458,132
Pendant numbers: F 40. G 40.
Adopted by: Guildford, Surrey.
Commanding Officer: Lieutenant-Commander W.F.E. Hussey appointed February
1941

Lookout
Second ship of the name.

Field: Per fess wavy white and blue
Badge: A man in the Crow's nest of a Whaler all
proper
Battle honours: Heligoland 1914, Dogger Bank
1915, Diego Suarez 1942, Malta Convoys 1942,
Arctic 1942, North Africa 1942–43, Sicily 1943,
Salerno 1943, South France 1944, Mediterranean
1943–45
Job number: J 1109
Builder: Scotts Shipbuilding & Engineering,
Greenock
Laid down: 23 November 1938
Launched: 4 November 1940
Completed: 30 January 1942
Contract: £458,000
Pendant numbers: F 32. G 32. D 232(1947)
Adopted by: Burnley, Lancashire
Commanding Officers: Lieutenant-Commander C.P.F. Brown appointed October
1941, Lieutenant-Commander A.G. Forman appointed August 1942, Lieutenant-
Commander D.H.F Hetherington appointed March 1944

Loyal
Second ship of the name.

Field: Barry wavy of four white and blue
Badge: A red rose barbed and seeded proper
charged with the Royal Crest
Battle honours: Sicily 1943, Salerno 1943,
Mediterranean 1943, Anzio 1944, Adriatic 1944
Job number: J 1110
Builder: Scotts Shipbuilding & Engineering,
Greenock
Laid down: 23 November 1938
Launched: 8 October 1941
Completed: 31 December 1942
Contract: £457,550
Pendant numbers: F15. G 15. D 94 (1947)
Adopted by: Cambridge
Commanding Officers: Lieutenant-Commander
H.E.F. Tweedie appointed September 1942, Commander G. Ransome appointed
October 1944, Lieutenant-Commander J.F.D. Bush appointed January 1945

Glossary

AIDAC	Signals information indicator 1939–42 'To be dealt with in accordance the Addressees standing Instructions for Deciphering and Circulation of message so prefixed.'
AA	Anti-aircraft
AB	Able Seaman
ACNS	Assistant Chief of Naval Staff
A-K Line	Cruiser Scouting Dispositions
A/S	Anti-Submarine
ASV	Aircraft/Surface Vessel
Capital Ships	Battleships or battle-cruisers
CG	Centre of Gravity
C-in-C	Commander-in-Chief
Controller	Controller of the Navy
CNS	Chief of Naval Staff
DC	Depth Charge
DCT	Director Control Tower
DCNS	Deputy Chief of Naval Staff
DDNO	Deputy Director of Naval Ordnance
Deep	Deep Displacement
D/F	Director Finder
D of C	Director of Contracts
D of P	Director of Plans
DNC	Director of Naval Construction
DNO	Director of Naval Ordnance
DP	Dual Purpose
DTM	Director of Torpedoes and Mining
DTSD	Director of Training and Staff duties
E-in-C	Engineer-in-Chief
ERA	Engine Room Artificer
Flotilla	At the period under review comprised eight

destroyers with either an enlarged Leader or one of the eight boats with larger office accommodation – has since been replaced (regrettably) by the American term 'Squadron'

FMO	Flotilla Medical Officer
FKC	Fuze Keeping Clock
FS	Fuze Setter
FP	Full Power
G	See CG
GIC	Gunner Information Control
GM	Metacentric height
GZ	Righting lever
HA	High Angle – guns designed principally for engaging aircraft
Hogging	Condition of hull stress when hull is centrally supported on a wave crest
HP Turbine	High Pressure Turbine
HCP	Hydraulic Control Power
IHP	Indicated Horse Power
IO	Illumination Officer
kw	Kilowatt
LA	Low Angle. Guns designed principally for engaging surface targets
LNT	London Naval Treaty
MTB	Motor Torpedo Boat (German-E-boat, Italian-MAS-Boat, American-PT-Boat)
mg	Machine gun
MF/DF	Medium Frequency Direction Finding
MV	Muzzle Velocity
OD	Ordinary Seaman
OOW	Officer of the Watch
OT	Oil Tight
PC	Propulative Co-efficient
Pdr	Pounder
PIL	Position in Line
PPI	Plan Position Indicator
QR	Quadruple Revolving
R/F	Range Finder
RDF	Radio Direction Finding
RPM	Revs per minute

RU	Ready Use
SHP	Shaft Horse Power
Standard	Standard Displacement as defined by Washington Naval Treaty
SAP	Semi-Armour Piercing shells
Sagging	Condition of hull stress when both ends of hull are supported with hull in a wave trough
TT	Torpedo Tube
TSDS	Two Speed Destroyer Sweep (for minesweeping)
TBI	Target Bearing Indicator
TS	Transmitting Station
TDS	Torpedo Deflection Sight
W/T	Wireless Telegraphy
VCG	Vertical Centre of Gravity

Index